VIEWPOINTS
THEORETICAL PERSPECTIVES ON IRISH VISUAL TEXTS

Viewpoints

Theoretical Perspectives on Irish Visual Texts

Edited by

Claire Bracken

and

Emma Radley

First published in 2013 by
Cork University Press
Youngline Industrial Estate
Pouladuff Road, Togher
Cork, Ireland

British Library Cataloguing in Publication Data
A CIP catalogue record for this book is available from the British Library.

ISBN-978-185918-496-7

Typeset by Tower Books, Ballincollig, County Cork
Printed in and bound by CPI Group (UK) Ltd, Croydon, CR0 4YY

www.corkuniversitypress.com

To Conor and Rezia
you let us see the world differently

CONTENTS

DISCOURSE

FORM

IDENTITY

LIST OF ILLUSTRATIONS

Contributors

Z<small>ÉLIE</small> A<small>SAVA</small>, U<small>NIVERSITY</small> C<small>OLLEGE</small> D<small>UBLIN</small> <small>AND</small> I<small>NSTITUTE OF</small> A<small>RT</small>, D<small>ESIGN AND</small> T<small>ECHNOLOGY</small>, D<small>UN</small> L<small>AOGHAIRE</small>

Zélie Asava is a Faculty Lecturer at University College Dublin and Institute of Art, Design and Technology, Dun Laoghaire. Her monograph, on racial representations in Irish film and television, is under contract with Peter Lang Ltd. She is the author of many articles on the intersection between race, gender and sexuality in Irish, French, African and American cinema. She completed her PhD on mixed-race representations in American and French cinema in 2009, and has also worked for Trinity College Dublin and the National University of Ireland Maynooth.

C<small>LAIRE</small> B<small>RACKEN</small>, U<small>NION</small> C<small>OLLEGE</small>, S<small>CHENECTADY</small>, NY

Claire Bracken is Assistant Professor of Irish Literature and Culture in the English Department at Union College, New York, where she teaches courses on Irish literature and film. She has published journal articles and book essays on Irish women's writing, feminist criticism and theory, and Irish cultural studies. She is co-editor of *Anne Enright* (Irish Academic Press, 2011) and her book *Irish Feminist Futures* will be published by Routledge in 2013 as part of their feminist series *Transformations*.

M<small>ATTHEW</small> B<small>ROWN</small>, D<small>EPARTMENT OF</small> E<small>NGLISH</small>, U<small>NIVERSITY OF</small> M<small>ASSACHUSETTS</small> B<small>OSTON</small>

Matthew Brown is an Associate Professor in the Department of English at the University of Massachusetts Boston. He has published essays on representations of political violence in twentieth- and twenty-first-century British and Irish fiction and film in journals such as *Éire-Ireland, New Hibernia Review* and *The Irish Review*. He is currently at work on a book project entitled *Perilous Pleasures: Fascination, Film and the Novel*.

JUSTIN CARVILLE, SCHOOL OF CREATIVE ARTS, INSTITUTE OF ART, DESIGN AND TECHNOLOGY, DUN LAOGHAIRE

Justin Carville is Lecturer in Historical and Theoretical Studies in Photography and Visual Culture Studies in the School of Creative Arts at the Institute of Art, Design and Technology, Dun Laoghaire. A former Government of Ireland Senior Research Scholar in the Humanities and Social Sciences (2003–4), he has guest edited a special Ireland-themed issue of *The Journal of Popular Visual Culture* and an issue of the journal *Photographies* on the photographic image and globalisation. His first book, *Photography and Ireland*, was published by Reaktion in 2011. He is currently researching the connections between photography, ethnography and the visualisation of Irish identity for which he was awarded an Irish Research Council for the Humanities and Social Sciences (IRCHSS) Government of Ireland Research Fellowship.

COLIN GRAHAM, DEPARTMENT OF ENGLISH, NATIONAL UNIVERSITY OF IRELAND MAYNOOTH

Colin Graham lectures at the National University of Ireland Maynooth. He is the author of *Ideologies of Epic* (Manchester University Press, 1998) and *Deconstructing Ireland* (Edinburgh University Press, 2001). He is co-editor of *Ireland and Cultural Theory* (Macmillan, 1999), *Irish and Postcolonial Writing* (Palgrave, 2002) and *Ireland and Europe in the Nineteenth Century* (Four Courts Press, 2006), and is also co-editor of *The Irish Review*.

CHERYL HERR, DEPARTMENT OF ENGLISH, UNIVERSITY OF IOWA

Cheryl Temple Herr teaches Irish and British fiction, film, music and culture at the University of Iowa. She has published *Joyce's Anatomy of Culture* (University of Illinois Press, 1986), *For the Land They Loved: Irish Political Melodramas, 1890–1925* (Syracuse University Press, 1991), *Critical Regionalism and Cultural Studies: From Ireland to the American Midwest* (University Press of Florida, 1996), *Ireland into Film: The Field* (Cork Univeristy Press, 2002), and many essays in a wide range of journals and essay collections. Current projects include a study of Joyce and phenomenology as well as a book tentatively called *Rock Britannia: World War II and Popular Music.*

HEATHER MACDOUGALL, CONCORDIA UNIVERSITY, MONTREAL

Heather Macdougall is currently completing her PhD at Concordia University in Montreal, Canada, where she also teaches courses on Irish and Northern Irish cinema. Her doctoral research, which is funded by the Fonds Québecois de Recherche sur la Société et la Culture, explores the role of language in Irish cinema, particularly within the short film format. Previously Heather worked as the coordinator of the short film programme at the Foyle Film Festival in Derry, Northern Ireland, and she is currently an active member of the programming committee for the Cine Gael Montreal Irish Film Society.

EMMIE MCFADDEN, SHEFFIELD HALLAM UNIVERSITY

Emmie McFadden teaches at Sheffield Hallam University. Her doctoral thesis was on film adaptation and Irish cinema, with a particular focus on representations of the Irish diaspora in England. She is co-editor and contributor of the forthcoming collection *21st-Century British Cinema*, and is currently preparing her monograph *'Hidden' Irishness: Visualising the Irish in Britain.*

AINTZANE LEGARRETA MENTXAKA, SCHOOL OF ENGLISH, DRAMA AND FILM AT UNIVERSITY COLLEGE DUBLIN, AND ST PATRICK'S COLLEGE, DUBLIN CITY UNIVERSITY

Aintzane Legarreta Mentxaka teaches literature in the School of English, Drama and Film at University College Dublin, and in St Patrick's College, Dublin City University. She was postdoctoral fellow of the National University of Ireland in 2012. In 2007 she was awarded a PhD in English, having completed an MA with a thesis on popular culture in 2004. She was Scholar of the Irish Research Council for the Humanities and the Social Sciences in 2005–6 and in 2006–7. Between 2003 and 2005 she was coordinator of the 'Dublin Queer Studies Group', and organiser of the annual conference 'An Evening with the Writer Kate O'Brien' between 2003 and 2006. Her main research interests are: modernist and twentieth-century literature, Irish literature and culture, intermedial studies, philosophy and critical theory, women's writing, popular culture, and early film. Mentxaka has published extensively, in English, Basque and Spanish. Her book *Kate O'Brien and the Fiction of Identity* was published by McFarland in 2011. She is currently working on a book on Modernist writing by Irish women, and, together with F. de Juan, she is also co-writing a book on silent film.

BARRY MONAGHAN, ENGLISH DEPARTMENT, UNIVERSITY COLLEGE CORK

Barry Monahan has been a College Lecturer at University College Cork since 2007. His monograph *Ireland's Theatre on Film: Style, Stories and the National Stage on Screen* (Irish Academic Press, 2009) considers the relationship between the Abbey Theatre and cinema from the beginning of the sound period until the 1960s. He has published on contemporary Irish cinema from different theoretical and aesthetic perspectives in several collections of essays, including chapters in *Screening Irish America*, Ruth Barton (ed.) (Irish Academic Press, 2009) and *Genre and Cinema: Ireland and Transnationalism*, Brian McIlroy (ed.) (Routledge, 2007). He contributes regularly to *Estudios Irlandeses, Spanish Journal of Irish Studies*.

ANNE MULHALL, SCHOOL OF ENGLISH, DRAMA AND FILM, UNIVERSITY COLLEGE DUBLIN

Anne Mulhall is a College Lecturer in the School of English, Drama and Film Studies at University College Dublin where she teaches and researches in critical theory, gender and sexuality studies, and Irish literary and cultural studies. She has published extensively on queer theory, psychoanalytic theory, contemporary Irish writing, Irish periodical culture, and contemporary Irish popular and visual culture. She has co-edited *Irish Postmodernisms and Popular Culture* (Palgrave, 2007), and *Women in Irish Culture and Society*, a collection of essays co-edited with Gerardine Meaney and Maria Luddy, is forthcoming with Irish Academic Press in 2012. She has co-edited a special feature on the work of Bracha L. Ettinger for *Studies in the Maternal*, has a co-edited special feature on the work of Lisa Baraitser forthcoming with *Studies in Gender and Sexuality*, and is co-editing a special issue of the *Irish University Review* on Queer Studies and Ireland, forthcoming in spring 2013. She is working on two monographs, *Anne Enright: Excavating the Present* and *Intimate States: The Biopolitics of Ireland 1970–2012*.

JENNY O'CONNOR, SCHOOL OF HUMANITIES, WATERFORD
INSTITUTE OF TECHNOLOGY

Jenny O'Connor received her PhD in 2009 from the School of English, Drama and Film at University College Dublin. Her research examined the way that film studies and Deleuzian philosophy interact. She has contributed to postgraduate publications, published a paper in the peer-reviewed online journal *Rhizomes*, and has had chapters in a number of books including *Screening Irish-America*, *Essays in Irish Literary Criticism*, and *Gender and Interpersonal Violence*. She is currently lecturering in Communications in the School of Humanities at Waterford Institute of Technology (WIT). She is a member of WIT's Centre for Excellence in Film Studies and Waterford Film For All, and is involved in several film-related activities in the city.

EMMA RADLEY, SCHOOL OF ENGLISH, DRAMA AND FILM,
UNIVERSITY COLLEGE DUBLIN

Emma Radley is Senior Research and Teaching Fellow with the Gender Research Education Programme (GREP) in Gender, Culture and Identity at University College Dublin. She teaches in Irish cinema and culture, psychoanalysis, and film studies. She has published articles on film and psychoanalytic theory, Irish cinema, and Irish cultural studies. She has co-edited a special issue of *Television and New Media* on reality television and national identity, forthcoming in spring 2013, and is currently working on a monograph on the intersections between postmodernism and psychoanalysis in contemporary cinema.

FINTAN WALSH, SCHOOL OF ENGLISH AND DRAMA, QUEEN MARY,
UNIVERSITY OF LONDON

Fintan Walsh is lecturer in Drama, Theatre and Performance in the School of English and Drama at Queen Mary, University of London. His research currently focuses on Irish theatre and cultural performance, performance affects and therapy cultures, queer theatre and performance practices, and theatre and performance in educational and community contexts. He is author of *Theatre & Therapy* (Palgrave Macmillan, forthcoming 2012) and *Male Trouble: Masculinity and the Performance of Crisis* (Palgrave Macmillan, 2010); editor of a special issue of the journal *Performing Ethos* on 'Queer

Publics' (vol. 2, no. 2 (2012)) and *Queer Notions: New Plays and Performances from Ireland* (Cork University Press, 2010); and co-editor of *Performance, Identity and the Neo-Political Subject* (Routledge, forthcoming 2012) and *Crossroads: Performance Studies and Irish Culture* (Palgrave Macmillan, 2009). His publications have also appeared in journals such as *Contemporary Theatre Review, Irish Theatre International, Parallax, Studies in the Maternal* and *Theatre Research International*, as well as in a number of book anthologies.

ACKNOWLEDGEMENTS

A huge thanks to all our contributors for their dedication, patience and intellectual vigour. We are proud of this book because of their wonderful and dynamic essays. In addition, we are grateful to all at Cork University Press, particularly Maria O'Donovan and Mike Collins who have provided invaluable support and guidance throughout the publication process. Susan Cahill and Mary McGlynn generously took time to read drafts of the collection's introduction and helped clarify and refine our focus and direction. We really appreciate their insights. Thanks to all our colleagues and students in the UCD School of English, Drama and Film, and the English Department, Union College. Particular mention also to Patricia Coughlan, Margaret Kelleher, Anne Mulhall, Diane Negra and Moynagh Sullivan, whose work consistently inspires our scholarship and who we are lucky to count as friends and mentors. And to Gerardine Meaney – for everything.

Thanks to our wonderful families and friends, who have always been there, providing care and support throughout the editing of this book, not to mention some very welcome distraction when needed! Special thanks to Susan Cahill, for years of friendship, stimulating conversation, and great fun. And of course to our partners Eoin Foley and Glen Wrafter, for their understanding, good humour and love.

The editors and publishers wish to thank the Museum of Archaeology and Anthropology, University of Cambridge for permission to reproduce 'The Bertillonage Method, Ireland', Lough Derg for 'Soul Survival' and 'Re-Kindle Your Spirit', Joe Duggan for 'Like

Father, Like Son (Kite)', 'Family Man No. 5', Hannah Starkey and Maureen Paley, London for 'Untitled – June 2007' and 'Untitled – May 1997', and Grand Pictures for the images from *Fergus's Wedding* and *Paths to Freedom*.

INTRODUCTION

Claire Bracken
and
Emma Radley

In 2010, Discover Ireland launched a new campaign aimed at the home market, focused on repackaging and remarketing Ireland as an attractive destination for those forced (by economic necessity or by Icelandic ash cloud) to partake in a so-called 'staycation'.[1] Set to the tune of Heathers' *Remember When*, the advertisement visualises an Ireland very different from the gloomy, humourless and disheartening recessionary Ireland of the newspapers and current affairs programmes. In this bright, multicultural, family-friendly, seductive and fun-filled visual space, Ireland is overwhelmingly active, no longer passively accepting its decreasing capital on the global stage. Here you can surf with blondes in barely-there bikinis in Donegal, second-honeymoon in gourmet Waterford, golf by a Mediterranean-looking beach in the west, indulge in spa treatments dispensed by handsome men in Kerry, and play the didgeridoo in artsy Galway. The visual register is bright, glamorous, uptempo and sexy, using quick cuts, panning shots and Dutch angles to indicate a space in transition, dynamic and changing. The traditional aesthetic, 'old' Ireland, is present – sweeping shots of beautiful, pastoral scenes, olde-worlde cobbled streets and pubs – but is insistently juxtaposed with 'new' Ireland, with luxury hotels and golf courses, cookery schools and activity centres, and is always presented as a backdrop for subjects in motion (kayaking, hiking, surfing), subjects taking charge of and rearticulating its representational space (Fig. 0.1).

Image matters in this image-saturated world. It is significant that this is a local campaign rather than an international one – while the

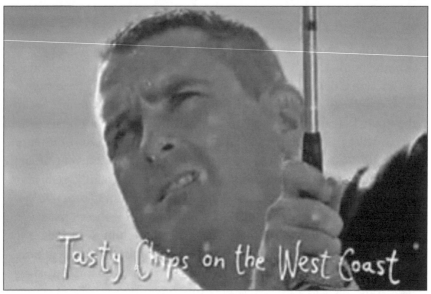

Fig. 0.1 'The Fun Starts Here': Fáilte Ireland, 2010.

space may be familiar as the picturesque, traditional 'Éire Álainn' from film and television, it is a skewed perspective. Despite the troubling and commodified versions of neo-liberalism that the ad presents, it is significant for the manner in which it persistently represents Ireland as a culture in flux. Citizens of the new Ireland are being urged to take another look at their cultural landscape, to see it differently. Over the last twenty years, Ireland has experienced transition into, as well as away from, the Celtic Tiger phenomenon and, as a consequence, notions of Irish identity and nationality have been in constant flux. For this reason, it is a timely moment to consider visual representations, both past and present, of Irish cultural life, and contribute to conversations about questions such as: What kind of iconic currencies does Ireland have? How should we see them? Are there specific ideological frameworks operating when we imagine Ireland? Can we imagine Irishness differently?

Viewpoints: Theoretical Perspectives on Irish Visual Texts seeks to build on and contribute to the rich and significant tradition of Irish scholarly work on image-based texts in the fields of art history and film studies,[2] as well as the burgeoning inter-disciplinary work on Irish visual culture (evident in the recent publication of two edited collections: *Ireland, Design and Visual Culture* and *Ireland in Focus: Film, Photography and Popular Culture*).[3] This collection shares an interest in inter-disciplinarity, bringing together scholars working in a variety of areas in Irish studies, using the visual as a focal point to demonstrate the importance and vitality of this register in Irish culture. The essays collected here are primarily concerned with cultural narratives that are visual, examining images as generative of different meanings in and of Ireland, both contemporary and historical. Given the focus on cultural narrative, many of the pieces are concerned with film; however, by definition, the image operates across a variety of media, and for this reason we also include essays on television, photographic art and advertising. While many of the essays consider the aesthetic qualities and functions of the visual in and of itself, at the heart of the authors' concern here is the ways in which image-based texts engage *with* questions of Irish culture, and the manner in which those texts are received, circulated and consumed *in* Irish culture. The essays create new perspectives and new frameworks from which to examine visual texts and the ideological and critical discourses in which they are produced.

Discourse

In order to intervene in the traditional frameworks that are used to analyse image-based texts, new paradigms must be established, new perspectives adopted, new lenses fashioned. The first section of the collection attempts to do just that: it constructs and positions new and alternative methodologies that have an effect on how visual texts are coded both in Irish culture and in Irish critical discourse. In the opening essay, Justin Carville dissects the notion of a unified field of 'Irish Visual Culture'. His essay examines the disciplinary border disputes in the study of the visual within the Irish academy, and considers the way in which the image has been deployed as a marker of cultural meaning. Carville's essay is a subversive intervention into the 'cultural politics of the visual' – rather than placing the emphasis on the visual image as an object that 'reveals' Irish identity, Carville advocates a focus on visual practice itself, the mechanics of looking and visualising. Through an examination of one of A.C. Haddon's late nineteenth-century ethnographic photographs, Carville considers how the terrain of the visible is a shifting one – a *terra infirma* constantly in the process of deterritorialisation – which cannot and should not be colonised, determined or contained by the practices of identity politics.

Cheryl Herr's essay also advocates a change in methodological approach in order to question the ways in which Irish cinematic representation has been received in critical discourse. Herr's piece deliberately sidelines explorations of plot and character, instead examining the relationship between Irishness and material, social and cultural practices. Using Pierre Bordieu's concept of 'habitus', and Thaddeus O'Sullivan's *The Woman Who Married Clark Gable* (1995) as a case study, Herr considers how social and cultural practices of everyday life produce knowledge and reality, and puts forward an alternative way of seeing the screen – looking to the 'banal' rather than at a 'bigger picture' in order to watch how Irishness is produced in embodied and embedded practices of living.

Barry Monahan's essay considers one of Ireland's most celebrated and innovative contemporary directors, Lenny Abrahamson, from a phenomenological perspective, and also suggests an alternative way of understanding narrative in Irish cinema. Like Herr's, Monahan's essay is interested in focusing not on narrative as meaning, but rather on narrative as experience, which has the similar effect of introducing a new type of interpretation to the conceptual framework of Irish cinema. Through an analysis of the change in narrative structure from a more traditional cause-and-effect system in *Adam & Paul* (2004) to a more open and existential system in *Garage* (2007), Monahan puts forward a relationship between spectator and text that is less determining and not as controlled by the forces of signification.

Matthew Brown's essay also considers the relationship between the camera and the spectator, and theorises it as one that is dominated by fascination on both sides, rather than by a desire for identification or narrative satisfaction. Looking at recent Northern Irish film, specifically *Hunger* (Steve McQueen, 2008) and *Bloody Sunday* (Paul Greengrass, 2002), Brown looks to the minutiae and silences, focusing on the aesthetic charge of particular objects, shots and scenes, and argues that the viewers' relationship with these moments are privileged over larger questions of ideology or representation. His essay challenges existing critical discourses, examining how post-peace process cinema deals with the lasting and insistent presence of the Troubles as spectacle.

Considering the interstices of critical discourse, ideology and culture, Heather Macdougall examines the relationship between occlusion and visual representation, between what is seen and not seen. Her argument is that there has been a marginalisation of Irish-language cinema in the establishment of an Irish national cinema and her essay works to reframe these terms through an analysis of the Irish short films by Daniel O'Hara: *Yu Ming is Ainm Dom/My Name is Yu Ming* (2003) and *Fluent Dysphasia* (2004). Drawing on theories of national cinema, Macdougall explores new vistas of Irish-language film to mobilise pluralist understandings of Irishness in the national cinematic context and calls for more inclusion of the Irish language in Ireland's national cinema of the future.

Form

The essays in the previous section establish a relational connection between the texts and the discourses in which those texts are read, in order to stage critical interventions. The essays here consider the specific and diverse ways in which the visual operates as a dynamic intertextual register. Emmie McFadden explores the theoretical possibilities of intertextuality in an analysis of the English film *Liam* (Stephen Frears, 2001), arguing that its theme and form are matched. Bringing together the theoretical discourses of diaspora studies, adaptation studies and narrative theory, McFadden argues that the subliminal message of *Liam* centres on the 'hidden Irishness' of the Sullivan family, while formally the film operates according to 'hidden intertextuality', as an unacknowledged adaptation of James Joyce's *A Portrait of the Artist as a Young Man* (1916). These 'hidden' elements of both theme and form work to unsettle fixed readings of origin, as beginnings are consistently presented as being oblique, which in turn has the effect of transforming the concept of national identity into something ambiguous rather than clear.

Emma Radley's essay is similarly interested in the concept of intertextuality. She argues that Irish genre films are critically excluded from the field of Irish film studies, as they are perceived to be 'impure' and 'contagious', carrying the viral markers of Hollywood commercialisation. However, analysing the burgeoning genre of Irish horror, Radley identifies a disruptive potential inherent in intersecting the representative systems of generic horror, national identity and national cinema. Deploying the psychoanalytic linguistic theories of Julia Kristeva, the essay interprets Irish horror as a semiotic force that enables a transformation of the dominant symbolic paradigms structuring Irish cinema.

Divisions between the visual and literary, between image and word, are deconstructed in Aintzane Legarreta Mentxaka's essay, which looks at visual practices in the literary form – the use of cinematic language (*mise en scène*, focus, cinematography) in printed language. Through an analysis of Kate O'Brien's modernist novel *Mary Lavelle* (1936), she considers the intersectional relationship between language and image as a queer intervention into both visual and literary practice, and positions this 'intermediality' as a political exercise aimed at rethinking aesthetic boundaries, and a way of mobilising 'hidden' or 'disguised' subtexts which run counter to the established narrative drive. Ultimately, she argues, the incorporation of cinematic language into *Mary Lavelle* is a device that contributes to the production of queer identity in the text, in addition to more generally configuring narrative form as queer.

Anne Mulhall deploys a paradigm of relationality in her analysis of the rebranding of two religious sites (Lough Derg and Krishna Island) in the early 2000s. Examining an assortment of visual texts (poster campaigns, fliers and marketing websites) in conjunction, Mulhall considers how their combined effects function to reposition the sites as therapeutic 'wellness' centres. While acknowledging the problematics indicative of late capitalist appropriations of eastern ideologies, Mulhall's analysis of the marketing documents reveal that the landscapes of Lough Derg and Krishna Island are not just representative sites of Western postmodernity transformed by Eastern ideologies; rather, they also signify the Celtic past and tradition. Through this, Mulhall makes the point that reading Irish landscape as having one singular meaning, as nationalist discourse tends to do, is necessarily disrupted in the contemporary period of globalisation, which has the effect of rendering multiple and contingent concepts such as 'tradition' and 'authenticity'.

Identity

The first two sections of the collection consider the visual text as a relational entity, and this final part continues an interest in borders and fluidity with essays that focus on representations of identity *within* the visual text of study. Colin Graham's essay analyses representations of modern identity in the work of Irish photographic artists Joe Duggan, Hannah Starkey and John Gerrard. Drawing on Adorno, he argues that all three artists, in different ways, reveal the vacuous category of identity in modern life, which is empty at the core. The illusion of identity, as represented in these photographs, is a marker of the modern self: a subject that is 'contingent' and internally divided, never able to realise its aspiration for coherent identity. Ultimately, this is an identity that traps the subject, fixing it in a repetitive and alienating desire for a sense of self that can never be achieved.

Claire Bracken's essay is also interested in constructions of modern identity, specifically in terms of gender. Examining actor Deirdre O'Kane's parts in two television series, *Paths to Freedom* (2000) and *Fergus's Wedding* (2002), she reads them as visual markers of post-feminist identity in Celtic Tiger Ireland, an identity that is deeply imbricated in capitalism and consumerism. Through an analysis of O'Kane's roles, Bracken argues that supposed post-feminist subjectivity is an empty category that fixes the feminine in its structures, structures that are maintained and regulated by late capitalist ideology. However, while the television series' critique of Celtic Tiger excess is both valid and worthy, the method is problematic, as the post-feminist woman functions as emblem of the negative face of contemporary Irish culture. In this respect, the feminist theories of Luce Irigaray are key, as the woman's body becomes appropriated as symbolic container for the representation of national concerns.

In a similar vein, Zélie Asava's essay on the intersecting contexts of race and gender considers the border trappings of identity, while also pointing to something more potentially fluid. She examines a new figure in Irish horror cinema – the mixed-race female heroine – through analyses of *Isolation* (Billy O'Brien, 2005) and *Boy Eats Girl* (Stephen Bradley, 2005). These two films, set in the context of the Celtic Tiger period, are considered, using various poststructuralist theories, in terms of their disruptions to fixed Irish national identity categories. However, Asava is cautious in her critique. While identifying the ethical potentiality of these two horror films, she also points to the way in which they display moments of racial stereotyping, thus signalling the power of established, containing norms to hauntingly return.

Jenny O'Connor's essay explores the hybrid category of becoming-woman in Neil Jordan's films, arguing that readings of Jordan's work have focused predominately on thematic issues such as nation, masculinity, and tradition versus modernity, with little examination of the philosophical nature of his work. To this end, the essay analyses *The Crying Game* (1992) and *Breakfast on Pluto* (2005), drawing on the neo-materialist philosophies of Gilles Deleuze and Félix Guattari, a strategy that facilitates an opening up of Jordan's films to a key concern of transformation, an exploration of 'becoming' in in-between spaces where change, rather than stasis, is the motivating factor. Shifting the terms of debate through and by which Jordan's films are read, O'Connor's consideration of the interstice also explores gender in this respect, as she makes the point that processes of change seem more available to male than to female bodies in the work.

Fintan Walsh's essay is also concerned with fluidity and identity, considering representations of the self in Lenny Abrahamson's films as a relational and coupling entity. Noting the absence of a dedicated treatment of sexuality in Irish film, his article seeks to counter this through an analysis of a 'queer representational aesthetic' in Lenny Abrahamson's two films *Adam & Paul* and *Garage*, which he reads with the theoretical work of Leo Bersani and Ulysse Dutoit. Walsh focuses on visual renderings of characters' material connections and couplings in the films, which articulate an alternative to normative structures of meaning, family and community. These configurations of relational selves create a 'partial signification' of the forgotten space of queerness in Irish culture, as well as enabling traces of its presence.

Positionings

Viewpoints follows on from, and is placed alongside, recent scholarship in Irish Studies that takes a holistic approach to Irish cultural representation and casts an interrogative eye on the discursive structures of the field itself. Works by Patricia Coughlan, Elizabeth Butler Cullingford, Colin Graham, Gerardine Meaney and Joseph Valente,[4] among others, have at their core a desire to complicate and disrupt established frameworks in the critical edifice of Irish studies. As Wanda Balzano, Anne Mulhall and Moynagh Sullivan perceptively note in their introduction to *Irish Postmodernisms and Popular*

Culture, the Field Day Project established a neo-Marxist and post-colonial approach as primary to Irish studies, which has led to a suspicion of theoretical paradigms that are outside these frames:

> Within this critique [. . .] it appears as if only certain theory can be legitimated, while other 'theories' are considered complicit with the corrupting influences of globalization itself. Although specifics are avoided in such denunciations, by a process of elimination it seems that what is in question are those versions of postmodernism, feminism and queer theory that have been influenced by psychoanalysis and poststructuralism.[5]

With this in mind, the essays here can be said to contribute to interventions in Irish cultural studies that seek to refashion, rethink and reimagine. By way of recourse to a range of theoretical positions that include feminism, psychoanalysis, phenomenology, philosophy and queer theory, *Viewpoints* presents multiple and variegated perspectives on Irish texts, culture, society and life.

With articles on theories of visualisation and early Irish photography, adaptation and memory in the diasporic image, identities in Irish photographic art, the advertising of therapeutic 'wellness' sites, as well as essays which read and focus Irish film and television 'differently', this book brings new critical readings to how we 'see' Irish culture. The voiceover of the Discover Ireland advertisement mentioned above advises us, 'Searching for a really fun place to get away from it all? Well good news, you're already there.' While the ad on some levels maintains a simplistic binary between old and new, it also effects a re-energised, re-articulated and, above all, re-animated vision of Ireland, open to different representative perspectives. Likewise, this collection sees Ireland as an image in process, a complex site of plural identities, traditions in flux, and dialogic exchange between past, present and future. The essays in this collection provide a diverse range of theoretical perspectives on this image in process, each inviting a new point of view.

DISCOURSE

Chapter One

TERRA INFIRMA: THE TERRITORY OF THE VISIBLE AND THE WRITING OF IRELAND'S VISUAL CULTURE

Justin Carville

The physical object is converted into a sign. Without ceasing to be part of material reality, such an object, to some degree, reflects and refracts another reality.[1]

In this essay, I want to address something of the anxiety surrounding the visual in Irish cultural production. This apprehension towards how to attend to the arena of the visual appears to have emerged over the last two decades in a range of literature on the subject covering everything from art history and cultural studies to contemporary art criticism and popular culture.[2] I employ the term 'anxiety' here with a degree of trepidation, cognisant of the fact that the ever-increasing body of literature on Irish visual culture suggests that the visual has become firmly rooted within scholarly analyses of Irish cultural heritage. It is not that I want to argue that there is an identifiable apprehension towards visual culture within the literature itself. It is more the case that the emergence of a sub-discipline of Irish visual culture appears to be a troubling one for the traditional disciplinary boundaries of the academy.[3] Throughout a number of studies of visual material in and of Ireland, there appears to be uncertainty of where and how to position visual culture within the broader field of cultural production. This is not, in itself, a cause for concern, let alone academic analysis. The most insightful discussions of visual representations and image-objects have often been those that have grappled the most with understanding and coming to terms with the sometimes baffling complexities of the visual in all its divergent forms. What is worth pursuing further, however, are

13

the disciplinary positionings and theoretical anxieties that circulate across the arena of what is defined either loosely or explicitly as *Irish visual culture.*[4]

What I intend to foreground in the discussion here is that the visual field of Irish cultural history has become a site through which contending theoretical perspectives have sought to wrestle with the parameters of the subject of their inquiry. The historical methods and theoretical frameworks of art history, Irish historiography and literary and cultural studies have all been mobilised in the establishment of an identifiable terrain of Irish visual culture with its own series of historically and culturally legible vernacular landmarks. Some of the more theoretically informed disciplines, particularly those that have combined the emergent methods of visual studies with postcolonial theory, have raised some significant and compelling questions about the place and role of the visual within Irish culture.[5] As I will suggest below, however, much of the literature on the place of the visual in Ireland has often overlooked some of the more nuanced relations between the materiality of Irish visual culture and the spaces across which the visual operates. It is these spaces – geographical, institutional, disciplinary, legal and economic – and their attendant discourses that have shaped not only the material forms of the visual in Irish culture, but also their circulation within and across different spheres of social life.

In what follows, I want to work towards a reading of a mundane example of late nineteenth-century anthropological photography to explore the social relations embedded within the materiality of Irish visual culture and the spaces across which image objects are distributed. The photograph, part of the ethnographer Alfred Cort Haddon's collection of Irish ethnography, emerged out of the incorporation of photography into the methods of colonial anthropology.[6] My interest in this particular photograph is how such an aesthetically dull image has the potential to reveal the complex networks of visual experience located within Irish visual culture. Before discussing this image, however, I want to turn to some existing discussions of visual culture in Ireland – from a range of differing discourses and methodologies addressed, to a diverse range of image objects and aesthetic practices – to identify some of the anxieties circulating around what constitutes a culturally specific Irish visual culture.

The paradox of Irish Visual Culture

The aim of this essay is a rather modest one, and the questions identified as appropriate to the task at hand have been conceived as the
most direct and functional for the scope of the subject of inquiry. Yet
the more uncomplicated the aims and questions posed to the field of
Irish visual culture have been, the more complex the visual objects
the questions are asked of appear to become. These questions are:
what is Irish visual culture? If it can be identified and defined as an
arena of material image objects, aesthetic practices, pictorial representations, discursive positionings and subjective ocular experiences,
then where is Irish visual culture? Or rather from where does Irish
visual culture emerge and to whom is it addressed? If it can be situated and located, across which spheres of Irish social life does the
visual circulate? And if we are to embrace visual culture studies as
not only a discipline that is concerned with representations and
image-objects but also with the material and technological subjectivities of vision, visuality and cultural practices of looking, can we ask:
do the Irish see differently?

These are deliberately broad questions proposed with a certain
degree of mischievousness. There is of course an Irish visual culture
in the same way that we could conceivably identify an American,
Japanese, Malaysian, Spanish or even a global visual culture for that
matter. Indeed Nicholas Mirzoeff, the most prominent advocate of
'visual culture' as a radical field of study of visual objects and experiences, has, in his early definition of the field, conflated visual
culture with the globalisation of the image world. For Mirzoeff, the
term visual culture designates an emergent academic discipline, or
what he argues might be properly defined as a 'tactic', as well as the
arena of the visual materials that it proposes to study. Within the
context of this definition, he has argued that it is precisely the globalised experience of visual media within postmodern everyday life
that characterises visual culture rather than the regional specificities
or national aesthetic practices of pictorial representation.[7] This
admittedly singular definition of visual culture would appear to be
contra to the aims of much literature on the visual within Ireland
that has addressed itself to the historical and cultural specificities of
Irish visual culture, or indeed to its absences. Irish visual culture as
an emerging sub-discipline of arts, humanities and social sciences

has become a bounded field circumscribed by the real and imaginary borders erected through theoretical models of identity politics addressed to the complexities of nation, race and gender. What is striking here are the problems that arise when the exclusiveness and inclusiveness of such criteria are put into practice. Who is to say, for example, that American, Spanish, Japanese or Malaysian visual culture is not as much part of Ireland's visual culture as indigenous cultural forms, not only through the many migrant communities who live within the nation's borders who access and distribute visual material through satellite broadcasts and printed material culture from their own homelands but also through such diverse material objects and discursive visual practices as commercial television drama, Manga comics, terracotta tiles and religious ceremonies and artefacts.[8]

Within recent discussions of visual representations of Ireland, however, a more polarised approach has emerged that posits two paradoxical conceptions of the territory of Irish visual culture. One suggests the formation of a sub-discipline of *Irish* visual culture studies, the other position (equally valid in its pronouncements concerning the place of the visual in Irish social life) proposes that Ireland does not in fact have a differentiated visual culture of its own.[9] On the one hand, then, there is an increasing number of published articles, specially themed journal issues, conferences, exhibitions and edited books which address Irish visual culture. Some are more rooted in the history of Irish arts, others with Irish cinema and popular cultural forms of advertising and tele-visual drama. These various publications and exhibitions, taken together in their entirety, would appear to suggest an emerging consensus that the visual is an important sphere of Irish cultural life worthy of scholarly attention. On the other hand, there is an expanding body of literature that argues that there exists several considerable historical lacunae in Irish visual culture. Indeed some commentators have gone as far as to suggest that Ireland has historically been a culture which has valued textual literacy over the visual, and does not have a visual heritage which might be qualified as being culturally differentiated. The paradox here lies in the mission to identify Irish visual culture as a distinct field of study bounded by geographic and ideological questions of nation and race, while at the same time admonishing visual cultural production for its gaps and lack of aesthetic specificity. In the introduction to *Visualizing Ireland,* for example, Adele M. Dalsimer and Vera Kreilkamp bemoan both the lack of scholarship by historians of what they term the 'Irish pictorial arts' and the considerable absence of artistic production from Irish cultural life.[10] In the same volume, one commentator, noting that Ireland's introduction to the European aesthetics of the Renaissance was interrupted by the process of colonialism, remarks that not only does 'Ireland have very little to show of graphic art from the middle ages to the second half of the seventeenth century, but there was not even much of any quality until a century later'.[11] Elsewhere another commentator has suggested that Ireland is not as visually literate a nation as it is verbally, reinforcing Maire de Paor's contention that 'the absence of peasant visual art is quite striking. Native Irish culture survived in words and in traditional music.'[12]

This last observation is one that I want to explore further in the discussion of Haddon's ethnographic photograph below; for what such statements demonstrate is a myopic approach to Irish visual culture, a constriction of the visual field to aesthetic production. Such narrowing of the territory of visual culture forecloses upon the visual field as site of cultural exchange, open to opposing practices of looking and visualising, focusing instead on the poetics of the image object as a marker for the modality of visual literacy. What is implied here is that the indigenous Irish, specifically the peasant culture of oral and aural communication, is visually primitive. Indigenous orality is identified as an event-based culture in which, as Walter Benjamin observed, 'memory is the epic faculty par excellence'.[13] Visual culture, on the other hand, is designated as object based which externalises mnemonic experience, objectifying the visual field through a process of aesthetic codification into atomised image objects. What I want to suggest through a reading of Haddon's photograph is that the visual field is itself an event-based culture, open to alternative practices of looking and visualising, and contending occular experiences, which have the potential to create space rather than myopically constrict the terrain of Irish visual culture.

The literary and cultural theorist Gibbons has made perhaps the most interesting observation on this issue. Writing in a book review in the mid-1980s, Gibbons remarked that 'the absence of a visual tradition in Ireland, equal in stature to its more powerful literary counterpart, has meant that the dominant images of Ireland have, for the most part, emanated from outside the country, or have been produced at home with an eye on the foreign (or tourist) market'.[14] Gibbons' admittedly brief remarks on the origins of representations of Ireland are deliberately pointed, drawing attention, as they do, to the legacy of colonial practices of visualisation and their incorporation into the postcolonial visual practices of commercial tourism. Although written over two decades ago, his remarks touch on two key critical issues that are at stake in the recent formation of a disciplinary field of Irish visual culture – firstly, the spaces and terrains out of and within which visual representations of Ireland circulate and, secondly, the place of visual culture studies within the academy. Although it may not have been the intention of his cursory remarks on the existence or lack of an indigenous visual culture, Gibbons' statement on the absence of what he terms a visual 'tradition' reveals the extent to which popular or everyday forms of visual culture have been largely overlooked within the broader field of Irish studies, and, as one recent commentator has observed, a tendency to favour a canon of visual art that is perceived to be illustrative of postcolonial theory.[15]

What is most striking about Gibbons' brief remarks is the recognition of the fractured territories of colonial and postcolonial visual cultures of Ireland, and his identification that the supposed bounded fields of vision within a national context are in fact elastic and porous, continually open to transgression and the collision of cultural politics. The terrain across which the visual operates, the sphere of social life in and through which visual materials circulate and distribute culturally meaningful practices of visualising and looking, are not passive bounded territories that circumscribe and contain particular visual practices. They are positional spaces from which vision is projected, colliding and coming into sometimes violent conflict with oppositional aesthetic ideologies and visual practices.[16] The detractors to the concept of an identifiable field of Irish visual culture briefly discussed above, however problematic their various positions may be, and however dated their statements may now appear, are significant in this context not least because the idea, the concept, the formation of an academic discipline of Irish visual culture that their collective work actively participates in forming, is grounded on specific geographic, national and ethnic parameters, within which visual representations are assessed, evaluated and written about. They are especially significant to the concerns of this essay, I would suggest, because they raise questions about the perspectives and disciplinary positions through and from which Irish visual culture is addressed. All writing is from a position – disciplinary, political, theoretical, autobiographical and reflexive – and it is clear from the examples quoted above that Irish visual culture is to be written from the perspective of the aesthetic discourses and ideologies of artistic movements and practices, without the slightest acknowledgement of the irony that had the aesthetic philosophy of the Renaissance entered Ireland unfettered, it would not in itself have brought about an indigenous Irish visual culture.[17] What such arguments overlook is that the introduction of an aesthetic philosophy such as the Renaissance into Ireland did not and would not have simply become acculturated into an Irish visual culture. Rather aesthetic philosophies and ideologies become altered and remoulded as a new cultural form through collision with indigenous cultural politics.

David Brett's development of Gibbons' remarks on the absence of a visual tradition, for example, is to suggest, through Barbara O'Connor's 'Myths and Mirrors' thesis, that 'the aesthetic values of the picturesque were internalised by Irish nationalism, which then projected them as ruralist policies during the Free State period'.[18] Charting the material cultural processes embedded in the clash between colonial and postcolonial aesthetic practices, Brett's discussion of the cultural politics and aesthetic ideology of the picturesque and the sublime remains one of the most thoughtful interventions into the debate on Irish visual culture. However, by limiting the terrain of the visual to the aesthetic and its attending ideologies, Brett provides a very narrow spatial configuration of Irish visual culture which has been subjected firstly to colonisation and then a cultural imperialism from which it cannot escape. The possibility of resistance and an oppositional visual politics is closed off because of the disciplinary perspective from which Ireland's visual culture is addressed, which contains within it an already prescribed colonial model of aesthetics. As Homi Bhabha was to complain of Edward Said, it is as if 'colonial power and discourse is possessed entirely by the colonizer',[19] what remains is a contracted model of Irish visual culture as a static field rather than an arena of conflicting perspectives and social struggle.

To move beyond this conception of Irish visual culture requires an epistemological shift not only of the conception of culture, but

also what constitutes the territory of the visible. To address epistemological shift, I want to extend both Gibbons' and Brett's
identification of visual culture as transgressive of boundaries and
borders, and as the space of collision and conflict, to a more
mundane sphere of social life which requires a vocabulary outside of
aesthetic discourse. From this perspective, I want to examine a case
study from late nineteenth-century anthropology where visual
culture is more grounded in social and subjective experiences of
practices and technologies of visual representation rather than aesthetic artistic production. In particular, I want to attend to what is
implied and explicitly stated in the examples cited above, that is, that
Ireland and the Irish were or are visually primitive or illiterate. In
exploring this supposed visual primitivism, I want to shift the debate
about Irish visual culture away from the pictorial arts and aesthetic
practices to a broader field of vision and visuality incorporating not
only visual technologies and material representations but also
textual, oral and everyday forms through which cultures have been
trained or socialised into looking at the world around them. In transgressing the myopic perspective of the territory of the visual as an
object-based culture, I want to suggest that everyday social encounters embedded in the material conditions of visual culture have the
potential to rupture preconceived conceptions of Ireland's supposed
visual primitivism. This requires re-conceptualising visual culture as
being as much an event-based culture as an object-based culture, a
space through which the visual field is ascribed agency and open to
contending ocular positionings and perceptual experiences.
Haddon's example of late nineteenth-century anthropological photography, a seemingly static visual exchange arrested by the
technology of the camera, is an example of how the visualising of
culture is open to transformative readings which may open up the
field of Irish visual culture rather than close it down.

Haddon's photograph and the excess of vision

Amongst the zoologist-turned-anthropologist Alfred Cort Haddon's
lantern slide collection of Irish ethnology, held at Cambridge
University's Museum of Anthropology and Archaeology, is a
photograph taken in the early 1890s depicting a seated man being
measured using the Bertillonage Method of craniotomy. The

Fig. 1.1 Alfred Cort Haddon Collection, 'Bertillonage Method, Ireland'
c. 1890.

photograph depicts the man being measured in the midst of several onlookers, including two Royal Irish Constabulary policemen, one of whom is writing in a notebook as he looks towards the camera's lens (Fig. 1.1).[20] Amongst the onlookers, several watch the spectacle of the measurement of the man's cranium, while others look towards the technological apparatus that is about to transform the spectacle of which they are part into the photo-chemical trace of the photograph.

Named after its inventor, the French policeman Alphonse Bertillon, the Bertillonage method is a form of anthropometry (the measurement of the human body), and was incorporated into physical anthropology from the late nineteenth century. Bertillon and his English counterpart Francis Galton combined anthropometry with photography in the 1880s, which was adapted as a rigorous method of visual anthropology for surveys of racial types across colonial nations through to the 1920s.[21] This particular photograph is unlikely to have been used as visual anthropological evidence, and its inclusion in Haddon's lantern slide collection of Irish ethnology, which he used for public lectures and anthropological instruction, was to visually illustrate his various anecdotes on the ruses employed to obtain photographs and anthropometric measurements of what he frequently referred to as native 'specimens'.[22] This is an example of how the visual is never experienced in ocular isolation but is rather 'braided', to use W.J.T. Mitchell's concept, with other oral and aural sensory experiences, as well as with language.[23] Projected in institutional and public spaces and accompanied by oral lectures of scientific merit or hyberbolic anecdote, lantern slides combined the static photograph with the dissolving flickering projection of the image in conjunction with auditory stimuli of orators. These extra-visual sensory experiences, and supplementary discourses outside the frame of the image, are important to understanding the agency of photography in producing meaning, but what I want to concentrate on in semiotic parlance is what is 'indexically' documented by the photograph.[24]

Haddon's photograph, on the surface, would appear in Foucauldian terms to demonstrate the disciplinary power of those 'apparatus' (in this example not just the discursive institutions of colonial administration, but also the material technologies of photography and callipers) 'in which the techniques that make it possible to see induce effects of power, and in which, conversely, the means of coercion make those on whom they are applied clearly visible'.[25] In visual studies, the prevailing discourse has interpreted similar images precisely within such a social power model.[26] However, Haddon's photograph reveals much that betrays the disciplinary paradigm of colonial anthropological photography, not least because through its ocular registers it renders visible what Foucault stated was exercised through its 'invisibility'.[27] The indexicality of Haddon's photograph lies not in its causality and modality of static 'realism'; rather what the photograph evidences is an encounter. To paraphrase Roland Barthes, it is evidence that what took place in front of the camera actually happened, and without which there would be no photograph.[28] The 'what happened' before the cameras lens, the performative aspect of the taking of the photograph, is what is significant in the context of the territory of the visual in Irish culture. If the photograph is an indexical trace of anything, it is not of the people whose corporeal physiognomy has been

transcribed photo-chemically onto the deadening surface of the photographic negative, but of an encounter between the photographer,
the photographed subject and the technological apparatus of the
camera. More importantly to the complexities of Irish visual culture
that I wish to tease out here, it is an encounter that is deeply
embedded within a perceptual field that is multi-dimensional in its
trajectories of embodied and technologically disembodied gazes.

There is much to the visual revelation of Haddon's ethnographic
photograph. The process through which the physical act of calibra-
tion is converted into the inscription of ethnographic data, which is to
be later transformed into the textual form of anthropological methods
of observation, is depicted in the photographically silent representation of information exchange between the ethnographer and
policeman who is engaged in the institutionalised practice of textual
'inscription' into his notebook.[29] The physical and ocular positioning
of the men, itself establishing the gendering of the perceptual field,
demonstrates the multi-perspectival experience of the photographic
act. Within the context of anthropological photography, Haddon's
lantern slide is unusual precisely because it depicts the social
encounter of the photographic act which was frequently erased
through the photo-mechanical flattening of social space in physical
anthropology into the mono-view of the 'type' photograph (Fig. 1.2).[30]

In the peculiar logic of photographic realism, the 'type' photograph functioned to conceal through its technical codification of the
body as a mute 'specimen' the subjective ocular experiences of the
photographic encounter. The anthropologists Martha Macintyre
and Maureen Mackenzie have argued that the physical proximity of
photographer and subject is an analogue of broader cultural differences, with portraits of subjects at a distance mirroring the cultural
chasm between the ethnographic photographer and the ethnograph-
ically observed subject-turned-object.[31] In Victorian and Edwardian
anthropology, however, it was the intimate proximity between photographer and subject that was deployed as a technical code to
collapse any trace of a social encounter. The 'type' photograph was
discursively positioned within physical anthropology as evidence of
a social sphere devoid of cultural exchange. In effect, what was con-
noted, to use Barthes' description of photographic communication,
was the photograph's denotative status.[32] The technical gaze of the
camera in turn required in its corollary the dispassionate gaze of the

Fig. 1.2 An example of the 'Type' photograph. Charles R. Browne, from
'Ethnography of Mullet' c. 1895.

scientific specialist. The 'type' photograph was established as a scientific document through the systematic ability of the photograph to
exhibit a particular kind of technical information, and for the viewer
to read that precise scientific information from within the frame of
the photograph. As Peter Galison and Lorraine Datson have demonstrated, photography was merely one of a number of visual
empirical practices that strove to repress the 'wilful intervention of
the artists-author' in modern science, the mechanical objectivity of
the camera becoming the idealised reflection of the disciplined eye of
the scientific observer.[33]

The position of the dispassionate gaze of the photographic document within the arena of Irish visual culture would appear to be at
the polar end of the aesthetic spectrum to the subjective ocular

experiences of the picturesque and artistic movements such as the Renaissance that have preoccupied much of the literature on the visual discussed above. The lowly document, despite having its own complex history, circulates within a very different cultural sphere to that which has been the preoccupation of Irish studies as an academic discipline.[34] Although the type portrait has its own poetic structure, its epistemological value was grounded in the dull, repetitive abstraction of human physiognomy into the geometrical photo-chemical form of the photographic image. The anthropological photographic document is the very antithesis of the aesthetic ideology of the picturesque that has dominated much of the discussions of the existence or absence of a differentiated Irish visual culture. The disjuncture created between the choice of these two image types is deliberate, because despite their obvious pictorial differences in terms of composition, codes, use and ideology, both were subordinated to a model of vision that privileged a static, monocular gaze, reducing all visual experience to a single point of view. Martin Jay, drawing from the Foucauldian model of 'regimes of truth', has identified Cartesian perspectivalism, based on Euclidean geometry, as the dominant 'scopic regime' of modernity. This was not simply a model of pictorial representation, but an abstract philosophy embedded in a scientific worldview threaded throughout religion, politics and an emerging system of global capitalism.[35] Although much has been written which is critical of the Cartesian model of vision, I want to abstract from it this one aspect of the valorisation of an absolute, single, disembodied point of view, for this Cartesian principle has its textual equivalence in the writing of Ireland's visual culture.

Haddon's photograph and the painterly renderings of the picturesque both share the codification of two-dimensional pictorial space as a window onto the world. It is a model of vision that presupposes a fixed, monocular gaze across a static, visual plane. Vision, if it has any political or cultural agency, is perceived to be monologic, in the eye of the beholder as it were. The writing of Ireland's visual culture, in its perception of the historical colonisation of the arena of the visible and the attendant lacuna in Irish aesthetic modernism and the avant-garde, has adopted a similar monologic perspective. Ireland's visual culture has been contained within a model that positions the territory of the visual as a static field of representations to be viewed through a detached optics that privileges a homogenous vantage point, a uniform point of view from which no oppositional or alternative visual experience can be tracked. Returning to Haddon's photograph of the man being measured by ethnographers, an alternative conception of the terrain of the visual might be identified: an immersive field, open rather than closed to oppositional and contending perspectives, subjective gazes and 'braided' sensory experiences.[36] The territory of the visible in Irish culture I am suggesting here might be something akin to Gilles Deleuze and Félix Guattari's re-articulation of the map as 'open and connectable in all its dimensions; [. . .] detachable, reversible, susceptible to constant modification'.[37]

While Haddon's photograph may at first appear to conform to the monological model of visual culture, I want to suggest that its photo-mechanical trace of the visual field as event has the potential to open it up to alternative reading, one that proposes to move beyond the myopic concept of Irish visual culture as constricted to a static arena of image objects codified by aesthetic ideology. Haddon's photograph, with its multiplicity of visual registers between the men and the camera, the ethnographer and ethnographic subject, and indeed the Cartesian constructed 'observer' and the photograph, projects visual perspectives and lines of sight within and beyond the frame of the image.[38] Despite the physically restrictive geometric frame of the photograph there is an 'excess of seeing', an excess of visibility that is present in every visual form and experience no matter how carefully composed the image may be.[39] The arena of the visual, the assemblage of material images objects, aesthetic ideologies, subjective and technological gazes and practices of looking that shift across the territory of the visible of Irish culture that Haddon's photograph illustrates, might be identified as forming the visual equivalent of what the Russian literary theorist Mikhail Bakhtin identified as 'heteroglossia', a poly-vocal space of conflicting visual perspectives and experiences. Heteroglossia was, for Bakhtin, a 'double-voiced discourse. It serves two speakers at the same time and expresses two different intentions: the direct intention of the character who is speaking, and the refracted intention of the author'.[40] Even that lowly photographic document, the anthropological 'type' portrait, includes within its ocular encounter between the technological apparatus of the camera and the subject an excess of vision. The seemingly static, mute gaze of the ethnographic subject staring out of the frame of the photograph had access to a visual horizon that the photographer and observer of the photograph did not, an excess of seeing, knowing and possessing inaccessible to others. As Bakhtin was to put it succinctly, 'As we look at each other, two different worlds are reflected in the pupils of our eyes.'[41]

Unlike the literature discussed above which seeks to restrict Irish visual culture to normative classifications of artistic styles, genres and aesthetic philosophies, identifying the alternative perspectives through which the visual field is experienced may allow for Irish visual culture to emerge as a fluid space in and through which dominant aesthetic ideologies are challenged and re-wrought. Moreover, such an approach challenges the paradigm of a visual primitivism in Ireland's colonial culture, instead ascribing agency to the transcription of vision embedded in the materiality of the image which transgresses the constricted boundaries of the terrain of Ireland's expanding visual field. Although the cultural politics of the visual outlined here are grounded within a specific reading of the photographic image, and a particular disciplinary model of anthropological photography for that matter, the displacement of the epicentre of the terrain of Irish visual culture I am proposing can potentially be identified in even the most abstract aesthetic ideologies of pictorial representation and visual experience. A useful analogy might be to envisage the large crowds who observed the religious, theatrical visual spectacles of the Eucharistic Congress held in Dublin in 1932; some from the streets, others from rooftops and bedroom windows.[42] Although the official pictorial record mobilised the photographic image to shape popular memory of the experience of the event, each individual, occupying a unique position within the visual field as event, had access to an excess of vision that the others did not. The visual spectacle of the single event experienced simultaneously by individuals who occupied different ocular vantage points was perceived differently within the same field of vision. As the sociologist Eamonn Slater has demonstrated, even the hegemony of the colonial aesthetics of the picturesque which physically and pictorially enclosed the territory of the visible in Irish culture had within it simultaneous oppositional 'visual' perspectives which manifested themselves in the orality of the indigenous Irish peasant.[43] The territory of the visible which much literature on Irish visual culture has striven to define and circumscribe is thus not a uniform, static space; it is a constantly shifting field of contending perspectives, oppositional gazes and 'deterritorializing lines of sight'.[44] If there is a 'pictorial turn' in Irish history, literary and cultural studies, to invoke Mitchell's now infamous term, the positions from which the visual is written need not only to be cognisant of this *terra infirma* of Ireland's visual culture, but actively contribute to its resistance to be bounded within the real and imaginary borders of disciplinary classification.[45] As Mitchell notes, what characterises a pictorial turn is not the existence of a dominant account of visual representation within a disciplinary field, but that the visual forms 'a point of peculiar friction and discomfort across a broad range of intellectual inquiry'.[46] For Irish visual culture to maintain its 'vitality and dynamism and the capacity for further development', to borrow Vološinov's description of the consequences of the multiaccentuality of the sign, its writing across various academic disciplines needs to see within the visual not another possible answer to questions of identity, but a problem never to be solved.[47]

Chapter Two

WORLD-MAKING IN THADDEUS O'SULLIVAN'S *THE WOMAN WHO MARRIED CLARK GABLE*

Cheryl Herr

I

Although Irish film has been the subject of over a dozen books and a great many articles, and although *The Woman Who Married Clark Gable* (1985) was nominated for a BAFTA Film Award for Best Short Film in 1986, this little gem has received almost no commentary apart from the initial responses in the canonical *Cinema and Ireland* (1988). There, both Kevin Rockett and Luke Gibbons provide economical readings of *The Woman Who Married Clark Gable* (*TWWMCG*) and these interpretations have remained, in print at least, unremarked upon over the years. In this essay, I argue that this received interpretation of *TWWMCG* – a primarily psychoanalytic reading characteristic of the period in which *Cinema and Ireland* was written – can be usefully supplemented by a reading grounded in the social practices displayed in the film. What is at stake here is the camera's focalising of a socially embedded way of being.

Rockett briefly summarises the narrative content of O'Sullivan's adaptation of a story by Seán O'Faoláin:

> [. . .] there is a stylish and witty representation of an Englishman (Bob Hoskins) and his Irish wife (Brenda Fricker). Set in Dublin in the late 1930s the childless couple's unstated oppression is displaced on to the woman's fantasy of her husband as Clark Gable in *San Francisco*. But fantasy is what it remains until the husband shaves off his newly-acquired moustache and they return to their humdrum artisanal class existence. By then her guilt at her inability to have children has been painfully exposed.[1]

Rockett thus places the woman at the centre of the drama and specifies the couple's problem as fundamentally owned by the wife, whose name is Mary.

For Gibbons, the thrust of O'Sullivan's short film is its depiction of the cinema as a 'magical world' that offers the wife, Mary, 'both the promise and the denial of a release from the constraints of Irish family life',[2] Gibbons explains:

> Mary's marriage to George [. . .] an Englishman, has come to a point where a gulf has opened up between them on account of her inability to live up to an idealised self-image of motherhood. [. . .] A night out at the cinema watching Clark Gable in *San Francisco* provides an outlet for her unfulfilled desires. [. . .] [T]he dividing line between the imaginary and the real becomes [. . .] problematic for Mary when she notices a resemblance between George (who has just grown a moustache) and the famous screen idol. Carried away by this 'discovery', the emotional plenitude of life on the screen spills over in her everyday existence, acting, as Christian Metz would have it, as a 'psychical substitute' for her maternal desire.[3]

Both Gibbons and Rockett, then, construe the trajectory of the storyline as guided by Mary's failure to have children and by the assumption that the couple's presumed infertility is Mary's fault. More recent commentators on Irish cinema and on O'Sullivan – such as Martin McLoone and Lance Pettitt – have mentioned *TWWMCG*[4] but have not in any way disturbed this psychoanalytic interpretation by way of a sceptical feminism.

Further, to my knowledge no film critic has returned in print to the source narrative, a short story by Seán O'Faoláin published in 1948.[5] This story usefully captures what was then a previous generation's foibles, and thus creates a screen on and against which O'Sullivan's vision is projected. While O'Faoláin prompts the reader to take note of the couple's lack of children, he does not position that circumstance as the rationale for the story or even the central issue in Mary's life. Instead, O'Faoláin sets out Mary's overriding desire for romance and excitement, a yearning that Irish culture in the 1930s seemed to her ill-equipped to satisfy. The story re-imagines Mary as she would have been had she inhabited Moscow and a Chekhov play:

> She would have said, 'I do not know whether life is angry with me because I do not live it, or whether I am angry with life because it will not let me live. Ivan Ivanovitch, for God's sake, meet me tonight by the frog-pond and tell me what is this pain in my heart.' And Ivan would have met her and told her in very simple terms.[6]

In this version of a wife's longing for adventurous lovemaking, Mary is ignorant of the nature of her problem but clear about her painful longing for something more. The narrator then strongly suggests that Mary's lack of romance is inherent in the way of being and the world that Mary inhabits:

> [. . .] she lived in Dublin (South Circular Road, small red house, red terrace, small garden, near the Old Woman's Hostel – full – and Kilmainham Jail – disused). She nagged her husband virtuously when she should have got drunk with him and poured her virtue down the drains. She went twice a week to the movies, hoovered the house until she had all the pile sucked off the carpets, bought a new knick-knack for the mantelpiece every week, washed the dog, polished the windows, slept after lunch, read *Chit Chat* and *Winifred's Weekly*, went for a walk, and then sat around waiting for her husband to come back from the job.[7]

The absolutely routine way that George and Mary live in the solemn, banal and somewhat shabby Dublin of the 1930s is laid out in wry detail as O'Faoláin sets us up for the small contretemps that emerges when George and Mary see the Hollywood film *San Francisco* (Woodbridge S. Van Dyke, 1936).

O'Faoláin is known for incisive portrayals of individuals in conflict with one or another of the repressive forces that he attributed to Irish society. However remote a given narrative voice may seem, a reader can detect various discourses converging in that voice, from homiletic rhythms to pedagogic repetitions and parental remonstrance. Priests, teachers and parents reinforce one another in delivering instructions about how to live and what to do. Underlying all such instructions – the givens of the squinting windows and the social superego – we can detect the cadences of indigenous storytelling, the give and take of intimate conversation, the careful staging of the naughty joke, and the nearly silenced heart cries of unformulated human desire.

The subtleties of O'Faoláin's characterisations stand in strong contrast to Van Dyke's *San Francisco*, which was nominated for five academy awards in 1936. This Hollywood spectacular was admired for portraying the famous earthquake of 1906 with stunning sincerity and bold special effects. Buildings collapse, the ground splits, the urban infrastructure sinks while seismic shifts and uncontainable fires prevail. Against the grain of everyday actions in 'The Woman Who Married Clark Gable', *San Francisco* helps its audience to visualise the totalising implosion of ordinary life that the earthquake represents. With the destruction of the city clearly in view from the beginning of the movie, Van Dyke tells the love story of conservative, small-town girl Mary and unscrupulous, irreligious Barbary Coast saloon operator Blackie. Blackie is overwhelmed and profoundly changed by the earthquake's effects. After days of searching for Mary in the rubble and ruin, he finds her at a Red Cross tent and offers up a prayer of thanksgiving.

In O'Faoláin's fiction, Mary, who at first disliked her husband's moustache, suddenly fancies the accoutrement. Simultaneously, she finds her sexual attraction to her husband returning to earlier pathways: 'For about two weeks they were happier than at any time since their honeymoon, in that little redbrick house on the South Circular Road.'[8] But George begins to be concerned when Mary asks him to see *San Francisco* repeatedly and wants him to perform activities depicted in the movie, places a picture of Gable on their parlour wall, and asks him to wear the turn-of-the-century cravat and three-cornered collar that the actor wore in the film. All too soon, George becomes unhappy with the collar, a distaste that Mary interprets – and this is the crux of the story – as *his* awareness 'that she was deceiving him with Mr Gable'.[9] O'Faoláin's Mary undergoes a split in behaviour so that she inhabits (that is, does things appropriate to) both *San Francisco* and the South Circular Road. O'Faoláin deftly displays Mary's ability to carry out behaviours characteristic of her social group in Dublin and also those that she has recently learned from studying the silver screen.

When, in distress, Mary consults her parish priest about whether her double living situation is sinful, he indicates that 'there could be no objection to her deciding that she was living with this Mr Mark Cable'. However, he counsels that she must always keep in view that the chief end of marriage is 'the bearing of children' and that 'what we call Love is, naturally, secondary to this great end'.[10] Strikingly, Mary seems oblivious to this nudge in the direction of mothering, and the narrator's mention of an earlier occasion when Mary had thought herself pregnant is the only indication in the story that her restlessness may result from her fears that she is infertile. The story's resolution therefore depends on George's actions. Throwing the collar into the canal and stopping by his barber's for a shave, George returns home and presents himself to his wife as a sort of new-born, upon which she faints, comes to, and returns to her former ways. O'Faoláin writes a fractured-fairy-tale conclusion to the story: 'They lived unhappily ever after in complete marital satisfaction.'[11] In a way that has been shown to be workable, if not ideal, George *is* her child, and his rebirth completes Mary within the given life-world of the story.

II

O'Sullivan brings O'Faoláin's story to the screen as a meditation on the phenomenology of social practices and the world-making potential of film. The first departure from O'Faoláin is immediately evident. Unlike the short story, *TWWMCG* opens in a pub where George, a British man living and working in Dublin, chats with his workmates in the snug. The first close-up shot shows George's beer, waiting by the shutter, and of George's face receiving this secular communion. We immediately learn that George is not a Catholic; he is, as he states, 'a non-conformist'. More important, when he orders his bitter, George fails to offer a round to his workmates. O'Sullivan's scrutiny of George as a misfit in the midst of fixed masculine pub-ways continues throughout the film. Whether at home or at work, George is almost always slightly thrown off by his failure to sit seamlessly in the workings of his corner of Dublin.

From the pub, the camera exits to the misty streets and follows George as he rides his bicycle homeward. At the back garden, a neighbour's lonely child waits with his football and calls out, 'Gi' us a kick.' George happily complies with some close-quarters footie until the boy's mother unmistakably issues her final demand that the child come in. George looks serious; in the mother's voice is not just exasperation but a desire to keep her son from fraternising with this pagan. Reassuming an adult demeanour, George says, 'You better go.' Towards the end of the film, there is a parallel scene in which George himself, having decided to forego his Gable lookalike status, closes the garden gate in the boy's face. This action signals his determination to stay within the known boundaries of the 1930s Irish everyday as lived by adults of his gender, class and occupation.

Another recurrent scene places George by the fireside across from Mary, as she does some darning. No part of their bodies breaks the frame; they are completely held in medium close-up. George notices that Mary looks tired, and she agrees that she feels fatigued, but she demurs when George suggests taking a stroll: 'You know how much I have to do.' Mary's internal script demands that the woman of the house is always busy at her work, that the true adult female takes responsibility for the home. Except for her preoccupation with films, Mary adheres to a strict domestic schedule. At this juncture, however, an otherwise refreshing stroll will not meet her needs, but nor does her bit of fireside mending. The next day, as always, she attends early mass and then turns to her dusting, vacuuming and other housework. There is nothing in her life for the camera to show except her daily practices. So it is that at one point O'Sullivan lets us watch Mary brushing her teeth while George literally makes conversation by telling her a stale joke. George's day is equally defined: he shaves before breakfast, compliments Mary on her meals, and then spends the day shaving excess paraffin off the machinery in the candle factory where he works. In many ways, George's life comes down to shaving versus not-shaving, a simple and childlike Manichaeism. That said, the filmmaker depicts these daily activities with loving care, always emphasising how Mary and George mirror one another.

The single area in which Mary and George are at odds is religion. We hear her prayer that George will find his way to the true faith; she asks God to grant 'the conversion of my husband'. We see her daily preparations to attend mass. There, she occupies the centre of the frame, surrounded by five faces at different distances, all listening intently to the off-camera priest. The identification between the pious Mary in *San Francisco*, eager to bring Blackie to God, and O'Sullivan's Mary is obvious. For O'Sullivan's Mary, that identification stands as a challenge to her mixed marriage. She is riveted by the first glimpse of the Hollywood film shown in *TWWMCG*. Before the earthquake, an apparently irredeemable Blackie explains himself to Mary: 'Did you ever taste the fog in your mouth, like it was salt? Did you take hold of someone and feel your blood rushing up like a river? What more does a man need, or a woman either? You know I never tried to kid you, Mary. You take me as I am, or you don't take me.'

While George puzzles out the 'hydraulics' of the earthquake special effects, Mary watches *San Francisco* multiple times in order to figure out how to move George. Before there can be a baby, it seems, there has to be an acceptance on her part of his spiritual non-conformism or an acceptance on his part of religion. George's coming to the faith would constitute, in Mary's eyes, his 'growing up'. Indeed, it is only after their second visit to the theatre (Mary's third, at least) that Mary begins to use the received script of *San Francisco* to mediate her marital issue. The camera cuts from Mary having tea to a dimly lighted audience shot. On the screen, a choir is singing 'Nearer, My God, to Thee' amidst the wreckage in which Blackie and Mary have found each other. Blackie's voice is heard over this shot until we get just a glimpse of his dirty, distraught face as he childishly tells God, 'Thanks, I really mean it.'

All boy, George is still wondering about the earthquake special effects as the two prepare for bed. Unusually, Mary hums to herself. She takes off her robe and is seen in the vanity mirror in an attractive sleeveless nightgown. As she settles in bed, she asks dreamily, 'Supposing this was San Francisco, you and me, the earth begins to shake . . . .' With his body, George vibrates the mattress to scare her a little, then reaches for her hand, and lovingly kisses it. In the universal language of cinematic sexual coupling, Mary reaches over and turns out the bedside light.

Insofar as Mary has a problem within her daily routine, it is to allow herself to make love, to feel like making love, with a man she knows not to be Catholic – a condition she regards as rather childlike and rebellious. The primary contradiction in her life is her love for her husband and her belief that she should not have a child with a non-believer, that non-belief is a form of not being satisfactorily grown up. In one compromise formation, she turns to the movies for help. Imposing the Clark Gable identity onto George, an identification enabled by his having grown a moustache, allows her to live both in Dublin's ways and in the ways of the Hollywood film. She integrates a bit of Hollywood-inspired romance into her life, and George responds in kind with a small bedstead tremor. The early critical reception of this film overlooked the scripted-but-improvisational skill with which both Mary and George attempt to grasp at a bit of fun in their lives, and how much of their relationship is contradictorily fixed within a parent–child asymmetry.

If we return to canonical summaries of *TWWMCG*, we can see that they leave an incorrect impression of the film. Essentially, Mary has been found guilty of not having a child: both Rockett and Gibbons state that this lapse, the woman's failure if you will, is the psychic kernel from which the plot unfolds. Everything else that happens on the screen becomes an epiphenomenon of Mary's pro-creative problem. However, there is little evidence in either the short story or the short film to indicate that Mary's lack of a child is the key to the rest of the narrative. In fact, her barrenness, whether temporary or permanent, is itself a red herring. A close reading of the O'Faoláin story shows that Mary's current lack of a child makes her desire for love and excitement all the more pressing. By the same token, Mary's viewpoint is only one element in a more complex and multifaceted envisioning of the story's world.

Again, what occupies most of the screen time is O'Sullivan's careful invention of life activities for Mary and George in Dublin in the 1930s. Riding a bicycle, making a meal, dusting a shelf, walking to the shops – these elements of world-making, which require engagement between an individual and a material realm – forestall the conclusions reached by Rockett and Gibbons in their attention to this film. The focus on everyday routines serves to destabilise a psychoanalytic, character-based approach by directing our attention to a specific way of looking at film, to an interpretive posture in which the diurnal and practical take centre stage, in which character can be read as emergent from a specific life-world, and in which conflicting worldviews create the cinematic conflict.

Further, *TWWMCG* gains in force and complexity when held up to O'Sullivan's widely demonstrated preoccupation with feminist themes. Just as important, this short film illustrates the complex entanglement of a psychoanalytic focus on subjectivity with a practice-based interpretation: the two approaches cannot really be teased apart. For example, in *December Bride* (1991) O'Sullivan tells the story of Sarah Gilmartin (Saskia Reeves), a woman who defied her Protestant community to live with two men while married to neither. Bearing these joint fathers a child, Sarah raises herself from servant to landowner. In one scene, we see the three adults dancing together in their cottage, milking pleasure from their circumstances, despite clerical and community disapproval. O'Sullivan sharpens the viewer's perception of everyday life in early twentieth-century Ulster precisely by foregrounding desire, its no doubt endlessly deferred satisfaction, and the altogether routine activities that a given world offers for human engagement. Rather than finding one man as her destiny, Sarah long refuses to declare herself a finished product. She merges two worlds to create her recalcitrant but gratifying lifestyle. At the same time, O'Sullivan's camera lingers lovingly over the ordinary farming and homemaking actions that come to constitute Sarah's life. A similar visual preoccupation and style can be discerned in Pat Murphy's *Anne Devlin* (1984), for which O'Sullivan was the cinematographer.

Like O'Faoláin, but under the sway of New Wave cinematography, O'Sullivan forces us to pause in our viewing. He makes the viewer question the apparent (and presumably universally recognised) destiny of all Irish Catholic women in the 1930s. He wants the audience to become aware of the ineluctable but unvoiced communications that have their place within the intimate material world of the encoupled state of being. O'Sullivan carefully deploys digressions (a scene in a greenhouse where Mary and George are both caught up in a shared visual pleasure that George disturbs by acting the clown with some playful lads; Mary's visit to the Shelbourne for tea where she sees a well-behaved little girl; George being teased by the men at work for his non-native behaviours) to interrupt the narrative line and to foreclose the viewer's expectation that a 'simple', localised failure to reproduce is the constant centre of Mary's experience. He forces us to see that everyday life accommodates these digressive experiences, these un-signalled lapses from linearity (whether in editing or in self-understanding) by virtue of the practical conservatism of our daily ways of acting. The materiality of film, like the experience of cinema-going, depends on rules as well as discontinuities, just as the society that O'Faoláin parsed depended on routines and repressions while slyly accommodating unexpected spaces of escape and improvised moments of release.

Hence O'Sullivan's rendering of O'Faoláin's story traverses the writer's ironic literary realism with wonderfully subtle, judiciously placed, and highly cinematic images of doing and being.

Kilmainham (disused), the terrace houses, the dog's bath, the Liffey, the factory, the pub, the Botanic Gardens, the cinema: these are not separate from the protagonists' being. Rather, these structures are all part of the characters' everyday life. The fuel in the fireplace and the rooms of their small home are part of the complex weave of dailiness in the Dublin of the 1930s; and they are inseparable from the urban infrastructure – the Liffey that George rides his bike along to get to work, the shops and theatres that Mary frequents, the pubs where the men drink. In fact, Mary rediscovers this infrastructure as the source of a reliable, workable contentment. The fling that she has had with Hollywood fantasy has proven far too taxing for her to survive within it for long. She retreats to ritual behaviours that have served her well – or well enough – in the past. For his part, George appears to have curtailed his childlike lapses so that marital balance can be maintained.

III

Over the past few years in various venues,[12] I have made a case for analysing narrative film from the perspective of a phenomenology of social practices. The principal aim of this methodology is to focus on everyday human activities – moments of performance in which an individual engages manually, physically, constitutively, with a given material environment – as depicted in cinema. Rather than place character or plot at the centre of our inquiry into a given film, we can provisionally bracket out the usual effort to discern motivation, feelings and thought processes. Ideally, the effect of switching our attention from character/story to the personal, domestic and social practices represented on screen is to de-famil- iarise our usual approaches to movies, to allow overlooked elements of the visual experience to come forward for study. The shift in what we attend to on the screen serves a focus on visual- ising the processes of world-making.

We make our worlds with others who are close at hand and who are trained from birth, as we are, to make use of a specific physical environment. In the case of cinema set in Ireland, a practice-based approach would cast light on the practical ways in which individuals are represented inhabiting and using Irish material culture in a given time and place. In the early days of modern Irish filmmaking,

O'Sullivan developed a cinematographic style that was highly pictorial and that radically foregrounded the processes that pertained to specific Irish sub-worlds. Similarly, Pierre Bourdieu persistently sought to define a sociology of practices. His distinctive turn towards putting customary behaviours forward as a category of analysis addressed the classic, deep dualisms played out in twentieth-century philosophy and ethnography. Is the subject – the seer – separate from the object – the thing seen? Does the individual precede the system into which she has been integrated, or does the system always show itself through the actions of the individual? Starting a film analysis from attention to practices means seeing both individuality and social structure emerging out of ongoing, shared, routine activity, something generally taken for granted.

Among the more revealing of Bourdieu's comments on his own anthropological work is a passage in *The Logic of Practice* in which he describes his efforts to tabulate in one diagram all the variants in the structuring oppositions of traditional life among Algerian peasants. Mapping onto a single chart rites of cooking, planting, the life cycle, the periods of the day, going out and coming in, and other recurrent activities led to many contradictions that could not be resolved back into fundamental oppositions. His fieldwork, that is, resisted the structuralist management of dichotomies that he had expected to discover in traditional Kabyle life. His synopsis of this cultural evidence showed him the need for a logic of social practices grounded in the notion of a generative habitus.[13]

The habitus always stands in dialectic with the often strategic, improvisational, fluid behaviour of individuals who perform tasks not only in space but also over time.[14] Repeated behaviours, routines learned by those brought up within those activities, habitual and un-theorised skills, routine sociation, taken-for-granted structuring mechanisms, un-interrogated kinetic knowledge, post-dualistic human-world interfaces – such terms are used by a wide variety of writers on 'practice' theory, from Anthony Giddens to Andrew Pickering, from Jeff Coulter to Stephen Turner. The effort to account fully for an individual's style, or for a society's symmetries and asymmetries, leads many of these writers, following Bourdieu, to appreciate the simultaneous over-determination and under-determination of social realities.[15]

Because my aim in this essay is to bracket primarily psychoanalytic assumptions in favour of one that foregrounds the embodied and embedded practices that we see on the screen, it is useful to cite Jacques Lacan here. Lacan's revision of Freud underlies not only Christian Metz's crucial work on cinema but also, and inevitably, the kind of thinking that prevails in *Cinema and Ireland*. In Lacan's essential piece called 'Of Structure as the Inmixing of an Otherness Prerequisite to Any Subject Whatever', he states:

> When I prepared this little talk for you, it was early in the morning. I could see Baltimore through the window and it was a very interesting moment because it was not quite daylight and a neon sign indicated to me every minute the change of time, and naturally there was heavy traffic and I remarked to myself that exactly all that I could see, except for some trees in the distance, was the result of thoughts actively thinking thoughts, where the function played by the subjects was not completely obvious. In any case the so-called *Dasein*, as a definition of the subject, was there in this rather intermittent or fading spectator. The best image to sum up the unconscious is Baltimore in the early morning.[16]

The sense that I take from Lacan's statement aligns with the insight of practice-based methodology, which posits that normative social behaviours literally bring persons into being. At the same time, the environment and its rules cannot govern every aspect of being, every nuance of identity, or every action that is performed. A degree of improvisation occurs, whether we are talking about people inhabiting a given social space or actors performing prescribed roles for the camera. Within a pre-set milieu, subjects mostly remain occluded to themselves and to the camera except insofar as these subjects are shown doing things. This is the insight that O'Sullivan furthers when he revises O'Faolain to illuminate Dublin itself – the factory where George is employed, the movie theatre, the streets and shops – along with the 'humdrum' and class-delimited activities of Mary and George. Even if we affirm Mary's biological drive to reproduce, a drive that would typically be highly stimulated in the Catholic culture of 1930s Dublin, we notice that her own desires are not entirely available either to herself, to her husband, or to the film's viewer. Dublin in the early morning, Dublin in the afternoon, Dublin in the evening: this is the infrastructural reality that we actually see on the screen. Rather than look first and primarily for characters' thoughts and motivations, I have found it useful to concentrate on the practical engagement between character and material world.

At the same time, social norms and practices positively shape and limit what Mary can do and think and say. The filmmaker, like the fiction writer, depicts the triumph of the everyday and of material circumstances over whatever so-called personal desires can be conceived within the given culture. So it is that O'Sullivan's final shots are of the uniform terrace cottages off the South Circular Road. It is evening, and through the darkness we hear a mother calling to a child. Once again, Mary and George mirror each other as they sit by the fire. Viewed from outside, their home glows in the darkness, a curtained window forming a screen. This, for the moment of projection, is Irish identity, an Irish world. The Heideggerian *Dasein* reminds us to understand Irishness not as a given condition but rather as continual participation in a world that is always being made and unmade before our eyes, a background that is always part and parcel of subjectivity and so-called identity. That said, the everyday that forms the background and basis for this narrative is undoubtedly banal. But it is what we have to turn to when we try to understand not only who film characters are but also why we are asked to watch them do what they do.

Chapter Three

THE PHENOMENOLOGICAL NARRATIVE SHIFT BETWEEN LENNY ABRAHAMSON'S *ADAM AND PAUL* AND *GARAGE*

Barry Monahan

I would like to narrate, here, a brief anecdote of coincidence that I believe relevant to what I discuss below. Travelling by train recently in Belgium, I was reflecting on the interesting historical, mechanical and aesthetic connections between the locomotive and cinema. It was there from the very beginning, first appearing in the early years when the Lumière brothers and Méliès represented the means of transport as either object of momentum coming forward through depths of field in *L'Arrivée d'un Train à La Ciotat* (1896), or phantasmagorical entity magically hurtling through space and time in *Le Voyage à Travers l'Impossible* (1904). Cinema was born only decades after the years of the development of underground networks in London (1863), New York (1869) and Paris (1900), whose temporal and spatial effects for the traveller were later duplicated for the film spectator by the editing table in various fades, cuts, wipes and dissolves. It occupied then a significant place at fairgrounds as early twentieth-century carnival rides, in much the same way that contemporary roller-coasters are linked thematically to blockbuster movies. Structural connections between train movement and narration are also evident across a diverse set of genres from the ominous inevitability of train journeys in films such as *Le Sang des Bêtes* (Georges Frangu, 1949) and *Nuit et Brouillard* (Alain Resnais, 1955) to opening sequence associations made in films like *Once Upon a Time in the West* (Sergio Leone, 1968) and *Dhoom:2* (Sanjay Gadhvi, 2006), to narrative bracketing devices such as the segment transitions used in *Peppermint Candy* (Chang-dong Lee, 1999). At times the relationship is sustained throughout the whole narrative structure in films as varied as *The General* (Buster Keaton, 1926), *The Lady Vanishes* (Alfred Hitchcock, 1938), *The Train* (John Frankenheimer, 1964) and *The Darjeeling Limited* (Wes Anderson, 2007).

As these thoughts occurred to me, I was distracted by a child's voice on the other side of the carriage. After a momentary flicker of darkness, a young girl – no more than four years old – said to her grandmother, 'On vient d'entrer dans un tunel.' In the light of what I had been thinking, this exclamation was opportunely fascinating in that it drew my attention to another functioning principle of cinema: the mode in which it thinks about and articulates its perceptions. As surely as I had *noticed* our entry into a tunnel, without affirmatively *thinking* about it, the girl had not only perceived this, but had felt the need, simultaneously and instantaneously, to state it. For her grandmother, it might not even have emerged as a moment of conscious thought. It struck me then that the language of cinema – its unique silent linguistic matter – and the particular expressive accent through which it articulates, operates in a way that seems to hover between the exclamation of the little girl and the invisible, unremarked realisation of her grandmother. The medium somehow, concurrently, notices and presents ideas and reflections on the universe and its living substance in a way that is connected to its animation and the way that it engages spectators. Like human perception, film somehow notices its environment by simultaneously uttering it, and saying nothing. Film has the capacity to say 'we have just entered a tunnel' without using any words; however, it still makes meaning, makes sense and invites conscious or unconscious thought that may call upon language.

For more than half a century, film theory has been stimulated by, and has contributed to, debates that address the notion of film authorship. Attempting to answer questions about film meaning-making, expression and comprehension, theoretical writing has been perennially interested in discovering the foundations of how communication works in the cinematic text. The terminology mobilised for this analysis is broad, and in time we have been asked to consider implied authors, focalisation, enunciation, invisible organisers and countless other narrative and meta-narrative qualities with a view to answering two key questions about film: does film have a consciousness and / or is it capable of representing human consciousness? By putting the spectator into the picture (as it were), assessing the way that films are watched and understood, many theorists have considered phenomenology as a useful analytical tool. Concerned with how pre-conscious perception and meaning-making work, phenomenology is used to explore the relation between the thinking subject and the perceived world, so it has been called upon by film theorists who posit a similar relationship between the film apparatus and the world. I would like, here, to develop this line of thinking to consider, specifically, how narrative operations may contribute to this sense of meaning-creation and to assess the precise cinematic relations established between the viewing spectator and the projected narrative, by proposing that meaning-making is not consistently evenly unilateral or fixed in every storytelling film. In order to concretise this theoretical abstraction, I will trace a specific stylistic development across two feature-length productions that have stimulated my thinking in this regard: *Adam & Paul* (2004) and *Garage* (2007), both of which were directed by Lenny Abrahamson.

I will propose that this alteration is one that involves a sense of cinematic communication using a visual and narrative syntax – a set of established codes and conventions – known to a typical film audience. While these are not necessarily related to spoken language, and my concentration will be predominantly of a cinematic semiotics, both *Adam & Paul* and *Garage* do actually place spoken language in an important position that reflects issues of characterisation, community and broader thematic concerns of each film. I do not want to offer a teleological reading that suggests that Abrahamson has somehow 'moved' on stylistically from his first to his second feature, or that in some way the change represents an aesthetic development in sophistication, as the shift occurs between the more syntactically regulated cinematic communication (of *Adam & Paul*) to an alternative form of expression that needs – or uses – fewer visual grammatical tools (*Garage*). Rather, I will propose that it is specific qualities of each film, relating to characterisation, *mise en scène* and thematic exploration – specifically presenting characters from a Celtic Tiger social underbelly in the first of the films and a socially awkward outsider in the second – that invite alternative modes of presentation that Abrahamson allows to function differently in each film. My consideration of *Adam & Paul* and *Garage*, therefore, will focus on the varying manifestations of narrative event as expressed through visual codes and conventions of cinema which are comparable with, but more silent than, the grammar and syntax of spoken language. While *Adam & Paul* is driven – like someone walking through the carriages of a moving train – through successive, carefully crafted leading beats, *Garage* operates more contrapuntally, through what French feminist theorists writing on the patriarchal nature of language would call 'fissures', or gaps between those same beats.[1]

It is not surprising that the operations of film, and the cinematic experience, were quickly associated with the way we perceive the world, and that the apparatus attempted a replication of mind-works from its earliest days. As soon as the logical inversion of this practice of replication was realised – and it was suggested that the mechanics of film could inform us about the workings of the human mind – there was also certain inevitability in the application to analytical film writings of a contemporaneous system of thought: phenomenology. In an attempt to understand how film stands before, regards and records its world, the study of mind-world, perceiving subject / perceived object relations seemed apposite. However, as a comment by Constance Penley and Janet Bergstrom attests, the phenomenological method was often applied to an ideological function of the cinematic apparatus, as it was understood to capture and encompass its object and in doing so establish an illusory omnipotence for the spectator: 'Cinema replays unconscious wishes the structures of which are shared by phenomenology: the illusion of perceptual mastery with the effect of the creation of a transcendental subject.'[2] Elsewhere, Daniel Herwitz acknowledged a similar capacity for the conception of subjectivity by the cinematic apparatus, this time specifically embodied by the camera. In reference to the earlier work of William Rothman, he noted that the camera is 'a full correlate of a human subject, its identity or "I-ness" involves the kind of capacity for self-reflection and for working through that the human being has'.[3] Even Christian Metz's 'The Imaginary Signifier' worked from an inferred connection between cinema and the conscious and unconscious functions of the human mind as its psychoanalytical premise, and explicitly proposed the benefits of its methodological application to a study of cinema: 'it is true that the topographical apparatus of the cinema resembles the conceptual apparatus of phenomenology, with the result that the latter can cast light on the former.'[4]

In all of these accounts, the comparison made between human subjectivity and the capacity of the film machine to grasp the world rests in a somewhat static, unilateral order, with emphasis on the 'receivers' of the image. In the different binaries – subject / world, spectator / film, and film / world – it is the second element in each set that is posited as evenly and unilaterally giving meaning to the first element. In the third category, for example, 'meaning' is contained in the world and is extracted by the film camera. A slightly different approach has read the recording apparatus dialectically in terms of what it captures of the world, and what it simultaneously adds to the meaning of that world. In this case the notion of intentionality may be usefully invoked, as the idea actively considers how the human mind – or for us here the cinematic apparatus – reaches out both to receive meaning from and bring meaning to the world. Central to this will be a consideration of the way in which the subject / film connection is cemented in a process of meaning-making based in narration. Following on from Vivian Sobchack's notion of the 'viewing view'[5] – the framed awareness by camera and film of their looking, and creation of meaning – Daniel Frampton invokes the phenomenological notion of 'intentionality' in his description of the recording moment: 'Cinema intends and creates at one and the same moment. Film owns the object it "sees", because the object is already included in the act of seeing.'[6] This acknowledgement of film's phenomenological capacity to 'intend' its conceived objects not only marks a certain purpose within its action of looking but also imbues it with a conscious ordering of the reality that it records and presents. Such a facility need not be ascribed solely to the conscious design of the *auteur* who makes the film in a certain way, but it should also be considered to be working at an elemental level of the cinematic apparatus. The very nature of its reaching out to grasp moments of time and space – its precise relationship with the world – is grounded in its capacity for phenomenological intentionality. The challenge is to find a way of allowing a phenomenological reading of film to elucidate the medium's capacity to invite meaning. This will entail a shift in the way in which we read how the spectator relates to narrative: no longer simply a passive consumer of meaning nor a wholly active participant in its construction, but whose 'viewing' position constantly fluctuates during the process.

When film is seen simply as message transmitted from sender to receiver, it is usually read as performing seamlessly, its narrative mechanisms acting invisibly. Citing Emile Benveniste, many narrative theorists have called upon the concept of 'enunciation', which was originally taken as 'the emphasis on the discursive relationship with a partner, whether it be real or imagined, individual or collective'.[7] However, as the notion was later evoked in the writing of film theorists, it came to imply, and eventually entail, an understanding of film narration that involved the effacement of the narrating *auteur*. The film spectator was deceived into a position of transcendental ubiquity and comprehension, and authorship maintained a position of invisibility. This ensured the quality – mostly evident in mainstream American cinema – of the illusory omniscience and ubiquity of the spectator within and around the story-world, and the resulting technical seamlessness which hides the operations of the apparatus.

Another theoretical take that emerged in tandem with this was the notion of the 'implied author' introduced in the writing of Christian Metz, a concept much more in line with later conceptualisations of how meaning worked in the cinema. The idea has been summarised by Edward Branigan as 'an anthropomorphic and shorthand way of designating a rather diffuse but fundamental set of operations which we sense as underlying what we do in making sense and in making patterns'.[8] The verbs that Branigan uses here – 'we sense', 'we do' – in description of the spectator's relationship with the text of the implied author expose a level of activity with which the viewer is expected to interpret and consolidate different levels of meaning in the process of cinematic narration. In effect, the concept of the implied author creates a narrative space between the actual author and a more anthropomorphic notional narrator that invites the spectator to assess degrees and values of presented truth claims or circumstances. The viewer is no longer taken to be a passive consumer, but as one who 'intends' meaning dialectically by a hermeneutic process, concurrently *from* and *towards* the encountered film. As both of these models show, there is a hermeneutic shift in the system of meaning-making in the process of narration whereby the spectator is increasingly empowered by greater activity in the reception of the film. This is not to say that the author has no role or even a diminished one: it merely emphasises – on the lines of phenomenological understanding – that the spectator's position as engaging consciousness should be recognised.

Inasmuch as narrative – especially, but not uniquely, mainstream – might be considered a linear condition of cause and effect coincidence, it may be understood as working through a series of 'beats', which lead the spectator in the sense-making process. These leading beats may be as concrete and blatant as evocative emotive music, or as amorphous and ephemeral as a transitional cut (that inherently, silently signifies a change in place or time), but there are certainly variants in the degrees to which such beats are applied in different cinematic texts. One useful way of conceptualising these narrative beats is through the notion of narrative schemas, systems of probability and possibility which the film viewer assesses with a view to creating coherence of meaning. Branigan reads them in this way: 'These schemas are a way of working through cultural assumptions and values. Thus "causes and effects" emerge, as it were, after the fact as explanatory labels for a sequence of actions viewed under a particular schematic description.'[9] Although spectators consciously undertake a process of meaning-creation through detailed selection, it is nevertheless inevitably the directing author who places the cues there – like clues in a whodunit – to facilitate narrative comprehension. One example of a typical set of beats relates to the idea of focalisation, whereby viewers are guided through the story epistemologically and emotively, by virtue of alignment with characters' points of view. This can be done by framing, focusing and in-camera effects (such as the double exposure used to signify dizziness), or through sound and music cues and editing (such as shot / reverse shot). Branigan sums up the idea:

> The narratological concept of *focalization* is meant to remind us that a character's role in a narrative may change from being an actual, or potential, *focus* of a causal chain to being the *source* of our knowledge of a causal chain: the character may become either a (high level) narrator or a (low level) focalizer.[10]

Although these beat systems – cause and effect and focalisation – may operate without recourse to language (we do not need to confirm vocally or linguistically in thought that a character on a train in a film 'has just gone into a tunnel'), they nevertheless function communicatively as transmitted epistemological codes from sender to receiver, with a view to establishing meaning. However, another type of cinematic representation exists which operates without such audience-leading beats, one that works, I will argue, in an indeterminate or *pre*-linguistic way cinematically speaking. Once I have examined below what this mode is, in consideration of how it might be working, I want to propose that there is a clear shift in Abrahamson's films stylistically – from *Adam & Paul* to *Garage* – in how narration invites audience engagement.

A cinema that works without the narrative beats already described requires a greater level of audience attention. This type of cinematic narration equates with the phenomenological modes described above in which certain procedures of filmmaking and film viewing require intentionality (of apparatus and spectator, respectively). The way in which consciousness comes into contact with the world perceived, and this world comes into contact with consciousness, is a manifest intentionality that is always a pre-linguistic processing: one that is also pre-cognitive and pre-conscious in the phenomenological sense. Conscious engagement with the narrative (thinking about its logic, weighing up various possible outcomes, and working it out) might be considered, in the words of Timothy Mooney and Dermot Moran, 'intentional fulfilment',[11] something to which all intentionality tends. In contrast, a cinema without narrative beats fosters a spectator's unconscious engagement through unrealised interpretation of narrative moments, something that we may usefully call, again after Mooney and Moran, 'thoughtless thought' in which the 'intending is intuitively unfulfilled'.[12] This intentionality in the comprehension of film scripts has found its way into the theoretical and analytical language of film studies in various incarnations. In his consideration of Buster Keaton's *The General* (1926), Noël Carroll speaks of 'visible intelligibility' and makes distinctions between 'believing that', 'seeing that', 'seeing how' and 'knowing that',[13] the last of which accords best with the notion of intentionality. Elsewhere, Edward Branigan explores the measures by which we come to acquire information about the narrative event and evokes the terms 'procedural knowledge' (knowing 'how') and 'declarative knowledge' (knowing 'what'), both of which relate to the system of intentionality in the spectator / text relationship.[14] While each of these concepts can facilitate our understanding of how certain films might be working pre-linguistically, the emphasis should rest on the absence of the *requirement* to apply a cinematic 'language' rather than the absence of a cinematic 'language' itself. Metz, too, struggled with this idea when he wrote about the narrating 'master of ceremonies' that is the film text 'who (before being recognised as the author, if it is an *auteur* film, or if not, in the absence of an author) is first and foremost *the film itself as a linguistic object* [. . .] or more precisely a sort of "potential linguistic focus"'.[15] This sense of an authorless film, which seems to articulate independently of its creator, actually implicitly underpins the functions through which spectators *intend* meaning in narrative comprehension. It suggests that on a basic ontological level the cinematic apparatus is capable of containing, and then expressing, a fundamental 'truth' about reality that is beyond the control of any director. This quality has been neatly articulated by Michelangelo Antonioni, referring specifically to *Blowup* (Antonioni, 1966), but also to his philosophy of cinema more broadly:

> We know that under the revealed image there is another one which is more faithful to reality, and under this one there is yet another, and again under this last one, down to the true image of that absolute mysterious reality that nobody will ever see. Or perhaps, not until the decomposition of every image, every reality.[16]

This expression may even be seen to echo a pre-linguistic Lacanian 'Real': the ontological position permanently lost to the developing infant at the psychological moment when it moves in the direction of a world of symbols and representation. Antonioni's statement may also find resonance in a statement about the non-linguistic musicality of cinema evoked elsewhere by Stanley Cavell: 'In the paucity of humane criticism dealing with whole films, and in the lack of fit between their technical description and a phenomenological account of them, movies have achieved the condition of music.'[17] If film uses spectator-leading beats to draw attention to how it is advancing its narration and presenting its world, then a 'pointerless' cinema offers substance to its spectators by inviting their interpretation or simply eschewing any answering of cause-and-effect questions. Common in avant-garde filmmaking, where spectators are given no clear-cut clues as to how to interpret the formalist play, the absence of guiding beats is all the more interesting in plot-driven cinema which requires that spectators follow narrative lines. In his work, Cavell takes up this position comparing what I have called 'narrative beat' films with those without:

> [I]t is equally a possibility of the medium not to call attention to [objects] but, rather, to let the world happen, to let its parts draw attention to themselves according to their natural weight. This possibility is less explored than its opposite. Dreyer, Flaherty, Vigo, Renoir, and Antonioni are masters of it.[18]

It is precisely this quality of letting 'the world happen' that underpins the significant shift in the tonality and style of Abrahamson's work from *Adam & Paul* to *Garage*, as he moves from a narrative that operates through leading beats to one in which his cinematic world has been 'intended' by the camera, and audiences are invited to 'intend' their understanding of the film's events and representations.

Abrahamson's minimalist style of cinematic silence began in 1991 with his award-winning short *3 Joes*, and his propensity to explore the idea of verbal inarticulacy and failure of communication that was evident in that film was to re-emerge in his later feature-length productions. With a minimum of dialogue, or spoken word, the film allows the three characters to develop through interactions over nothing more procedurally complicated than mundane shared household chores in a day-in-the-life way. While the lethargic, uninterested protagonists of the film go unhurriedly about a set of banal tasks in almost total silence, the film is nonetheless incredibly busy cinematically. Tasks performed by the three Joe characters are depicted in meticulous detail on screen, and many are imbricated in a way that distorts cause and effect expectations for comedy. The stretching and flapping of a bed sheet, for example, flicks a cigarette from the mouth of one character into underwear hanging on the washing line. The comical alteration of the cause and effect relationship disturbs linear narrative expectations, but it works by providing clearly defined narrative beats: cueing moments that lead the spectator through the story.

This leading of the audience by narrative beats also plays a central role in Abrahamson's first feature *Adam & Paul* and its structure is carefully honed along comical circumstances and lines that create these moments. One notable narrative strand moves along a series of these beats towards a pay-off gag, half an hour into the film. In order to demonstrate this, it is best to consider the sequence of beats in reverse. As outsiders, placed beyond the healthy functioning of a well-to-do society, the heroin addicts Adam and Paul must – by virtue of plot necessity – come into contact with another outsider (in this case a foreign immigrant) who will draw attention to, and question, their situation. And so it comes to pass that they meet a Bulgarian man on a bench in the thirtieth minute of the eighty-minute script. The logic of this progression works with a perfectly refined consequentiality. At a moment of narrative and character revelation, Adam asks the Bulgarian why he left his homeland, to which the man responds, 'I have to leave Sofia'. It is of critical importance then that Paul asks afterwards, 'Ah, right . . . Was she pregnant, like?' This heavily set gag-line pay-off reveals a way of thinking that is typical of the characters presented: namely that the only reason they can imagine the need to flee your country is because you are running away from the consequences of having made someone pregnant. The misunderstanding also motivates the following dialogue which culminates in the Bulgarian's asking the addicts: 'Why am *I* here? Did you ever ask yourself the same question?' Logically, the man must be Bulgarian because its capital can be confused with the name of a woman: following on this line, therefore, Adam's jacket must have been made in Bulgaria, something that Paul points out to the foreigner on another comical beat. In order for this to function, and so that Paul knows the provenance of the jacket, he must have seen the 'made in' label on it. This occurs at the beginning of the film, as he reads aloud from the jacket's label once he has torn it off the mattress to which it and Adam were glued at the beginning of the film. To complete this line of plot design, by necessity Adam must be stuck to the mattress in the opening sequence of the film, forcing Paul to tear the jacket from it, read the label and instigate the chain of narrative events along specific beats that lead to the pair's encounter with the Bulgarian, and the gag-line about Sofia.

Up to the point of the bench meeting, *Adam & Paul* has a definite linear quality through which its narrative works in a syntagmatic way, across sequential cause and effect beats. The clarity of this syntagmatic progression is upset after the bench sequence, which brings about a more fragmented narrative in which beats are paradigmatically stacked. Narrative moments are heaped so that they become less important as consecutive instances, and more like interchangeable set pieces. It does not matter, for example, which characters they meet, or in what order. That they have stolen the television amounts to no more than a convenient and extraordinary coincidence which leads them back to the flat next door to the one where they tried at the beginning of the film to get work to obtain money for drugs. In the end, the attempt to sell the television is unsuccessful and does not provide leading plot progression. Sitting outside the same block of flats, in another astonishing coincidence, two bags of heroin fall from a window above them and, amazed by their luck, they return to the city centre where they spend the next part of the evening getting high. While these beats are not completely removed in the latter half of the film (as I will mention below), it is significant that when the causal narrative beats are replaced by consecutively disconnected beats, the level of narrative coincidence escalates considerably. Without a 'cause and effect' justification giving the film narrative forwardly progressing momentum, significant and fabricated moments work through convenient coincidence. Following the conversation with the Bulgarian, the fragmentation of narrative progression echoes their mental condition, so that the man's question – 'What are you doing here?' – takes on threefold significance where it can be understood as (1) in Dublin, on a bench (2) in the mental, emotional and physical condition that you are both in, and (3) at this point in the narrative.

Both *Adam & Paul* and Abrahamson's second feature length film, *Garage*, present some mode of struggling with language – a moment or phase at which linguistic communication has failed – and in each case this is used for thematic exploration and character development. However, the cinematic language of each film varies considerably in each of three registers of semantic construction: on the level of spoken language (screenplay dialogue), on the level of functional signification (including props and *mise en scène*), and on the level of filmic coding (the cinematic event). In respect of these categories, *Adam & Paul* works through its beats with an unambiguous positioning of spectator. It displays a greater diversity of linguistic competence and performance across its characters, whose colloquial Dublin dialect and accents are rendered strangely poetic as iterations and repetitions flow in musical cadences and tones. *Garage*, on the other hand, is limited in its use of dialogue and works through and frames moments of silence, repetition and the inability of characters to connect meaningfully through language. The narrative of *Garage* is straightforward. It presents Josie, a middle-aged social misfit who lives in and runs a garage on the outskirts of a small Irish village. The butt of locals' jokes and sarcastic remarks, and ostracised because of his intellectual simplicity, he befriends David, a teenager who comes to work in the garage at weekends. He shares cans of beer with the youngster after work and when a truck-driving customer gives him video pornography he shows it to David. A formal complaint is made, and the police take Josie to the station, after which a tragic series of events occurs. Tonally and structurally, *Garage* works like a short film, inasmuch as its *fabula* may be interpreted by spectators on myriad layers of complexity even though its *syuzhet* is very simple. This simplicity of story, stillness of action and bareness of *mise en scène* may also be read as the kind of cinematic performative silence that comes from 'structuring absences':[19] ideological and framing elements that become important for audiences' reading of a given text by virtue of their ostensible omission. In *Adam & Paul*, things are 'there' and actions 'occur' blatantly, and these are meaningfully representative – metaphorically or symbolically – of other ideas. The television becomes a commodity that can lead to money for a score but also symbolises affluence; the mattress provides a place to sleep but also, as I have shown, contributes to specific cause-and-effect narrative progression; the stolen milk fails in functionality as it cannot be used without the missing straw but because of this, as a tool, it helps instigate the addicts' conversation with the Bulgarian; and, ultimately, the drugs are the absolute extreme of functionality as they have motivated all of the preceding action. In *Garage*, by contrast, items and actions are exaggerated beyond their use and their presence is rendered pointless. The reiteration of the need to move the 'oils' into view in front of the garage; the awkwardly manipulated yellow tubing that Josie carries; the time that Josie gives to collecting beer cans only to throw them into a ditch; and his careful winding of a cable before he tosses it carelessly on the ground are some of the many elements that have no 'beat' function within the film.

On the level of cinematic coding, *Adam & Paul* uses narrative conventions that direct spectators. The most sustained is the one already detailed above, but other minor cases occur throughout. A notable example works across two shots, the first of which presents a homeless young man in a sleeping bag asking Adam and Paul for a cigarette, while the second shot comically places the same character in the background lighting up a cigarette which we were already led to believe he did not have. Other informative beats occur along the plot line that culminates in Adam and Paul's meeting Clank. Various moments punctuate the plot at which other characters wrongly understand that the addicts are looking for him. This confusion is resolved when Clank appears, punching Paul in the face and demanding that he and Adam get into his car in order to act as lookouts at a petrol station he intends to rob. This section of the narrative is also carefully structured along leading lines and progressive moments that result in the addicts' return to the apartment blocks where their story began.

In *Garage*, a remarkably limited number of these beats are used in its cinematic communication. Space and time are emptied of symbolically constructed signification in favour of allowing spectators to intend meaning into the seemingly self-unfolding events. Not only are musical cues kept to a minimum, but there is also notable restraint when it comes to shot / reverse shot revelations, so that the reverse field shot that follows a character's sight line rarely entails moments of heightened dramatic revelation or the provision of significant information for our continued reading of the film. When shot / reverse shots can be avoided they usually are, so that otherwise busily cut head shots of conversations are replaced with a more still frontal shot in which conversing characters both sit facing the camera, or stand still in profile in a set framed shot. The cinematic silence that emanates from this respect for the ontological wholeness of the moment invites the spectator's participation in meaning construction, and it is this quality that allows phenomenological intentionality. One of the more significant scenes in this regard is the noteworthy restraint in epistemological provision when Josie, sitting alone at his kitchen table, his back to the camera, stops eating and puts his hand up to his face. Evidently, we are to believe that this marks a moment of personal enlightenment for him, where he realises the implication and gravity of having shown the pornography to David. However, all speculation of the impact this has for him is withheld by Abrahamson, and the viewer is drawn closer to the situation and granted free interpretation of the event.

Perhaps the most important, and memorable, example of the cinematic silence of *Garage* is the one that occurs at the end. Early in the film, an emotional connection is made between Josie and a horse which he finds tethered in a field on his route to the village. In one scene, he feeds the horse apples and he talks quietly and gently to it. At the end of the film, immediately after he has committed suicide, there is a shot of the same horse – now no longer tethered, and perhaps freed by Josie – walking along unused train tracks towards the camera. The horse turns slightly to screen right, and after a short pause the screen cuts to black. It is essential for the functioning of this part of the film that the spectator's moment can, and perhaps should, remain non-linguistic: the horse and the shot of it should not be read symbolically or metaphorically, they and their narrative 'position' should not connote anything if they are to be successful as cinematic effects. The non-linguistic style that has provided the fabric for the rest of the film is maintained here, and it serves as another example of how the film invites audience intentionality.

Linguistically, and in terms of cinematic coding, where *Adam & Paul* is replete with an absurd Beckettian epistemology and play with language as poetic game, *Garage* is underscored by a more existential quality of emptiness that haunts the works of Camus and Sartre. While both bear similarities in their address of the uses and functions of language within community, there is a dramatic shift from conventional cinematic coding and narrative structuring as Abrahamson moves from his first to second feature-length production. With this shift, a certain empowerment of spectatorship takes place as a heightening of film consciousness – the deliberate framing of the film's thinking relationship with the world – invites a novel type of audience engagement. Ironically, perhaps, it is the medium's capacity to iterate without language, its ability to think about and represent the world in such a non-linguistic way that invites a differently engaged contemplation by the viewer. Like Truffaut's still shot of Antoine at the end of *Les 400 Coups* (1959), Antonioni's fading of his fashion photographer protagonist at the end of *Blowup* (1966), and any number of Joan's framed faces in Dreyer's *La Passion de Jeanne d'Arc* (1928), the capacity of the medium for thought evident throughout *Garage* is specifically that which engages spectators by stimulating intentionality and inviting alternative profound reflection.

Chapter Four

FASCINATING STATES:[1] SCREENING NORTHERN IRELAND

Matthew Brown

If the degree of fascination with a nation can be gauged by the number of films produced about it, Northern Ireland has emerged, in the last twenty years, as an exceedingly fascinating place. The recent release of two films about the history and legacies of political violence, *Hunger* (Steve McQueen, 2008) and *Five Minutes of Heaven* (Oliver Hirschbiegel, 2009), caps a remarkable run of films produced about Northern Ireland after 1992, the year *The Crying Game* (Neil Jordan) hit theatres, including *Cycle of Violence* (Henry Herbert, 1998), *Divorcing Jack* (David Caffrey, 1998), *Bloody Sunday* (Paul Greengrass, 2002) and *Omagh* (Pete Travis, 2004).[2] During this span, moviegoers were confronted with images of the Troubles through cinematic masterplots of political struggle, bigotry, sectarian violence, and tenuous attempts at reconciliation – evidence enough that the film camera remains fascinated by the changing states of Northern Ireland. Without question, some instances of visual fascination invite a cynical response. Consider two Hollywood productions from the 1990s, *Patriot Games* (Phillip Noyce, 1992) and *The Devil's Own* (Alan J. Pakula, 1997). In the former, the screen mythology of an atavistic nation rendered even more chaotic by the 'bloodthirsty Irish Republican Army (IRA)' remains the dominant filmic image;[3] in the latter, the sexualised, quasi-heroic allure of the isolated IRA gunman (Brad Pitt) is the signal motif, one that recalls the agonised wanderings of Johnny McQueen (James Mason) in Carol Reed's *Odd Man Out* (1947). In these films, violence is doubly nationalised but differently valued, for it represents the complexity of Northern Ireland through the shorthand of terrorism and curtails its alternatively psychotic and alluring appeals through the sanctioned violence of an American bellwether (i.e., the characters played by Harrison Ford, who stars in both films). Though not a sovereign state, Northern Ireland is nevertheless a fascinating one on screen, projected as a zone of violence, betrayal and dangerous liaisons – it has become, in other words, a means to screen the more lurid pleasures of movie going.

Among contemporary filmmakers, however, some radical experiments with the nation's screen image are underway. Recent films that screen Northern Ireland, such as *Hunger* and *Bloody Sunday*, are not only fascinated by the histories of political violence, but also explore the role played by fascination in shaping visual narratives of the Troubles. Consequently, a new way to theorise the politics of visuality in Northern Ireland is being wagered by filmmakers who explore the structures of fascination in film, which can be analysed in terms of the general history of cinematic fascination and the more localised, political force of each production. *Hunger* and *Bloody Sunday* are here exemplary, insofar as both films dramatise transitive and intransitive modes of cinematic perception and focus our critical attentions on affect and embodiment within the Troubles film. To clarify, I begin with a brief history of fascination, before moving on to discuss the structures of fascination and 'pensive spectatorship' in *Hunger* and *Bloody Sunday*, films that diagnose the appeal of visual propaganda in Northern Ireland without being able to fully escape its call.

*   *   *

At first glance, one might concede that fascination, if taken as a Hollywood byword for the pleasures of watching manipulative violence on screen, has ruined film: it creates a situation in which the majority of films produced or marketed by Hollywood are, first and foremost, pornographic spectacle, in the sense that each film's visual pleasures are insidious seductions (Murder! Sex!), each film's ends bound by what Frederic Jameson terms 'rapt, mindless fascination'.[4] Hollywood's ability to construct the ocular pleasures of sexuality and violence underwrites this established view and, as Laura Mulvey notes, the two motifs are routinely conflated in mainstream films, in which attention falls on 'the female star as ultimate spectacle, the emblem and guarantee of [a film's] fascination and power'.[5] The itinerary of *The Crying Game*, from a little-viewed art house film in Europe to a feted blockbuster in the United States, testifies to the ways in which this type of fascination is commercially manufactured. By the end of 1992, *The Crying Game* attracted some mixed reviews from the British and European press, grossing about £300,000. After it was bought by Miramax and shown at various film festivals, it garnered significant acclaim. Miramax's advertising campaign had much to do with the film's reception: its US release was accompanied by a black-and-white poster depicting Miranda Richardson (who plays Jude, an IRA member and sexpot in the film) as a forties femme fatale. She holds a smoking gun next to her face while staring out from the poster with the signature come-hither gaze of film noir; the top edge of the poster provides the obvious caption, 'Sex. Murder. Betrayal. In Neil Jordan's new thriller, nothing is what it seems to be'.[6]

Fascination, of course, bears a more complex relationship to the history of film and to representations of the Troubles on screen, beyond these risqué trailers and Hollywood taglines. A brief history of the concept illuminates some of these correspondences. The serendipitous emergence of psychoanalysis and film in 1895 forecast a century of theorists captivated by their shared affects; within this body of work, fascination remains a premier site of overlap. From Sergei Eisenstein's interest in conjuring powerful emotions in the viewer through bodily movements on screen to Slavoj Žižek's claim that what 'fascinates us [about *film noir*] is precisely a certain gaze, the gaze of the "other"',[7] fascination has traditionally signified the intense rapport between the cinematic image and the spectator. But fascination does not simply denote, within twentieth-century film theory, the passive gaze of the spectator on the screen, but all the corresponding affects produced in the viewer by this gazing, therefore becoming 'less a theory of fantasy (psychoanalytic or otherwise) than a theory of the affects and transformations of bodies'[8] – broadly put, fascination signifies the 'materiality of sensation'[9] produced by film and, in this respect, calls to mind the earliest OED definition of the term, provided by Francis Bacon: 'Fascination is the power and act of imagination, intensive upon other bodies.'[10] Within psychoanalysis, the term was given some initial exposition in Sigmund Freud's *Group Psychology and the Analysis of the Ego*, in which Freud introduces the concept during a discussion of G. Le Bon's *Psychologie des Foules* (1895), which defines fascination as an extreme state of suggestibility, similar to being hypnotised: 'The conscious personality has entirely vanished; will and discernment are lost. All feelings and thoughts are bent in the direction determined by the hypnotiser.'[11] As the root causes of fascination remain 'plunged in obscurity' for Le Bon, Freud seeks to lay them bare during a later discussion of identification. During identification, the ego appears to 'enrich itself with the properties of the object' it identifies with, while during fascination the ego seems to be 'impoverished, it has surrendered itself to the object'.[12] Here, fascination is a mode of heightened identification, an ocular, *transitive* phenomenon characterised by the actions one subject exercises upon another, and by the affective states of paralysis, docility and absolute dependency.[13] It also arouses some powerful effects, for the 'fascinator' awakens in the subject an 'archaic heritage', Freud continues, which simulates the subject's compliance towards 'the idea of a paramount and dangerous personality, towards whom only a passive-masochistic attitude is possible'.[14] Not only is transitive fascination mad, bad and dangerous, but it is also, in Freud's final analysis, uncanny, an affect in which the return of a familiar 'paramount and dangerous personality' elicits feelings of masochistic self-perception.

That these distinguishing affects share some family resemblances with fascism produced, in the mid-twentieth century, a healthy suspicion of mediums that powerfully solicit and manipulate the senses, such as propaganda designed to transform individual perception into collective belief. As many post-Freud, post-fascist writers have rightly pointed out, fascination as fascist lends itself to an at best flaccid relationship to culture, 'disparaged as a state of illusion and passivity [. . .] [and] associated with sexual fetishism and the fetishism of commodities', or it signals the hypnotic seductions of aestheticised politics, a state Theodor Adorno refers to as 'will-less fascination'.[15] After Freud's diagnosis, the pleasures of gazing, of visual fascination itself, became politically suspect.

In the early to mid-twentieth century, however, Walter Benjamin and Maurice Blanchot separately gazed at fascination to resist its transitive summon, cultivating instead, within the theory of fascination itself, an intransitive mien. A premier form of embodied spectatorship, fascination represents to Benjamin the 'willingness to be drawn to phenomena that attract our attention yet do not submit entirely to our understanding'.[16] Fascination does not signal masochistic self-perception but offers, like allegory, an 'image of transfixed unrest' through a dialectic of seeing in which there appears to be a collision or, at the very least, a lack of coordination between the different representational and material orders of the aesthetic phenomenon.[17] Further, for Benjamin, fascination precipitates a critical reflection on the dialectical relationship between image and narrative, through motifs of suspension, captivation, enthrallment and wonder. As Stephen Connor avers, fascination so defined transitions it from a transitive to an intransitive phenomenon, in which we are fascinated 'with *things*, the susceptibility to becoming fascinated now being converted into a positive power [. . .] a desire for arrest, but of a certain enlivening kind'.[18] Fascist no more, intransitive fascination names the self's desire to engage wilfully and be enthralled by something that is not the self but, nevertheless, ramps up self-perception. Similarly, Blanchot defines fascination as a kind of 'radical passivity', in which 'whoever is fascinated doesn't see, properly speaking, what he sees. Rather, it touches him in an immediate proximity; it seizes and ceaselessly draws him close, even though it leaves him absolutely at a distance.'[19] Here, Blanchot identifies a key difference between transitive and intransitive modes of fascination: in the former, the gazed upon object is equipped with claims to mastery and domination over the gazing subject; in the latter, with feelings of suspension, reflection and mystification that emanate from fascination's ability to 'contact at a distance'.[20]

These early-to-mid twentieth-century views on fascination reverberate through the later writings of film theorist Laura Mulvey, for whom fascination has been encoded into film theory primarily as a transitive phenomenon, as that Freudian-Lacanian play of subjective domination made to signify scopophilia or feelings of mastery generated by the ability to identify, in a highly gendered way, with the images projected onto the cinema screen. Mulvey's widely influential essay 'Visual Pleasure and Narrative Cinema' connects the many looks in a Hollywood film to the masculine gaze – aggressive, voyeuristic, fearful of castration – and to the ways in which the camera directs this gaze towards a displayed, to-be-looked-at woman. In Mulvey's scenario, the 'fascination of the human form' is produced by the cinema camera, which hypnotises the viewer into an ideology of representation that mimics the perception of the male subject, the 'conscious aim being always to eliminate intrusive camera presence and prevent a distancing awareness in the audience'.[21] To avoid this hierarchy of vision, Mulvey advocates for the spectator to cultivate a 'passionate detachment' from, and not visual or visceral pleasure with, the world presented on film – one way for the viewer, in Mulvey's estimation, to inoculate gazing itself from the blandishments of visual fascination.

Cultivating a 'distancing awareness' to ward off fascination's charms is, of course, precisely how Blanchot and Benjamin define fascination itself – enthrallment at a distance – and so Mulvey considers this alternative in her more recent work, one that has become more apparent since the 'digital revolution' of the 1990s changed the perceptual situations of film and promoted the rise of the 'alternative' film industry. The dynamic between the stillness of fascination, what Blanchot elsewhere names a 'passion for the image',[22] and the progressive movement of narrative captivates Mulvey, who is careful to argue that a new mode of cinematic spectatorship has emerged from this dynamic between image and narrative, what she names the 'pensive spectator'. Mulvey ascribes the rise of this pensive spectator to contemporary shifts in the material practices of watching film, namely the prevalence of the individual viewer watching a film in isolation through a medium over which she or he has a different kind of mastery, such as the ability to pause or break down a film viewed on DVD into individual frames. For Mulvey, this new kind of filmic gazing represents the pensive spectator, who might pause the film at any moment, and, in so doing, interrupt the narrative flow by juxtaposing the frozen time of the image with the narrative time progression of the film: this juxtaposition provides a Benjaminian moment of 'transfixed unrest', for, as Mulvey concludes, 'in any halt to a film, a sense of the image as document makes itself felt as the fascination of time fossilised overwhelms the fascination of narrative progression'.[23] By gravitating towards an intransitive mode of spectatorship, Mulvey's pensive spectator comes to realise that 'out of a pause or delay in normal cinematic time, the body of narrative film can find new modes of spectatorship'.[24] Reducing the movie viewer to an isolated wing-nut with a fetish for the pause button is something Mulvey presumably wants to avoid and so we should take her 'pensive spectator' to be more arch and suggestive about the internal and external structures of fascination at work in *Hunger* and *Bloody Sunday* – films that dramatically reconstruct, and pause over, two iconic events in the long history of political conflict in Northern Ireland and the seminal role the varieties of fascination played in both events.

* * *

Hunger and *Bloody Sunday* are typical of many experimental films about Northern Ireland, to the extent that they bring into focus the intense politics of visuality within Troubles narratives. Screening the politics of visuality, apparent in the H-Block protests in *Hunger* and the civil rights march in *Bloody Sunday*, is by no means apolitical: both films deliver cinematic interventions into the Northern conflict yet stay sceptical about the politics of this cinematic act, for both remain aware that intransitive modes of fascination on screen have been historically consigned to, or co-opted by, the transitive beckon of propaganda. Consequently, these films are fascinating because they outline the political limits of screen fascination in the Troubles film. *Hunger* meditates, for example, on how fascination, filmically rendered as a 'passion for the image', has been variously implicated into narratives of political representation in Northern Ireland's urban politics. Directed by British visual artist Steve McQueen, *Hunger* is a powerfully stylised take on a familiar tale: Bobby Sands and the protests he spearheaded at HM Prison Maze in the late 1970s and early 1980s. *Hunger* is loosely divided into three parts: the first images of prisoner abuse in Maze, the second an extended-take conversation between Bobby Sands (Michael Fassbender) and a priest (Liam Cunningham) about the symbolism of hunger striking, the third a chronicle of Sands starving to death during his final, fatal hunger strike. To capture visually the ways in which bodies were historically politicised at Maze, McQueen uses the camera to create a field of spectatorship that is simultaneously intimate, critically distanced, and viscerally charged: his camera lingers over visual metonyms for the abused, starving body. Bleeding knuckles and bloody wounds are intercut with images of crumbs scattered across a napkin, uneaten food organised on a cafeteria tray, clean but unworn clothing, and waste-covered prison walls. The viewer's degree of fascination with these shots – of food, faeces, clean clothes and soiled blankets – depends upon a willingness (per the pensive spectator) to subordinate the desire for narrative development to the strange temporality of the film. In such a way, McQueen's camera allegorises the protests in Maze as a metonymic struggle between these stunning, momentary shots and the implicit, long-term narratives that give them meaning or, at the very least, a meaningful force of feeling within the republican community.

In the first third of the film, McQueen's camera plots Maze as a space choreographed by the confrontations between the prisoners, who refuse to wear prison uniforms, bathe or shave, and the prison guards, who labour to deprive these 'blanket protests' of any symbolic import by forcibly cleaning the prisoners while also beating them: hygiene has become micropolitical work. Early in the film, this dramatic tension is on display when a prisoner enters Maze for the first time. Dressed in his street clothes, the prisoner, Milligan (Brian Milligan), declares before a prison official, 'I will not wear the uniform of a criminal. I demand to wear my own clothes', a declaration that rehearses the stance taken by many prisoners at Maze to distinguish themselves as 'political prisoners', not 'ODCs',[25] through clothing. Moments later, Milligan is forced to strip naked and is escorted down a long corridor. As he walks the camera focuses on a detail we have not yet noticed: a fresh wound appears on Milligan's head and blood trickles down his face. The wound is fascinating precisely because it deprives the viewer of any felt sense of narrative mastery over the scene, for the camera here gestures to an off-camera, extra-diegetic visuality, which we cannot make exact sense of in terms of the film's narrative temporality. From the moment he strips to the moment he walks down the hallway, it appears that only a few seconds have elapsed on screen. But somewhere beyond what the camera is able to see, Milligan has come to possess this wound. Previous scenes in the film are suggestive: an opening shot focuses on a prison guard's bloodied knuckles. But Milligan's wound, deprived a direct, visual origin, indexes the abiding tension in *Hunger* between the progressive, diegetic world of the film and an extra-diegetic mode of pensive spectatorship that requires the viewers to coordinate McQueen's still images with historical statements about political protest, which, until the middle third of the film, are articulated through the materiality of screen sensations (e.g. the shock of Milligan's wound) rather than through narrative testimony.

This cinematic play – between fascinated wonder, elicited by the visual assortment of wounds and totems, and the narrative strategies of political expression in Northern Ireland – informs the extended conversation between Sands and a priest in the middle third of the film. In this remarkable extended shot, McQueen's camera frames the two men sitting across a table from each other in what the priest notices to be a very 'clean room', as if to provide the audience with a clinical view of the debates coursing through Belfast's Catholic community in the 1970s and 1980s. In this static sequence, the cinematic camera switches gears, using narrative as a means to explain the film's internal structures of fascination. Their conversation centres largely on the question: How can the politics of visuality in Maze, ostensibly hidden from public view, register any meaningful effects in Belfast's Catholic community? In response, Sands tropes fascination as political inspiration: 'You need the revolutionary, you need the cultural political soldier to give life a pulse, to give life a direction.' Dubbing the planned hunger strike a 'suicide mission', the priest summarily dismisses such claims: 'Freedom fighter? They're the men and women working out there in the community [of west Belfast]. And that was you, once upon a time, am I right? [. . .] That's where we need you, Bobby, and you know I'm right.'

By contrasting Sands' commitment with the priest's view, McQueen cinematically renders a pragmatic civic-mindedness amongst the republican community without diminishing the iconic, emotional appeal of Bobby Sands himself, who remains a monumental object of public fascination on the streets of Belfast today. Otherwise put, McQueen screens the transitive appeal of the hunger strike for Sands – once he dies on strike, another striker will take his place – while maintaining for the viewer an intransitive approach to the event through a series of camera shots that are at once visceral and clinical. The final section of *Hunger*, populated with jarring images of the emaciated body of Sands, however, raises some concerns about the relation between the film's formal experiments with screen fascination and its political content. In *Cinema and Ireland,* John Hill observes that films about the Republic and Northern Ireland are not up to the task of capturing the social and political complexity of the Troubles, for movies such as *Angel* (Neil Jordan, 1982) and *Cal* (Pat O'Connor, 1984) empty cinematic violence of political content by reverting to genre conventions or metaphysical speculations about the individual conscience. 'The ability to respond intelligently to history, and the willingness to engage with economic, political and cultural complexity', Hill writes, 'would need to be considerably greater that that which the cinema has so far demonstrated.'[26] Following Hill's analysis, Sands' isolation positions his agony within a genre convention in the Troubles film: the 'metaphysics of suffering'. With the political narrative transformed into a somatic event on screen, the viewer's fascination with Sands is similarly transformed into a mode of affective witnessing that evokes, but does not resolve, the film's shuttling among transitive and intransitive modes of fascination, the viewer ultimately unable to divest the visceral shock of McQueen's final shots of Sands from the republican iconography of suffering that the priest's civic-mindedness cannot abide. In turn, graphic shots of the body in pain are formally inaccessible to the collective or civic politics screened earlier in the film.

Much of *Hunger*'s fascination with Sands, then, resides in its narrative negotiation of the same debates (e.g. violent vs. non-violent protest) that have defined collectivist, public demonstrations undertaken by the republican community, debates that predominate in *Bloody Sunday*, a film that stages a historically based fictionalisation of an iconic event in the history of political struggle in Northern Ireland: the shooting of civilians during a non-violent protest march in Derry on 30 January, 1972.[27] Like *Hunger*, the film considers how fascination has been visually politicised through a cinematic gaze that is pensive like McQueen's but differently stylised, the film bypassing McQueen's still lives for the 'reality-effects' of docudrama and 'dramatic reconstruction'.[28] Hand-held camerawork, natural lighting, amateur or unknown actors, and improvisation are the key features of the docudrama, perhaps the least fascinating genre of film in the traditional sense, for its aesthetic gains momentum by reacting against the pleasures provided by CGI pyrotechnics. But it is fascinating in the terms outlined by Blanchot, Benjamin and Mulvey, for it submits entirely suspect political narratives such as the Widgery Report, the 'official' report on 'Bloody Sunday' until

the 2010 issue of the Saville Report, to the gaze of the pensive
spectator, a gaze in which 'the future looks back with greedy
fascination at the past', a gaze meant to deliver a cinematic
autocritique of Troubles narratives by reflecting and critically
suspending the perceptual-political submission to sectarian
iconography and inculcating the spectacle of non-violence into the
urban scene.[29]

Indeed, the politics of collective non-violence are the film's focal
point: its protagonist, the Civil Rights Association activist and
Protestant MP Ivan Cooper (James Nesbitt), speaks out for non-
violent solutions to sectarian division: championing civil rights. The
film's script remains suspicious of both the IRA and the British
government for their continued devotion to retaliatory violence; the
camera aspires to unsettle the hard-line positions that have
historically zoned urban Northern Ireland and to arrest the
transitive, hypnotic appeals of visual propaganda within the
cityscape. Fittingly, the camera itself plays a lead role in the film.
The opening sequence of *Bloody Sunday* shows an assortment of
media cameras gathered for two different press conferences. In one,
Cooper explains why the association has chosen to march through
the city: 'We're marching because ever since the partition of Ireland,
Catholics here in the North have suffered discrimination in a
Protestant-dominated land. That's why we're marching.' In the
other, Major General Ford (Tim Piggot-Smith), in command of the
British army stationed in Derry, cautions that the march represents
an illegal gathering. 'The law is the law and must be respected,' he
reminds the Civil Rights Association just before delivering this
warning: 'Any responsibility for any violence which may take place
must rest fairly and squarely on your shoulders.' With the cinematic
camera shooting each press conference as if it were a media camera,
Bloody Sunday plots a central conflict between the visual symbolism
of protest and the narratives that lay claim to these symbols in the
court of public opinion, a conflict that plays out on the
claustrophobic streets of Derry.

Derry's geography provides visual backing to these ideological
claims. On screen, it is a city of borders, of ossified boundaries and,
before the march begins, hand-held cameras trail after Cooper as he
navigates this contested terrain, meeting with his constituents on the
street, sparring with British soldiers, and imploring a leader within

the IRA to cooperate with the Civil Rights Association. Cooper desires for the march to be a fascinating affair, one that aspires to imaginatively cut across Derry's sectarian fault lines. But the British military has another spectacle in mind – the film intercuts Cooper's movements with the military's coordinated efforts to treat the march as an opportunity to conduct a mass arrest operation. The camera gazes on the First Paramilitary Unit (the 'paras') preparing for the march by studying grids of the city and interior shots of military headquarters, where a strategy is mapped out to catch two or three hundred of the 'Derry young hooligans' among the marchers, a strategy of 'maximum aggression, maximum arrests', in which the physical space of Derry's narrow streets will be used against the marchers. Roving amongst these views, the camera plots the march through Derry as doubly fascinating: for the marchers it aspires to transform the tenaciously ideological ways of moving through the city via the intransitive display of non-violence; for the military, the appeal is purely transitive, the march a means to stage publicly the state's continuing authority.

When the march begins, the camera captures two collective views, that of the marchers as they walk through the city and that of the military as they watch the marchers – the film leaves no doubt that the latter seeks to claim perceptual mastery over the former, evident when the cinematic camera catches sight of a military helicopter swirling overhead. Though aerial surveillance does not merge with the perspective of the cinematic camera (i.e. Greengrass does not screen any shot of the city from the helicopter's vantage), the view is nevertheless implied in the radio transmissions sent and received by the British commanders, who chart the progress of the march based on these reports. But the implied master shot of the helicopter's eagle eye does not confer mastery, its absence on screen auguring a conceptual breakdown within the military's field of vision. Enter the cinema of delay, in which we witness something happen on the street, and then, a few moments later, we listen as the event is transmitted back to the British brigade, where a decision must be made about how to proceed. These delays in transmission stall the narrative lines of development between the brigade and the paras, who listen to events unfold on the streets from a walled-in courtyard. Accordingly, the film deprives the helicopter's 'master shot' of its transitive powers while simultaneously providing the viewer with an intransitive gaze at the imagistic and narrative mix-ups that preceded 'Bloody Sunday'.

During the march, the film's other collective perspective is that of the marchers, captured by a small hand-held camera operated by a member of the Civil Rights Association. Directed by Cooper, who it follows, this diegetic camera strikes a remarkable contrast with the army's cinema of delay, for it realises a cinema of immediacy, in which the audience is directed by Cooper to gaze at events the moment they happen and to be fascinated into the bargain; in these scenes, the film's internal and external structures of fascination begin to merge. Gazing into the diegetic camera, for example, Cooper enjoins the viewer to be pensive spectator, one who visually shuttles back and forth between the specific images he points to and the overall symbolism and progression of the march. As Cooper approaches the flatbed truck that will lead the marchers, he points at the Civil Rights Association banner and remarks to the cameraman, 'Make sure you got that'; moments later, Cooper instructs the camera to document the number of people marching – both the diegetic camera and the cinematic camera obey this cue by panning across the mass of people assembled behind the truck. Later, we see Cooper pointing to something off screen: 'See that there', he says to the camera, 'how provocative is that.' The camera cuts to what he witnesses: soldiers positioned atop a concrete wall, their guns trained on the crowd below. Until this moment in the march, the diegetic camera has, from Cooper's point of view, testified to the collective, symbolic strength of non-violent protest. But this image of the soldiers shifts its narrative direction, from non-violent protest to furious confrontation, evident when the cinematic camera splits off from the diegetic camera and positions itself amongst the marchers, who are collectively outraged. The call of 'Brits go home!' is taken up while youths rush to confront the British army at the next barricade.

But what seems like an affront to the fascination enjoined by the non-violent protest – this image of the 'Derry hooligans' splitting off from the march to confront the British military – is, in fact, a re-articulation of it. In his speech to the crowd after the march concludes, Cooper holds the narrative of non-violent protest intact by incorporating this image of youth rioting into a larger story about non-violence. In this speech, he frames the march not in terms of its shared goals (i.e. the end of unionist domination, the emergence of a shared civic space) but in terms of the choices it symbolically represents, between non-violent and violent solutions to political problems. Pointing to the youths rioting in the background, Cooper tells his audience, 'If we are going to give a future to the children of this city [. . .] we have to show them that non-violence works.' 'Civil rights,' Cooper concludes, 'isn't the soft option', though it certainly is the difficult one, given the reactionary violence apparent in this scene. This speech centrally articulates the politics of fascination at work in the film – for Cooper, the visceral image of violence inspires the difficult working out of alternative narratives of non-violence, a narrative that Cooper frames for the crowd in terms of the global civil rights movement. This is the alternative he conjures when he asks the crowd to envision themselves as part of a shared community whose other members include those who marched for civil rights in America and those who marched for independence in India: this is the alternative visuality the film asks the viewer to juxtapose to the spectacle of youth rioting in Derry and of paratroopers storming into the Bogside and opening fire on the crowd.

But Greengrass concedes that the collective fascination with these alternatives has not had the same kind of purchase in Northern Ireland as has the fascination with violence – this is due, in large part, to the status of the image. When the paras storm the Bogside, we see other diegetic cameras at work: photographers take pictures of soldiers beating civilians and firing into the crowd. After the event, the brigade radio reports that media photographers are taking pictures of a civilian casualty who is covered in a blood-saturated civil rights banner. We have seen this image before, once in the film, in which the camera explains that the victim was shot by the paras while trying to help an injured man, his body later covered with the banner, and once in historical photographs of the event, for the image of Bernard McGuigan shot dead, his body partially covered with a blanket, is an iconic one for 'Bloody Sunday'. As such, the prominence of the image as political iconography informs the final scenes of the film. Though the camera in *Bloody Sunday* aspires to document the attitudes and the errors within Britain's military leadership that precipitated the shootings, and though it sympathises with the victims and, more generally, the civil rights movement, it cannot escape the conclusion that non-violent protest ironically managed to rationalise violence as the only viable political option in Northern Ireland. This is the explicit message Cooper delivers to the assembled press corps after the event, in which he states straight into the camera, 'I just want to say this to the British government [. . .] you have destroyed the civil rights movement and you've given the IRA the biggest victory it will ever have.' In this final prognosis, Cooper references the ascension of bad fascination (read transitive) to the exclusion of his narrative bid for civil rights, further evidence of which is provided by the final shot in the film showing young men in Derry joining the IRA.

Hunger and *Bloody Sunday* formally experiment with screen mythologies of Northern Ireland, the morphology of both hostile to cinematic renderings of the 'atavistic nation' yet unable to revise entirely this projection – both films acknowledging that the projection, through its iconography of suffering, maintains a sure traction within sectarian self-representation. Thus Cooper's concession at the end of *Bloody Sunday* voices a salient point about fascination and historical habits of memorialisation in Northern Ireland: the distance between 'transfixed unrest' and 'hypnotic gazing' widens significantly when screen memories cathect Bloody Sunday and the hunger strikes into the blunt-force appeal of propaganda. Though these films resist this conversion for the most part, they nevertheless recognise the pressure to be fascinating without being politically 'hypnotic' in visual work about the Troubles. Northern Ireland has long been a fascinating state to European and American audiences: hopefully, this cinematic effort to avoid the more salacious pleasures of fascination and to screen more radical ways of gazing at the nation will continue.

Chapter Five

FINDING A VOICE: IRISH-LANGUAGE FILM IN THE TWENTY-FIRST CENTURY

Heather Macdougall

Film and television *as Gaeilge* has benefited from growing theoretical and critical attention over the past decade, but it may at first appear curious that an essay on this subject would be included in a collection on visual culture. After all, the films and television programmes produced in Irish are distinguished more by an aural characteristic – the language that is spoken – than by a visual one, given that the cinematography has so far displayed no fundamental differences from English-language media. And yet the visual nature of the media itself is crucial. Even a very superficial comparison of the impact of Raidió na Gaeltachta (RnaG), which began broadcasting in 1972, and Teilifís na Gaeilge (TG4),[1] which aired its first programmes in 1996, demonstrates that the visual medium has succeeded in reaching a much larger national audience than the strictly oral one. While RnaG has been an important cultural resource for the Gaeltacht communities in the west of Ireland, its impact has been limited to its audience of fluent Irish speakers, by far the minority population: the 2011 census in the Republic of Ireland found that only 1.8 per cent of the population self-reported as speaking Irish on a daily basis (outside of instructional settings). The visual nature of television, however, has allowed TG4 to broaden its audience because visual cues make the material more accessible to those with an imperfect knowledge of the language, including the approximately 40 per cent of residents who reported having (at least some) knowledge of Irish.[2] More importantly, perhaps, subtitling technology made it possible to disseminate Irish-language culture beyond the Irish-language community.

One reason that TG4 was founded was because the national broadcaster, RTÉ, had failed to incorporate a meaningful amount of Irish-language material within the mainstream programming: Iarfhlaith Watson notes that while 6 per cent of RTÉ's radio and television broadcasting was in the Irish language in 1965, even that meagre figure had dropped to 2 per cent by 1985.[3] Similarly, as will be demonstrated, the Irish Film Board focused overwhelmingly on English-language production until a partnership with TG4 brought new funding to encourage Irish-language projects. In short, as Ireland has begun to develop an increasingly vibrant national cinema and television culture over the past few decades, the incorporation of the 'national language'[4] within this project has a chequered historical record, but is now potentially on the cusp of a revitalised future.

What follows in this essay is a theoretical examination of what Irish-language film might offer to Irish national cinema in the twenty-first century. At stake in this discussion is the place of the traditional spoken language – which at times has been associated with a narrow nationalism – as Ireland increasingly makes its own voice heard through the modern visual and international language of cinema, often associated (especially in predominantly Anglo-phone markets) with the particular 'dialect', if one might call it that, of Hollywood. I argue that contemporary Irish-language film complements English-language indigenous production and is crucial to the development of a national cinema in Ireland that expresses the specificity and uniqueness of Irish culture, while also reflecting a national identity that has plural rather than homogenous articu-lations. This argument is supported by an examination of competing theories of both nation and national cinema, which will serve to illuminate the seemingly paradoxical situation of Irish-language film: despite the fact that the language is an integral part of the official national identity, it has been marginalised within the development of an Irish national cinema. The application of theories of national cinema is complicated by the fact that the 'national' language is spoken fluently by only a small minority of citizens. The existing linguistic situation also raises further theoretical questions: new research in the field of screen translation, for example, has demonstrated that choices in subtitling and dubbing, like in all forms of translation, are not value-neutral decisions. Additionally, theories from the field of sociolinguistics contribute useful insights into the ways that popular culture and modern media can help to revitalise a threatened language. Given the unique position of the Irish language with respect to the Irish nation, then, the theorisation of Irish-language film as part of Irish cinema requires theories of national cinema to be combined with work from these other disciplines. The theoretical paradigms of national cinema are therefore necessarily extended and renegotiated when applied to the Irish context, as a result of their intersection with theories from other fields.

While an in-depth discussion of attitudes towards the Irish language is beyond the purview of this chapter, it will suffice here to repeat Ruth Lysaght's claim that when TG4 began broadcasting in the 1990s, it 'had to take on the almost completely negative image that was the heritage of the Irish language'.[5] In order to contest that negative image, the station has consistently emphasised high production values by commissioning quality drama, documentary, and current affairs programmes and by broadcasting hit international shows – such as American animation *South Park* – in translation. In short, it presents an aesthetic that differs little from mainstream television and certainly has none of the low-budget public access feel that many early detractors said would be unavoidable with a minority-interest station. Furthermore, TG4 provides a positive, 'trendy' view of life in the Irish language (which does not preclude a critical look at various aspects of Irish-language ideology or tradition). It has been so successful in its task that it was credited in the national press with single-handedly changing the language's image from 'scary to sexy, backward to modern, conservative to chic'.[6]

As well as broadcast television, TG4 has also facilitated the sustained production of films in Irish, often by partnering with other film institutions such as the Irish Film Board. When asked where film fit into TG4's vision of Irish-language media, deputy CEO of TG4 Pádhraic Ó Ciardha replied that:

> [I]t is clearly a badge of honour or a symbol of maturity in a minority-language broadcaster, in any broadcaster really, that you make film, and drama particularly [. . .]. When we were

> founded in 1995 our ambition was, like our Welsh cousins, to
> make a feature film that would show that the language was alive,
> could deal with the narrative form, could come alive in that art
> form.[7]

Beyond the perceived prestige of film over television, film also has a
greater potential to reach international – in addition to domestic –
audiences, and for that reason I would like to focus primarily on
film in this chapter.

National Cinema – theoretical arguments

The sheer volume of scholarly work on the subject attests to the
enduring appeal of the nation as a lens through which to categorise,
examine, celebrate and theorise the medium of film. The concept of
'national cinema' as a theoretical framework is alluring in its apparent
simplicity. The diversity of approaches and opinions, however, belies
what might otherwise seem to be an intuitively straightforward
concept. Richard Abel et al begin their collection of essays on *Early
Cinema and the 'National'* by asserting that ideas about the nation(al)
have provided a means for categorising films since the very dawn of
cinema. As early as 1896, for example, the Lumière brothers
organised the films in their sales catalogue by country of origin.[8] Since
that time, the nation has been employed as a way of grouping films
together for various purposes, such as festival or awards programmes,
historical narratives, and (not insignificantly) academic publications
and film studies curricula. Stephen Crofts confirms that in academia
most writing on film prior to the 1980s adopted 'common-sense'
notions of national cinema, with various publications on particular
national cinemas focusing simply on the films produced within a
given nation-state. Furthermore, nation-based research on films
tended to read these films 'as expressions of a putative national spirit'
rather than analysing the industrial frameworks that influence film
production differently in different states.[9]

Since the 1980s, however, scholarly debates that question the
very concepts of nations and of national cinema have provided
fertile ground for new understandings of both the role of cinema in
nation-building and the influence of nationalism in the production
and study of film. Benedict Anderson's publication in 1983 of
Imagined Communities, as well as the ongoing work of Jürgen

Habermas and Eric Hobsbawm among others, have refocused the attention of scholars onto the socially constructed nature of modern nations and the importance of the various media in nation-building projects. In the field of film studies, Andrew Higson's watershed essay 'The Concept of National Cinema' was published in *Screen* in 1989 and laid out an argument for an expanded theory of national cinema(s) which included a more comprehensive appreciation of film culture within a given nation. One of his most ground-breaking suggestions was that a theory of national cinema could not ignore the nation as a site of consumption as well as production; that is, he argued for a fuller consideration of the film-watching culture of the nation, including the 'naturalised' role that Hollywood films play in many national cultures.[10] He also identified two conceptual methods of establishing the specificity of a national cinema. The first was to create a contrast against other national cinemas, thereby producing 'meaning and identity through difference'.[11] The second was to link the cinema to other, pre-existing nationally specific cultural practices.[12] These concepts can be productively applied to the Irish example, where the use of the indigenous Irish language could satisfy either method of establishing a unique national cinema, since it asserts its difference against other (Anglophone) cinemas, while also creating a close connection between the medium of film and a pre-existing indigenous culture.

Meanwhile, Benedict Anderson's stress on the popular press and mass literacy as key factors in fostering the perception of interconnectedness (or 'imagined community') was extended by other scholars to include audio-visual media, which similarly has the capacity to create a feeling of shared culture among members of a nation who, in practice, never meet the vast majority of their fellow citizens personally and may actually have very little in common with them. Anderson points out that even for two people in opposite ends of the country, with 'no necessary reason to know of one another's existence', the circulation of printed material throughout the nation enabled them to 'visualise in a general way the existence of thousands and thousands like themselves'.[13] Anderson's focus is on print-capitalism, but his theories are also very applicable to the intra-national communication that occurs through nationally distributed film, television, and other modern media. Higson's and Anderson's theories, when taken together, complement each other by confirming the role that cinema might play in building national identity: by encouraging the perception of a shared culture intranationally, and by asserting difference from other nations. What is included or excluded within a given nation's cinema, then, becomes of utmost importance in the construction or affirmation of a national cultural identity.

Just as film scholars have found the nation to provide a useful framework for writing about cinema, many national governments have implemented policies to encourage filmmaking as a medium for national cultural expression, often influencing the direction of that expression. In the introduction to his 1996 volume *Film Policy: International, National and Regional Perspectives*, Albert Moran confirms the power of cinema 'for generating and spreading ideas'[14] and that films made in (or indeed about) particular communities 'cumulatively produce a mental landscape, a world view, a particular way of thinking about reality'.[15] Again, what is included or excluded in the cumulative cinematic representations of a given national culture have real-world implications in the construction of identity. In this light, it is clear that the use of the Irish language in film bears important implications in identity formation for both native Irish speakers and for English-speaking Irish citizens who still consider the language to be an important part of their national heritage. The perspectives of these two groups, however, have not always been aligned, as will become clear throughout this chapter.

The Irish language on screen

In terms of Irish cinema, the key agency for funding indigenous production is Bord Scannán na hÉireann/the Irish Film Board (IFB). The IFB was first established by government statute in 1980, but was under-funded and was then dissolved in 1987. Since its reinstatement in 1993 (with a more substantial budget), the IFB has remained the cornerstone of the Irish film industry. After decades of minimal and sporadic indigenous production, the importance of state support became clear as the annual number of Irish-made films increased rapidly following the board's re-inauguration: there were three Irish films made in 1992 (the year before the IFB was re-established), twenty in 1997, and over fifty by 1999.[16] As Ruth Barton notes, 'ten years after its inception, the Board was able to lay claim to having supported the making of nearly a hundred feature films as well as several hundred short films and documentaries, this in a country that produced 18 feature films during the 1980s'.[17] Furthermore, the films supported by the IFB display a wide array of approaches towards representing Irish culture and identity; they have included literary adaptations, explorations of contemporary social issues, popular genre films, and fresh perspectives on Ireland's past. Clearly, the IFB supports a pluralist approach to cultural expression. The record on including the Irish language in that project, however, has been somewhat inconsistent.

While the focus of this chapter is on contemporary Irish-language film, a brief look at earlier, pre-Film Board projects is instructive in illuminating the competing ideologies that provide some background to the current issues surrounding the place of language within a national film culture, as well as the place of film within the language movement. From 1956 to 1964, a non-governmental language promotion group called Gael Linn made a series of Irish-language short documentary newsreels. Máiréad Pratschke explains that by using the Irish language in film, Gael Linn linked the language to 'a form of modern media associated with popular entertainment and success' and was attempting 'to eliminate the link between the Irish language and rural poverty in the public consciousness'.[18] The success of these newsreels inspired Gael Linn to pursue more ambitious film projects. In 1960, the organisation commissioned filmmaker George Morrison to produce a feature-length documentary about the events leading up to the 1916 Easter Rising. The resultant film *Mise Éire* – which is a collage of historical footage and photographs, accompanied by an Irish-language voice-over and an orchestral score – presented a heroic view of the Irish people themselves and as such was, according to Harvey O'Brien, 'a crowd-pleasing portrait of centuries of struggle against English occupation'.[19] It was followed by a less popular sequel, *Saoirse?* (1961), which employed an identical aesthetic formula but examined the contentious period following independence, including the civil war.

Looking back now, the films may seem slow and ideologically heavy-handed, but it is important to remember that the use of archival footage linked by photographs and newspaper headlines was 'a format that was novel at the time'.[20] While it was certainly novel for Irish filmmaking, O'Brien is quick to point out that it had two important precedents: first, the Soviet montage movement including Sergei Eisenstein and Dziga Vertov, but especially Esfir Shub's archival compilation documentary *Fall of the Romanov Dynasty* (1927); and second, the National Film Board of Canada short *City of Gold* (Wolf Koening and Colin Low, 1957) which used archival still photographs as the sole visual accompaniment to a spoken recollection of the Klondike gold rush and which Morrison may have seen when it screened at the Cork Film Festival.[21] Morrison echoed and combined these techniques in his own filmmaking, which was nonetheless completely novel in terms of Irish cinema. While the director wrote the script and had full creative control over the film's aesthetic, the decision that it be presented through the Irish language was a stipulation of funders Gael Linn rather than Morrison's own preference. He was in fact quite keen to release the film in English, but Gael Linn was adamant on the language question.[22] It would be very difficult to argue, then, that the visual style employed by Morrison grew out of any intrinsic qualities of the Irish language, beyond perhaps Martin Doyle's suggestion that the shots of newspaper headlines in English were chosen intentionally 'so as not to alienate non-Irish speakers' in a film that was presented without subtitles yet targeted to a broad national audience.[23]

Film scholar Jerry White is critical of the unproblematised use of Irish-language narration in *Mise Éire*, noting that 'the complex ideology and history of the decline of the Irish language is smoothed over and obscured'.[24] We will see echoes of this kind of criticism again below in relation to the 'trendy' films associated with TG4 in the 1990s and 2000s, particularly those that have no narrative engagement with either the communities where Irish is actually spoken or language politics in the rest of the country. The Gael Linn films, like the newsreels, promoted a normalised view of the language while both the filmmakers and their audiences were well aware that an Irish-speaking nation was a distant goal rather than a contemporary reality. Martin McLoone points out, for example, that exhibitors felt compelled to hand out a written summary in English so that audiences might be able to follow the action; even so, he argues, the propagandistic style and content of the films[25] work to exacerbate the view of Irish as the 'private discourse' of a narrow kind of nationalism, and the choice of language 'severely curtailed the impact that the films could have made, especially in Britain and America'.[26] This was, then, national cinema for a national(ist) audience.

While Gael Linn was a Dublin-based organisation, a different kind of Irish-language cinema emerged in the Connemara Gaeltacht in the 1970s. Bob Quinn, a disgruntled television director, had left his job at RTÉ to establish himself in the west of Ireland where he began working on community-oriented film and video projects. His work was given a boost when the Arts Council established a Film Script Award and, in 1978, chose Quinn's Irish-language feature *Poitín* (1977) as the inaugural recipient. This could be read as an early recognition of film in Irish as more 'artistic' than in English; in Ireland, as elsewhere in the Anglophone world, films made in languages other than English are normally considered more suitable for 'art houses' or cultural festivals, regardless of the content of the films themselves.

Martin McLoone notes in relation to the Connemara-set *Poitín* that 'its study of the grim realities of rural life [. . .] is neither Flaherty nor Ford'.[27] Contributing to this de-romanticisation was Quinn's choice to shoot the film inland, away from the picturesque mountains and crashing sea that feature so heavily in Robert Flaherty's *The Man of Aran* (1934), and in drab colours that bear no resemblance to the bright greens of John Ford's *The Quiet Man* (1952). Quinn's work was more regional than national. Writing of his own work in 2000, Quinn commented, 'I seem purposely to have been making my oeuvres as obscure as possible, in a language little known outside Ireland, in a community equally rather despised by progressive Irish people.'[28] Quinn himself lived in Connemara and spoke Irish, the natural means of everyday communication for the local community (although it was not his own mother tongue). It is perhaps for this reason that his films did not fit easily into an idealised view wherein the language was being held up as an emblem of traditional Irish identity; visually, this is matched with a refusal to romanticise the landscape of the Irish-speaking region. McLoone perceptively concludes that Quinn's films 'exist in an ironic relationship with both tradition and modernity, on one hand castigating cultural nationalism's use, or abuse, of Gaelic Ireland while at the same time being deeply suspicious of the modernity represented by Dublin'.[29]

Irish-language film since the beginning of TG4

Since its inception in 1996, TG4 has worked self-consciously towards offering a young, hip image of the language within an audio-visual medium. Its focus on sports, drama, travel shows, children's programming and even soap operas stands in stark contrast to the heavy-handed nationalist and documentary films of Gael Linn, the gritty independent Quinn pictures, the occasional educational reels available previously through the school system, or even the 'art house' aesthetic that is often associated with non-Anglophone European cinema. In addition to commissioning its own television programmes, the station has also partnered with other institutions in order to promote Irish-language film projects. The *Oscailt* funding scheme for short films was launched in 1998 as a cooperative effort with the Irish Film Board, while the year 2000 brought a complementary programme, the *Lasair* initiative, which supports Irish-language shorts shot on digital media. The latter is a joint project of TG4 and FilmBase, an organisation that provides low-cost training and equipment to emerging filmmakers. The films made through these two initiatives are guaranteed a broadcast on the station and a screening at the Cork Film Festival, and most of them have also applied successfully to other Irish and international film festivals, thereby bringing a more heterogeneous cinematic representation of Irish identity to both a global and domestic audience, while also employing a unique aspect of Irish heritage (the indigenous language) to assert Ireland's difference against other national cinemas. In terms of visual style, the Irish-language short films more or less match the films made through comparable English-language schemes of the IFB; there is a great deal of variety within both languages in terms of aesthetic objectives and technical accomplishment, but the differences are apparent only between individual filmmakers rather than between the two linguistic systems.

One of the most celebrated products of the Irish-langauge short film initiatives is Daniel O'Hara's *Yu Ming is Ainm Dom/My Name is Yu Ming* (2003), which was funded through the *Lasair* scheme. The narrative follows a young Chinese man who randomly chooses a country to visit (Ireland) and diligently studies up on what the encyclopaedia informs him is the national language of that country

Fig. 5.1 Yu Ming (Daniel Wu) has trouble finding someone who speaks Irish in Dublin. *Yu Ming is Ainm Dom* (Daniel O'Hara, 2003).

(Irish). When he arrives in Dublin, he has no trouble reading the bilingual signs but believes his poor command of Irish is to blame when no one understands him (Fig. 5.1).

Eventually, an old man at a pub overhears him trying to communicate with the bartender and explains, much to Yu Ming's surprise, that people in Ireland generally speak English. *Yu Ming* took both the Best Irish Short and Best First Short awards for its debut screening at the Galway Film Fleadh, and then went on to win several other awards at international festivals and an IFTA (the Irish equivalent of an Oscar). The film balances a deliberate departure from traditional representations of the Irish language against the current reality in Ireland; in the words of director Daniel O'Hara, audiences responded to the film because 'so much of the drama in Irish had either been set in the Gaeltacht or, if it was set in Dublin, everyone was speaking Irish and it was unrealistic'.[30] The film uses gentle humour to make its point. It also pays tribute to the survival of Irish as a living language, however, as our protagonist settles happily in the Gaeltacht at the end of the film.

O'Hara's success with *Yu Ming is Ainm Dom* led to a second short film, *Fluent Dysphasia*, through the *Oscailt* scheme in 2004. In this film, Stephen Rea plays a man ('Murph') who suffers a head injury that leaves him unable to speak or understand English, yet he is now miraculously fluent in Irish. As with the first film, O'Hara gently questions assumptions about the Irish language. For example, after the accident Murph's monolingual friend believes him to be possessed and speaking in tongues. Meanwhile, when the camera adopts Murph's point of view, his friend's English is rendered as unintelligible gibberish. This is a very effective cinematic technique to remind viewers that English and Irish are linguistically equidistant, and it should theoretically be no harder for an English speaker to learn Irish than vice versa. Furthermore, some hope for a linguistic revival is provided by younger characters; the two men are able to communicate through their daughter and nephew, respectively, who have mastered the language at school (Fig. 5.2).

Most importantly, both *Yu Ming* and *Fluent Dysphasia* use the visual medium of film constructively to explore, through humorous fictional narratives, the role of Irish for different segments of contemporary Irish society – Dubliners, foreign visitors, Gaeltacht residents, and students of the language. Each of these groups has a different linguistic identity with respect to Irish, and it is one of O'Hara's strengths to be able to bring them together creatively within his short films.

These two short films are unquestionably part of Irish national cinema, no matter how one would choose to define that concept. They are funded through national agencies, their diegetic content contributes to a contemporary debate of national interest, and they were widely seen throughout the nation: at festivals, on broadcast television, in schools, and in the case of *Yu Ming* in mainstream cinemas when it was packaged with Jim Sheridan's *In America* for Irish theatrical release. Theoretically speaking, then, films such as these have a very important role in influencing notions of national identity. This can be seen by looking at how the films might function with respect to Anderson's and Higson's theories on identity-building through a combination of shared intra-national communication and affirmation of difference against other nations. On one level, the comedy of the film relies on a wink and a nod to Irish audiences who recognise the complexities and ironies of their official national language; this recognition, at least, is shared across the nation regardless of the linguistic identity of individual viewers, and therefore creates among the audience members a sense of collective experience at the national level. On another level, it

I can't talk to anyone else.

Fig. 5.2 Murph (Stephen Rea) is grateful that his daughter (Jayne Stynes) has learned to speak Irish at school. *Fluent Dysphasia* (Daniel O'Hara, 2004).

signals to both Irish and foreign viewers that Ireland has something different from other nations – its own language. This is particularly important within the cinematic sphere as it operates to differentiate this kind of Irish cinema from the dominant Anglo-American representations in mainstream global culture. In short, the use of the Irish language in addition to English positions these examples of Irish films as national texts that nonetheless recognise a plural articulation of national identity.

Linguistic identity – filmmakers and audiences

It is necessary to consider both filmmakers and audiences in terms of how their interests or potential contributions might depend on their linguistic identities. Ruth Lysaght expresses the frustrations of many native Irish speakers when she complains that 'English-speakers make their *Oscailt* in order to break through into the [film] industry in general, and disregard the language as a tool for expression'.[31] This comment hints at charges of cultural appropriation, and raises doubts about the premise that the national language belongs to all members of the nation. It also reinforces the idea that to date the only difference between English- and Irish-language production is language, rather than any visual or aesthetic characteristic that may be associated more with one tradition than the other (other than subtitles, for which the visual impact is discussed below).

Responding to criticism that its *Oscailt* scheme encourages simple translations of English texts from filmmakers who might perceive the level of competition to be lower for Irish-language submissions, the Irish Film Board discontinued the programme. As reported in *Film Ireland*, the major trade publication for the Irish cinema industry, in December 2007:

> Concerns about the Irish language short being 'ghetto-ised' have resulted in the dedicated scheme Oscailt being discontinued. Instead, all five short schemes have been opened up to Irish-language submissions. The thinking behind this is to give those writing *as Gaeilge* as much scope as possible and also to discourage shorts being translated purely for the purpose of funding.[32]

The involvement of Anglophone creative talent in the Irish-language production process is hotly debated, but controversy over the linguistic group targeted for consumption is also lively. Cathal Goan recalls that in the early planning stages of TG4:

> [T]he debate became sharply focused on the choice between a national service available to everyone in Ireland through the medium of the Irish language, or a service devoted exclusively to the Gaeltacht. A consensus emerged that a national service, based in the Gaeltacht, was the preferred option.[33]

Having decided to market itself to the entire Irish population, and keeping in mind the variable linguistic abilities of its potential audience, TG4 therefore has chosen to subtitle nearly all of its Irish-language programming. Lysaght welcomes this policy, calling it the station's 'most innovative feature' and noting that 'people from a non-Irish speaking background can see something of how life may be lived in this language [. . .] providing the first real opportunity for one group to communicate with the other on an imaginative and expressive basis'.[34] Media theorist Aodán Mac Póilin also applauds targeting a broad national audience, noting that in a more insular broadcasting environment, the 'opportunities to influence that [majority] community towards a better appreciation and under-standing of the minority culture are decreased'.[35]

The policy, however, has drawn fire from minority-language activists such as Eithne O'Connell, who argues that the visual linguistic information is privileged over the aural. She points to studies that have demonstrated that 'viewers who have no need of subtitles find it hard to avoid reading them'.[36] This can have dire consequences in the Irish situation, she claims, because adding English subtitles 'critically undermines the original monolingual relationship between broadcaster and viewer and potentially poses a real threat to the already beleaguered language community of Irish speakers'.[37] While O'Connell focuses on broadcast television, the parallels with subtitled films are obvious. In addition to the concerns of reduced value for native speakers, there are theoretical implications for non-speakers as well. Michael Cronin notes that, in general, the reading of subtitles:

> [c]onfers a sort of omniscience, as if the all-seeing eye of the camera was paralleled by the all-understanding ear of the reader of subtitles. The spectator takes on the role of interpreter experiencing the joy of connectedness without the pain of connection, the time and effort necessary to master languages. However, the very availability of the subtitles themselves indicates the limits to any omniscience that might be assumed by their readers.[38]

In the Irish context, the twin effects of subtitles both to connect and to distance the viewer from the action on screen is heightened: for English-speaking Irish viewers, subtitles allow access to cultural products in their own national language while at the same time constantly reminding them of their separateness from that linguistic heritage. The consequence of this is that the cinematic medium has brought a new dimension to the discourse surrounding the official national language, one that brings together Irish speakers (on the audio track) and English viewers (through the visible subtitles), thereby facilitating the kind of intra-national communication that Anderson speaks of while avoiding a homogenising view of Irish identity. In other words, not only is the Irish language a valuable asset to Irish national cinema, but the cinema itself is an important asset to the construction of a plural articulation of Irish national identity.

Conclusion

The breadth and depth of scholarly and popular attention to the confident indigenous Irish national cinema that has developed since the re-launch of the Irish Film Board in the mid-1990s is testament to the fact that cinema enjoys a prominent role in the way that audiences, both from within and without the nation, make sense of Irish cultural identity. Despite Kevin Rockett's claims that indigenous productions initially failed to challenge foreign cinematic stereotypes, Irish national cinema has developed a distinctive voice that is increasingly recognised both at home and abroad. However, as film theorist Toby Miller argues, 'no cinema that claims resistance to Hollywood in the name of national specificity is worthy of endorsement if it does not actually attend to sexual and racial minorities and women, along with class politics.'[39] In a bilingual nation, this same argument is easily applied to language as well. While there is no overwhelming consensus for the comparative roles of the Irish and English languages within Irish national cinema, either in terms of production or consumption, it is clear from films such as those of Daniel O'Hara that the tensions between the two languages can be creatively explored through film; given the visual nature of film and the capacity for subtitling, cinematic texts such as these have the potential to reach a broad audience and thereby inform crucial debates on the construction of both national identity and a national cinema.

Advocates for a more cohesive bilingual national film and television industry, one that unites the two linguistic traditions, have many reasons to be optimistic. Several notable Irish actors, including Stephen Rea, Brendan Gleeson, Colm Meaney, Cillian Murphy, Gabriel Byrne and Fionnula Flanagan have all appeared in both English- and Irish-language productions. The cross-over appeal of these and other celebrities, as well as thematically bilingual programmes such as those of Daniel O'Hara, may encourage greater collaboration between filmmakers working in both languages. It may also help to promote interaction among Irish speakers along the full continuum of fluency, rather than perpetuating a notion of two completely distinct linguistic communities. Finally, international acceptance of Irish-language film may yet also come. Tom Collins' 2007 Irish-language feature *Kings* screened at Toronto and other important film festivals, picking up several awards, and distinguished itself as the first Irish film ever submitted for consideration in the Oscar competition for best foreign-language film. Ultimately it would not secure a nomination, but the submission itself marks an important step in the Irish film industry's strategic positioning. While maintaining the advantages of the cultural affinities it shares with mainstream Anglo-American cinema, Ireland is also beginning to recognise the potential of marketing itself among the prestigious European film cultures that generally dominate the foreign film category. Whether *Kings* will be an isolated example or whether it will be followed by more Irish-language features that strengthen the presence of the national language within Irish cultural identity as it is expressed through the national cinema remains to be seen.

The research leading to this paper was made possible by funding from the Ireland Canada University Foundation as well as the *Fonds Québécois de Recherche sur la Société et la Culture*. I would like to thank Haidee Wasson and Michael Kenneally of Concordia University for their direction and encouragement. I would also like to thank the editors of this volume for their invaluable suggestions and insight.

FORM

Chapter Six

MEMORY TO FILM:
REVIVING THEIRISH DIASPORA
IN STEPHEN FREARS' *LIAM*

Emmie McFadden

Ego credo ut vita pauperum est simpliciter atrox, simpliciter sanguinarius atrox, in Liverpollio.[1]

Adaptation studies and diaspora studies are two interdisciplinary subjects that are fundamentally concerned with the notion of 'origin'. However, *Liam* (Stephen Frears 2001), as an adaptation and as a film about Irish diaspora, constitutes an exploration of origins in which the origin is at once signalled as being important and traceable, but then also found to be contradictory and confusing. *Liam* centres on the story of the Sullivan family living in Liverpool during the 1930s depression. Although Sullivan is an Irish surname, we are never explicitly told that the central characters in *Liam* are Irish; however, when we watch *Liam* we get the distinct impression that this is a film that is undoubtedly about Ireland and Irish identity. One of the ways in which the film signals a genetic kinship to Irish ethnicity is by drawing on the cultural memory of James Joyce's *A Portrait of the Artist as a Young Man*, published in 1916. However, like the Sullivan family's unavowed Irish origins, *Liam* does not explicitly declare that it is an adaptation of Joyce's text. Thus, the film's story offers an analogy between the film's status as an adaptation and the ambiguous national identity of its characters.

In Irish diaspora studies, those who conceal their ethnic origin from the census are despondently referred to as 'the lost Irish': descendents who do not want to be associated with 'the old country'.[2] At the same time, ethnic identifiers such as surnames and maiden names connect migrants to their country of origin. Similarly,

93

in film adaptation studies, not all adaptations acknowledge their status as an adaptation and by extension they conceal their story origins from the spectator. Adaptation theorist Robert Stam points out that film adaptations get 'caught up in the ongoing whirl of inter-textual reference and transformation, of texts generating other texts in an endless process of recycling, transformation, and transmuta-tion, with no clear point of origin'.[3] This implies that film adaptations can effectively hide, conceal or indeed become detached from their sources, that the origins of the story become buried in the film.

Narrative theorist Gérard Genette argues that there are many dif-ferent ways of identifying a text's relationship with other texts, and he offers the term 'transtextuality' to account for 'all that sets the text in a relationship, whether obvious or concealed, with other texts'.[4] Genette further subdivides the concept of transtextuality into five organised types: intertextuality, paratextuality, metatextuality, hyper-textuality and architextuality. Each of the five types accounts for the different relations one text can have with the text proper, while collec-tively they draw attention to all of the texts that are linked to the text proper. The omnisciency of Genette's transtextuality has prompted Catherine Grant to declare that there is no such thing as a '"secret" adaptation', but rather all adaptations, whether manifest or covert, 'draw attention to their status as adaptations'.[5] Further inspired by John Ellis who argues that an adaptation 'trades upon the memory'[6] of an anterior text or texts, Grant stresses the act of 'recall' as one of the ways the spectator identifies the film's 'reproductive act'.[7]

In order to draw attention to the way in which *Liam* complicates traditional notions of 'origin', this article will use two of Genette's transtextual concepts: intertextuality and paratextuality. Together intertextuality and paratextuality incorporate discourses from both inside and outside the text proper. Intertextuality deals with the presence of other texts inside the text proper, and it is defined by Genette as a relationship of 'co-presence' between two or more texts. The intertextual presence of another text can be acknowledged or unacknowledged: it can appear in the manner of direct 'quotation', indirect 'plagiarism', or through the more ambiguous form of 'allu-sion'. The acknowledgment of an intertextual relation to another text is often found in the paratexts of the text proper. In the case of film, these paratexts include the opening and closing credits, the film's publicity material, such as the promotional posters, trailers and press packages as well as interviews and critical reviews.[8] Although the paratexts lie outside the text proper they are inextricably tied to the text's overall meaning.

This article is divided into the separate yet interconnecting phenomena that constitute both the film's form and theme: 'hidden intertextuality' and 'hidden diaspora'. The first section will examine the film's intertexts and paratexts, while the second will discuss the film's ambiguous presentation of Irish diasporic identity. The article argues that the film's simultaneous treatment of 'hidden intertextuality' and 'hidden Irishness' functions to critique notions of 'fixed' origins.

Recognising the original

The critical paratext is often the spectator's first encounter with a film, and paratexts that come in the form of reviews can radically shape a spectator's expectations and experience of a film. Prior to the theatrical release of *Liam*, reviewers repeatedly compared the film to British director Alan Parker's adaptation of the Irish novel *Angela's Ashes* (1999). Neil Smith stated, 'If you've seen *Angela's Ashes* you'll have some idea what to expect from Stephen Frears' film';[9] similarly, Charles Taylor commented, 'This is the film that *Angela's Ashes* should have been';[10] *The Guardian*'s Peter Bradshaw remarked that scenes from *Liam* 'look a lot like sequences from Alan Parker's underrated *Angela's Ashes*,'[11] and Steve Rhodes added that *Liam* is 'an *Angela's Ashes* type story'.[12] At the same time, American critic Roger Ebert compared *Liam* to the British realism of Ken Loach, specifically *Raining Stones* (1993),[13] while Charles Whitehouse drew comparisons between *Liam* and the 'flat-cap social realism' of Terence Davies, in addition to the scripts of Jimmy McGovern.[14]

It is clear from the paratextual reviews that Frears' *Liam* is extremely referential, but what exactly *Liam* is referencing varies amongst the reviewers. At the same time, it is evident from the critical responses that *Liam* evokes memories of both Irish texts and English texts; and indeed, given that the English Alan Parker directed the Irish *Angela's Ashes*, it could be argued that *Liam* specifically recalls films that explore filmic interrelations between the English and the Irish. Indeed, each of these English directors/writers has worked on Irish or Irish-related films such as Frears' *The Snapper*

(1993), *The Van* (1996) and *Mary Reilly* (1996); Loach's *Hidden Agenda* (1990), *Ae Fond Kiss . . .* (2004) and *The Wind that Shakes the Barley* (2006); McGovern's *Priest* (1995) and *Sunday* (2002); and of course Parker's *The Commitments* (1991).

Although the film *Liam* was not promoted as an adaptation, we are told in the paratexts of the closing credits that the 'story was inspired by the book *Back Crack Boy* by Joseph McKeown'. Set in the Irish quarters of 1920s and 1930s Liverpool, *Back Crack Boy* (1978) recounts the 'fleeting impressions' of the young male protagonist, Liam Sullivan, from the earliest days of his life through to his development as a maturing teen.[15] The adult Liam, who is both the homodiegetic narrator and external focaliser, informs the reader that the first sense of identity he learned in life was his name, 'Liam', while the second was that he was 'Catholic'.[16] Given that all the dialogue in *Back Crack Boy* is rendered in a working-class Liverpudlian accent, the reader is also constantly reminded of Liam's Liverpudlian identity. The narrator recounts childhood memories of his brother Con, and his sisters Teresa and Bernadette, and his 'legions' of aunts and uncles, including Uncle Mick and Uncle Matt.[17] He remembers his mother's illness with appendicitis, the death of his aunt Aggie, the bully Dinny Devlin, his school teacher Miss McIlroy, who had a class 'full of sinners to work on',[18] and his parents' volatile relationship with his eldest sister Bernadette, which was 'strained to breaking point'[19] on account of her dating an 'Orangeman'.[20]

In particular, McKeown's Liam recounts his childhood observations of the economic hardship in Liverpool during the 1930s. He remembers when his father began to return home 'less and less with the oil and grease of the shipyard on him';[21] he recalls the introduction of the National Economy Order in 1931, which brought about the Means Test; he remembers the house calls from the means test inspector, his visits to the pawnshop, mass unemployment, hunger marches, the suicide of one neighbour, the deaths of other neighbours of influenza, and the day his mother had to sell their pawnshop ticket for food.

Despite the fact that *Back Crack Boy* is an acknowledged intertext for *Liam*, the novel's story is not easily recognisable in Frears' film. Elements such as the knocker-up tapping on the window, Liam's move to Con's room, and Liam sneaking into his mother's bedroom for her morning breakfast once his father has left for the shipyard are all included in Frears' adaptation. Furthermore, the school teacher, Miss McIlroy in the novel, Ms Abernathy in the film, also has a class 'full of sinners to work on',[22] albeit in Frears' film the school teacher is assisted by the local Catholic priest, Father Ryan, who helps prepare the children for their First Confession and First Holy Communion. The names of the Sullivan children remain Con, Teresa and Liam; however, Liam's eldest sister in McKeown's novel, Bernadette, is not included in Frears' film. In McKeown's novel, Bernadette's courtship of, and eventual marriage to, a Protestant man functions to expose the prejudicial and sectarian attitudes of the heads of the Sullivan household. Hostile comments towards Protestants ('Me mother'd turn in 'er grave is she knew one 'f mine'd married an Orangeman';[23] 'They're trouble makers' [. . .]. 'That's what I've gorr against them')[24] are omitted from the portrait of the Sullivan family in Frears' adaptation.

The story that is easily recognisable in Frears' film is, ironically, one that is unacknowledged in the film's paratexts, namely *A Portrait of the Artist as a Young Man*. Aspects of Joyce's literary classic that appear in *Liam* gradually become apparent to the 'knowing spectator' and Joyce's text emerges as the film's central intertext. In order to evoke an intertextual relation to *Portrait*, Frears' film demonstrates many of the themes of Joyce's novel, specifically themes of religion and politics. Like Stephen Dedalus, Liam Sullivan is the son of a devout Catholic mother and a resolute nationalist father. Both boys witness feuds between neighbouring Catholics and Protestants. Both observe their father quarrelling against the Catholic Church and favouring extreme nationalist politics over religious dogma. Both struggle with the English language – as Stephen gets older he becomes increasingly conscious of the fact that English is not his native language, while Liam, on the other hand, is burdened with a speech impediment that foregrounds his troubled relationship with language. Both characters experience strong emotional reactions to the hellfire sermons delivered in their school by their local Catholic priest; and both find a renewed spiritual state when they finally confess their sins: sixteen-year-old Stephen confesses that he has been sleeping with prostitutes, while seven-year-old Liam confesses that he has seen his mother naked.

The tagline on the promotional poster for *Liam*, 'Big Heroes Come In Small Packages', can be seen to allude to the antecedent text for Joyce's *Portrait*, namely *Stephen Hero*, which was published

posthumously in 1944. Interestingly, while one of the film's paratexts, in this case the opening and closing credits, omits the
acknowledgment of *Portrait* as an intertext, the paratext of the promotional poster alludes to the text that was the 'origin' for Joyce's
Portrait. The link between Stephen and Liam is re-emphasised in the
text proper when at the beginning of the film Liam (Anthony
Borrows) is approached by a police officer who gruffly asks him his
name. Impeded by his stammer, Liam replies, 'Sssssss Sssssss Sssssss
Liam'. The involuntary prolongation of the S sound during Liam's
verbal block suggests a hesitation to utter the name Stephen.
However, although Liam's response evokes the name Stephen, the
connection between Liam and Stephen is literally left unspoken.
This muted dialogism between *Liam* and *Portrait* is characteristic of
the film's paradoxical enunciation of its sources.

The notion of an intertextual dialogue between *Liam* and *Portrait*
is amplified by Frears through a series of verbal cues that draw attention to *Portrait* as the central intertext for *Liam*. As mentioned,
throughout *Portrait* and *Liam* we respectively witness Stephen
Dedalus and Liam Sullivan struggle with the English language.
Joyce's reader first witnesses Stephen's engagement with language
through the story of the 'moocow' and 'baby tuckoo' as narrated to
him by his father. As he grows older, Stephen responds to the
acoustic pleasures found within the rhythm and repetition of language: 'pull out his eyes, apologise, apologise, pull out his eyes';[25] he
experiments with the power of language to signify identity: 'Stephen
Dedalus is my name, Ireland is my nation';[26] and he enquires into
the arbitrary nature of language: 'God was God's name [. . .] *Dieu*
was the French for God and that was God's name too.'[27] Later, when
Stephen is attending university he becomes considerably distressed
after the dean fails to recognise his word 'tundish', and instead uses
the word 'funnel', unknown to Stephen. Given that the dean is an
Englishman, Stephen accepts the word 'funnel' as the correct word,
and consequently he not only becomes suspicious of 'tundish', but of
all English words he uses. Stephen laments:

> The language in which we are speaking is his before it is mine.
> How different are the words home, Christ, ale, master, on his lips
> and on mine! I cannot speak or write these words without unrest
> of spirit. His language, so familiar and so foreign, will always be
> for me an acquired speech. I have not made or accepted its

words. My voice holds them at bay. My soul frets in the shadow
of his language.[28]

A maturing Stephen becomes aware that the language in which he
speaks and writes has been imposed on him by the colonising power,
and for Stephen, English becomes the language of oppression. At the
same time, Stephen views Irish as a language of repression; it has now
been put in the service of Irish nationalism via the Gaelic League. For
Seamus Deane, Stephen's struggle to engage with his national tongue
reflects the 'traumatic experience of having lost a language'.[29]

Although Stephen views these languages as 'nets' designed to
'hold [him] back from flight',[30] he spends the majority of his time in
Portrait quoting writers, philosophers, Latin phrases, hymns and folk
songs, and paradoxically his 'voice' takes creative flight via the borrowing of other voices. In Joyce's works we get not the articulation
of a national text or the national experience but texts about the difficulty of producing the national text. Similarly, *Liam* is a film that is
not so much about 'speaking' the Irish diaspora but about the difficulties of speaking the Irish diaspora: and one of the ways that
Frears suggests the difficulty of speaking the Irish diaspora is
through Liam's speech impediment.

Liam's involuntary pauses and verbal blocks, prolongations of
single sounds and repetition of syllables, all of which become
heightened in moments of anxiety, become so severe that they
impede his oral communication altogether. Twice he endures cor-
poral punishment in the attempt to avoid speech: once by Ms
Abernathy who catches him writing 'dickey-bow' during class, and
later that day his Aunt Aggie strikes him for refusing to repeat the
word 'dickey-bow'. Liam's expectations of his own inability to utter
words correctly or coherently increase his anxiety about speech,
and consequently his confidence with language is shattered.
Language, and in particular the difficulties of language, preoccupies
Liam's daily life. He too 'frets' at the thought of speaking and he
too experiences 'unrest in spirit' when he is required to speak in
front of others. The spectator witnesses both the pawnshop broker
and the priest grow impatient with Liam's speech impediment, and
optical point-of-view shots capture Liam's fellow students staring at
him when he becomes trapped in moments of collapsed speech. As
in *Portrait*, English is made foreign, and with respect to language
Liam is no freer than Stephen.

Frears continues to trade upon the memory of Stephen's relationship with language, as rhythmical sounds of language are shown
to fascinate Liam. Despite his stutter, Liam achieves verbal fluency
when he sings his words: 'dickey-bow, dickey-bow, me mom wants
the loan of a dickey-bow'; 'seven-and-a-tenner, seven-and-a-tenner,
me mom said seven-and-a-tenner'; 'My name's Liam Sullivan [. . .] I
went to nine o'clock mass and Holy Communion – nine o'clock
mass and Holy Communion'. Although Liam suffers a verbal breakdown during his confession with Father Ryan he is able to sing his
sin. Indeed, Liam does not take 'flight' through the spoken word,
but like Stephen he takes 'creative flight' by singing his words.

A further intertextual complication arises in that while Joyce's
Portrait emerges in the narrative details of *Liam*, the origins for *Liam*
are also detectable in American director Joseph Strick's 1977 adaptation of Joyce's classic. During Strick's construction of the scene at
Belvedere College, one of Stephen's (Bosco Hogan) classmates
removes some mildly pornographic photographs from inside his
jacket pocket and passes them around the class while their Christian
Brother teacher reads aloud Stephen's prize-winning essay (Fig. 6.1).
To the annoyance of his classmate, Stephen retains the photographs,
and continues to listen to the Brother. Later as Stephen sits with his
parents in a tea-room, a montage of optical point-of-view shots
reveal Stephen voyeuristically gazing at the lips, chests and legs of
different women in the restaurant, an act his mother (Rosaleen
Linehan) notices. Following this, Stephen privately revisits his classmate's photographs, which at this point he has hidden up the
chimneybreast in his bedroom.

Similarly, Frears' camera captures Liam and his classmates examining pictures of nude women; in this case the pictures are
reproductions of Jean-Auguste Dominique Ingres' oil paintings *The
Turkish Bath* (1862) and *Venus Anadyomene* (1848). Their voyeurism is
interrupted when their teacher, Ms Abernathy (Anne Reid), arrives
in the classroom with Father Ryan (Russell Dixon), before asking,
'Can anybody tell me what sin does?' At this point, the book containing the nude reproductions is still open on Liam's desk, and with
a guilty look on his face he closes it as discreetly as he can. Later at
home, Liam opens the bathroom door and accidentally sees his
mother (Claire Hackett) standing naked in the washtub. Plagued by
thoughts that his mother is suffering from a physical abnormality,

Liam, out of a Ruskin-like anxiety, returns to an empty classroom and re-examines the reproductions of Ingres' nudes.

Interestingly, when Liam revisits the art book containing the reproductions of the female nudes it becomes noticeable that the images and the titles of the images do not correspond with each other. While the presentation page reads 'View of Delft' by Jan Vermeer, the corresponding page shows Jean-Auguste Dominique Ingres' 'Venus Anadyomene' (1848). As Liam continues to turn the pages the presentation page signals Vermeer's 'Lady at a Spinet', yet the corresponding page reveals 'Lucretia' (1524) by the German painter Lucas Cranach. The discrepancy between the titles and the images not only draws the spectator's attention to the idea of the presence of one text in another, but it also reminds the spectator of the unreliability of reference.

When Liam and his classmates are voyeuristically examining these pictures in an earlier scene, it is clear that the page they are inspecting

Fig. 6.1 Visual allusion to Joseph Strick's *Portrait of the Artist* (1977) in *Liam* (Stephen Frears, 2001).

is loose and not actually part of the book. Just like Stephen's classmates, Liam's classmates have also hidden nude pictures of women in
their classroom, which they surreptitiously view under the presence of
a member of the Catholic clergy. The scene in which the nude pictures are being passed around the classroom does not actually occur
in Joyce's *Portrait*, rather it is an additional scene in Strick's adaptation
of Joyce's *Portrait*. Thus, the corresponding scene involving nude pictures in the classroom in Frears' film reveals that origins in *Liam*
emerge not only through affinities to Joyce's *Portrait* but also via
Strick's adaptation of Joyce's *Portrait*. As we track the references in
Liam, we find that the 'route' to the origin does not necessarily lead to
the origin's 'root': in *Liam* the route to Joyce is via Strick, yet it is the
Joycean root that brings us to the Sullivan family's ethnic origin. In
particular, the 'co-presence' of one text in another text, as previously
outlined by Genette, emerges here to disrupt notions of fixed origins.

Recognising Irish identity

Despite the seemingly certain signifiers of Irishness in *Liam*, such as
the surname Sullivan and the forename Liam, the political and racial
attitude of the Sullivan patriarch wholly contradicts the likelihood
that the family is in fact Irish. After the father loses his job at the
Liverpool docks, he engages in a series of aggressive confrontations
with the newly arrived Irish immigrants and demands that the Irish
'Get out of [his] country' – 'his country' being England. Working as
a source of cheap labour, the new Irish immigrants pose a threat for
the local casual labourers, many of whom are second- and third-gen-
eration Irish immigrants. As such, there develops a complex, and
somewhat contradictory, set of 'race relations' between the newly
arrived and the long-established Irish immigrants.

In order to distance himself from the newly arrived immigrants,
the father joins the Blackshirts led by the British fascist Oswald
Mosley (interestingly, Mosley himself was of Anglo-Irish descent)
and participates in violent campaigns to fight against the immigrant
Irish and Jewish communities that have descended on Liverpool.
The father's decision to join the Blackshirts and to wear the
Blackshirts' uniform symbolises his desire for a 'secure' and 'stable'
identity, one that displays national uniformity and sameness;
however, as Paul Gilroy reminds us, such uniforms merely compel

an 'illusion of sameness'.[31] In *Liam*, not only do we discover that not all adaptations have a desire to signal their sources, but we also find that not all Irish immigrants have a desire to signal their country of origin. Indeed, as Patrick O'Sullivan says in regards to research in the field of Irish diaspora studies, 'a simple methodological point: not all people want to be "Irish"'.[32]

This contradictory identity is again illustrated in the scene where Liam and his sister go to the cinema to watch a Western. Whilst inside the film theatre, the children actively take part in the action on screen by cheering the 'cowboys' and booing the 'Indians'. They playfully aim their pointed index fingers at the Indians and shout 'bang-bang'. When the film is over, the children run home through the courtyards imitating both the cowboys and the Indians. In this scene, as well as many others, we can see Frears actively critiquing notions of 'fixed' origins. The children at first assume the role of the 'cowboy'/ the 'settler' / the 'oppressor', then switch to the role of the 'Indian' / the 'native' / the 'oppressed'. The children, many of whom are descendants of Irish immigrants, are shown to be conscious of their own hybrid identity as they freely perform the dual roles of 'settler' and 'native'.

Liam's role as cowboy is abruptly interrupted after he accidentally bumps into a member of Mosley's Blackshirts standing guard at a rally. At this point, Frears cuts to the speaker of the rally who informs his listeners that 'hundreds and thousands of Irishmen are flooding this country'. If Liam is of Irish decent, then at this rally Liam instantly slides from the role of the settler (the cowboy) to the oppressed (the Irish immigrant). In this case, Liam as second-, possibly third-, generation Irish in England is both 'native' to England and 'oppressed' by extreme right-wing English politics. As the voice track transmits the rally speaker's warning that England is 'being overrun by Jews and Irish', Frears cuts again, this time to accommodate Liam's point of view, and shows Liam's father standing amidst the crowd during the rally's anti-Irish hate speech. A parallel emerges here between the children's game in which they are shown to slide fluidly between two identity poles, the cowboys and the Indians, and the Sullivan family patriarch, who, although he has a surname that signifies Irish descent, assumes an English identity. The father is, to borrow Declan Kiberd's expression, 'playing at being not-Irish', and rather than moving between his two identities he establishes a relationship of opposition between the Irish immigrants – a relationship that recalls the coloniser/colonised binary and one which haunts English-Irish relations.[33]

Within the novel *Back Crack Boy* there is crucial background information about the Sullivan family that Frears' film leaves out, which is the fact that Liam's father's father was shot dead on his doorstep in Ireland by the British Black and Tans. The Sullivan family's genealogical connection to Ireland is again mentioned with news of Teresa securing employment while staying with relatives in Ireland. Interestingly, in favour of using a series of indirect clues that remind the spectator of *Portrait*, Frears overlooks background information from *Back Crack Boy* that directly reveals the Sullivan family's Irish origin. On the one hand, Frears alludes to the family's ethnic origin by using Joycean material, while on the other Frears suppresses the family's Irish origin by not using story material from *Back Crack Boy*. Although *Back Crack Boy* is the only source that is referenced as an intertext in the credits for *Liam*, it is merely used by Frears as another clue to the Sullivan family's Irish origins.

The importance of Irish origin is again signalled when the song 'I'll Take You Home Again, Kathleen' is sung at the New Year's gathering at the Sullivan family home. Traditionally, ballads trade upon nostalgia for the homeland, and in *Liam* the 'homeland' that the ballad 'I'll Take You Home Again, Kathleen' evokes is specifically Ireland. This is noted when the singing of the ballad by the Sullivan family's Irish immigrant neighbour prompts the intolerant remark, 'If it's that bleedin' good over there, what are you doing over here?' However, written in 1875 by Thomas Westendorf in Plainfield, Illinois, USA, neither the composer nor the song is of Irish origin. Therefore, the cultural memory, and the sense of nostalgia the ballad invokes, works on the omission of the ballad's origin. While there are seemingly overt references to Irishness in *Liam*, the exact origins for some of the references disrupt readings of the Sullivan family's Irish ethnicity. On the one hand the origins are signalled, but on the other these origins are also found to have an indirect connection to Irish cultural life.

The film's parallel between the notion of 'hidden Irishness' and the concept of 'hidden intertextuality' is forged in the metaphor of fire. Whereas in Joyce's *Portrait* fire symbolises hell, in *Liam* fire is associated with the working-class labourers, many of whom are Irish immigrants. Frears employs a series of close-ups of fire in *Liam*: fire is the source of the labourers' work in the shipyards; it is their source of heat in their homes, and on the street corners. But fire is also used as a weapon to attack the supposed enemy, and in two cases a Jewish home and Jewish pawnshop are targeted. If *Portrait* used fire as a symbol of hell then *Liam* extends the metaphor of hell to the experience of Irish immigrants in 1930s England. The notion of hellfires becoming the immigrant hell is continued until the end of the film when Liam's sister is accidentally set on fire by their father (Fig. 6.2).

Unknown to the father before he throws an ignited bottle of petrol through a Jewish family's window is the fact that his daughter is inside their house. In the attempt to rid England of immigrants the father's violent actions are inadvertently executed on his own child. Through the fire imagery the contradictory nature of the father's racism is exposed, and his racial hatred against immigrants

Fig. 6.2 *Liam*'s allusion to Joyce's Icarus/Daedalus metaphor of the father setting fire to/curtailing the freedoms of his child.

is shown as self-destruction and self-immolation. Again, what is effectively recalled here is the Icarus/Daedalus myth utilised by Joyce, with the father's actions literally incinerating the child. This scene is particularly horrific given that out of all the people, objects and furnishings in the house his daughter is the only thing that actually catches fire. The Joycean mixed metaphors of flight and freedom, which are also about burning and falling from the sky, are actively recalled in *Liam*, and the use of fire in the ending shows not only the hell of immigrant poverty, but also the dangers of trying to 'silence' or bury one's origins. The act of burying one's origins is shown in *Liam* to be an act of self-destruction and self-hatred. Liam's verbal passivity contrasts sharply with the verbal violence and hate speech executed by his father. In particular, the father's violence disables the son's verbal act and the spectator witnesses Liam struggle to locate his utterance in time to tell his father that Teresa is inside the house targeted by the Blackshirts. The 'father', the 'artificer',[34] appears in Frears' film in the form of the casual dock labourer, and it is through the Icarus/Daedalus myth that the father in *Liam* is equated with the self-destructive father, Dedalus, in Joyce's *Portrait*.

The scenes that follow the traumatic visuals of Teresa being set on fire by her father are marked with a noticeable absence of verbal speech. At the same time, although silence dominates the soundtrack, the words from Joyce's *Portrait* are evoked in the visuals. The image of the father with his finger over a burning match stick vividly recalls the fire and brimstone passage delivered by the priest in Joyce's *Portrait*. As Joyce's *Portrait* reads:

> Place your finger for a moment in the flame of a candle and you will feel the pain of fire. But our earthly fire was created by God for the benefit of man, to maintain in him the spark of life and to help him in the useful arts, whereas the fire of hell is of another quality and was created by God to torture and punish the unrepentant sinner [. . .] [T]he sulphurous brimstone which burns in hell is a substance which is specially designed to burn for ever and for ever with unspeakable fury. Moreover, our earthly fire destroys at the same time as it burns, so that the more intense it is the shorter is its duration; but the fire of hell has this property, that it preserves that which it burns, and, though it rages with incredible intensity, it rages for ever.[35]

Indeed, the scene does not use the novel's words overtly, but rather it trades upon the language of *Portrait* by realising its implied images. Upon recognising Joyce in this image, the spectator gains the ability to interpret the father's unspoken feelings of sorrow and regret. By prompting the knowing spectator to recall the passages of prose from Joyce's *Portrait*, *Liam* thus involves a constant transition from one text to another. This kind of interpretative activity requires the spectator to connect the image from the film back to the word in the novel, then uses the words of the novel to read the images in the film. The conceptual flipping back and forth results in the two texts – that is Frears' *Liam* and Joyce's *Portrait* – being experienced simultaneously. At the same time, the notion of 'origin' continues to be disrupted given that in Joyce's damnation scene he is drawing on the words and imagery from Dante's *Inferno*. The allegory of rejecting sin that structures Dante's descent into hell is equated with the burying of origins evident in *Liam*. Thus the visual allusion to Joyce, via Joyce's use of Dante's imagery, functions to simultaneously link to and move away from our experience of Joyce's *Portrait* as a secure source of origin for Frears' *Liam*.

After some time away, the father returns to the Sullivan family home for the first time since the incident with Teresa. The house he returns to is silent, and as he climbs the stairs to Teresa's room, the sound of his footsteps against the floorboards paradoxically draws attention to the silence. Upon entering Teresa's room, the father looks at Liam, but does not declare his presence to Teresa who at this time is looking out the window. Liam, who has not overcome his stammer, is unable to tell Teresa that their father is standing in her room. Liam's attempt to speak grabs Teresa's attention, and as she turns to look at her father she reveals her blistered and disfigured skin. The words from Joyce's novel ghost the interpretation of the image of Teresa as she sits by the window. Permanently scarred by 'the ravenous tongues of flames'[36] that haunted Stephen in Joyce's *Portrait* – the red, raw blisters trail down the sides of her face, tightening her skin – she turns to a side profile signifying a life that is now half – 'never to be free from those pains',[37] 'they are ever lasting [. . .] intolerably intense, unbearably extensive':[38] they are a direct result of her father's 'unspeakable fury'.[39] The severity of Teresa's burns impedes her physical mobility; confined to an armchair at the film's close, Teresa's immigrant 'flight' is shown to have been cruelly compromised by the racist and violent hellfire fuelled by her father.

The notion of hellfires burning 'eternally in darkness'[40] as conveyed in Joyce's damnation passage is further stressed in Frears' conflicting visuals. When the father enters Teresa's room, she is sitting next to window and daylight is clearly visible; seconds later when the father leaves through the front door of the Sullivan family home, he walks onto a darkening street. Frears' camera immediately returns to a close-up of Teresa again showing the light of day shining on her face as she watches her father walk away. The splitting of visuals into day and night serves as a metaphor for the 'physical torments' and the 'spiritual torments' of hell as narrated by Father Arnall in Joyce's *Portrait*. Although the father does not experience the intensity of fire in the same way as Teresa, Joyce's passage reminds us of the internal torment – the 'perpetual remorse'[41] – to which the damned, in this case the father, is subjected. Thus the interconnection between words from Joyce's *Portrait* and images from *Liam* provide a framework that enables us to interpret the father's suffering.

In his review of *Ulysses* (1922) in '*Ulysses*, Order and Myth', T.S. Eliot draws our attention to Joyce's use of the 'mythical method'.[42] Eliot notes that the parallel use of one text to another, as in the case of *Ulysses* and the *Odyssey*, enables the retelling of a classic story in a renewed and innovative way. Eliot's idea of the 'mythical method' is similar to Genette's concept of intertextuality. For Genette, intertextuality 'launches [old] works into new circuits of meaning', and he stresses that old stories not only need to be 're-read' but also need to be 'rewritten'.[43] *Liam* as an adaptation is a rewriting of *Portrait*, and it is by linking adaptation, that is, re-writing, to the concept of diaspora that enables the retelling of an Irish national text. Intertextuality functions in *Liam* to make new connections across national boundaries, and the film achieves textual transcendence in the transposition of *Portrait* to a diasporic milieu. Indeed, it is out of the paradox of origin and transcendence that newness emerges.

Chapter Seven

VIOLENT TRANSPOSITIONS: THE DISTURBING 'APPEARANCE' OF THE IRISH HORROR FILM

Emma Radley

Mid-way through Paddy Breathnach's slasher flick *Shrooms* (2007), an American teenager, on a hallucinogenic-mushroom-hunting trip in an Irish forest, finds himself in the grip of a strange, drug-induced vision. Bluto, the quintessential all-American jock, follows a young woman into the woods in the belief that he has been invited to partake in a sex game. Instead, while searching for the woman's car, Bluto comes across a cow. The cow, perhaps unsurprisingly given the amount of 'magic' mushroom tea Bluto has consumed, can talk: he warns Bluto against following the girl, that he will not only be 'fucked' but 'dead fucked' if he does. Bluto disregards the advice – what could a cow, even a talking one, know about the delights of dogging? – to predictably disastrous consequences: he is castrated and beaten to death by the woman he followed, who is revealed to be the spectre of the haggard old druid killing off the group of teenagers one by one.

Bluto's fate is not unexpected: anyone familiar with the horror sub-genre of the slasher will know that not only is a midnight walk alone in the woods a bad idea, a walk combined with the twin evils of drugs and sex is a quick passport to a grisly death. However, what is curious and significant about this scene is Breathnach's oddly whimsical and surreal use of the talking cow, which, glowing white against the blue-black backdrop of the sinister forest, appears to be a trespasser in the generic, narrative and aesthetic landscapes of the film: talking cows aren't usually a feature of stalk-and-slash cinema, which tends to prefer monsters of the human variety – and *Shrooms*, despite its vaguely supernatural premise with a ghostly killer, ultimately sticks quite closely to the individual-as-psychopath narrative trope.

On closer inspection, however, perhaps the cow is not such an anomalous signifier, if one pays attention to the cultural specificity of the *Irish* horror film. Drawing on discourses beyond or outside the primary generic sensibility of the film reveals a space in which more localised meanings intersect with the globalised meanings of the genre, where interior gradations interrupt and rearticulate the exterior shell. Firstly, there is the matter of the cow's voice – instantly recognisable to a modern Irish audience as that of Don Wycherley, veteran actor best known for his role as Raymond in Celtic Tiger-era drama series *Bachelor's Walk* and, at the time of the film's release, providing the voiceover for a series of radio ads for a property website. Although Wycherley himself does appear in *Shrooms* (he plays one of the 'mountain men', Bernie), the voice he uses for that character is disguised and mutated – a flat rural monotone. As the cow, however, he uses the distinctive, honey-toned, vaguely south Dublin drawl that, through his portrayal of the upper-middle-class landlord Raymond and his aural personification of the boom-time preoccupation with property, marks his voice as indelibly associated, for the knowing spectator, with Celtic Tiger money, class, confidence and consumerism.[1]

In addition, there is the matter of the 'cow': why not some other animal, a more cinematic horse, perhaps, or a more horror-appropriate wolf? The trite answer would direct us towards the historical and cultural association of the cow with Ireland: the dairy farm is an important feature of the Irish agricultural landscape. This is certainly true, though the animal takes on another local significance in the light of the outbreak of bovine spongiform encephalopathy (BSE), more colloquially known as mad cow disease, that gripped the UK and Ireland in the preceding decade, engendering the resignification of the dairy farm site of contamination, decay and death. Indeed, the burgeoning field of Irish horror cinema has frequently reconfigured the cow as a signifier of terror: in Conor McMahon's *Dead Meat* (2004), an infection that causes the dead to come back to life spreads initially from cows to humans, creating a localised zombie apocalypse that eradicates much of Irish society; in Billy O'Brien's *Isolation* (2005) the cow is the host of a failed genetic experiment that creates mutant and parasitic bovine offspring, passing the species barrier from cow to human through bite. The cow, when read from an Irish context, is certainly a horror-appropriate animal. For the knowing (national) spectator then, the talking cow in *Shrooms* functions as an interruption to and a rearticulation of the generic (transnational) space of the slasher: a short-circuiting of the structures of meaning that create the meaning of the film across formal, aesthetic and contextual lines. The cow brings with it its own signification, which intersects and combines with the already-loaded language of the generic, resulting in a 'cross-border circulation of meaning', a 'heterogenous generic fertility'[2] that complicates the film's acquiescence to structured readings based on either generic or national association.

Accounting for the complex relationship between genre and national cinema requires more than identifying, tracking and indeed accepting generic structures in Irish film; it requires a radical destabilisation and re-articulation of the discursive construction of Irish cinema itself. This involves pulling back the 'thin sheath of the sign' to reveal a more 'complex architecture'[3] beneath – a change in the manner in which this sign is read (how we see Irish cinema) certainly, but also something more: an alteration at the level of the signifier – a change in the manner in which the sign is constructed and maintained (how we speak about Irish cinema). Focusing specifically on the horror genre, this essay considers the signifying space that emerges when the aesthetic and ideological languages of genre and nation are put into conversation. What happens when national and generic sensibilities are combined? When the 'received system of generic seamlessness is reopened and a dialogue based on incongruities occurs throughout the text'?[4] Genre, within the context of national cinema, is refigured here as a dynamic force that insistently disrupts the symbolic discourse of Irish cinema. Through this rupture, a new discursive site is articulated: one that is intertextual, heterogeneous and profoundly 'in-process'. This space is not just 'double-voiced'[5] but tripled, quadrupled: the Irish genre film functions as, to borrow Julia Kristeva's term, a 'transposition' – an intratextual leap from one signifying system to another, and a point at which traditional understandings of representation and meaning (national, cinematic and indeed generic) are transformed and remade. Here, 'through the destruction of an old position and the formation of a new one',[6] a rearticulated subject of Irish cinema can emerge.

The 'sudden' appearance of the Irish horror film in the last decade makes it a solid position from which to examine the impact, affect and resistance to generic development in contemporary national production. While the historical 'purity' of Irish filmmaking in terms of generic sensibility pre-Celtic Tiger can be, and indeed has been, interrogated,[7] there is little doubt that contemporary film-makers are interested in genre as a representative strategy.[8] The horror genre, as noted, in particular: Breathnach's *Shrooms* premiered in 2007, at the mid-point of a decade that produced a significant number of horror films in Irish national cinema, with barely a year passing without one or more feature releases, as well as many shorts.[9] McMahon's darkly comic zombie film *Dead Meat* in 2004 was fol-lowed in 2005 by O'Brien's *Isolation*, Patrick Kenny's *Winter's End*, also set on a rural farm, and Stephen Bradley's 'rom-zom-com' *Boy Eats Girl.* Justin O'Brien's *Ghostwood* (a supernatural horror about an Irish-American who comes to Ireland to investigate his father's death) was released in 2006; 2007 saw the limited release of Ivan Kavanagh's Michael Haneke-inspired *Tin Can Man*, a violent explo-ration of psychosis (re-released in 2012). In 2008 came Eric Courteney's *Seer*, a psychological 'haunted house' horror, and *The Daisy Chain*, Aisling Walsh's story about a grieving couple who adopt a child that may or may not be responsible for horrific events in their rural village. In 2010, Conor McPherson's ghost story *The Eclipse* was released, followed in 2011 by David Keating's *Wake Wood*. Carrying the distinction of being the first feature from Hammer Films (famous for its horror productions) in thirty years, *Wake Wood* is another 'evil child' story – after the death of their daughter, a couple move to a rural Irish town (the eponymous Wake Wood) and discover that the inhabitants are capable of bringing the recently deceased back to life for a few days, a procedure which goes predictably and disturbingly awry. 2012 brought a further three Irish horror features to cinemas: Eoin Macken's psychological thriller *The Inside*, and two horror comedies, Conor MacMahon's, *Stitches*, and Jon Wright's *Grabbers*.

The traditional associations of the horror genre with ideological anxiety[10] means that, in a country undergoing significant socio-cul-tural transformations in the Celtic Tiger and post-Celtic Tiger period, it is perhaps not surprising that Irish filmmakers turn to horror as a representative strategy. However, the discursive preoc-cupation of the genre – its excessive generic reflexivity – positions it as uniquely affecting the structural language of Irish national cinema. By way of its formal construction, its 'violent awareness of itself'[11] as a textual construction, the contemporary horror film is always already a vehicle of transposition. Its transplantation into Irish cinema multiplies this force: these new Irish horror films 'transpose the violence of their subject matter into the field of representation, exerting violence against previous artistic forms and demolishing traditional pictorial codes'.[12] They do not just copy or mimic generic codes, they resignify them, transforming the monologic and monolithic 'body' of Irish cinema as they go.

The body that matters

Genre and Irish cinema, in general, are not happy bedfellows. Despite the publication of Brian McIlroy's edited collection of essays on the topic in 2007, there has been a certain reluctance to properly interrogate both the term and the form of genre (the system and the structure) as it acts on the terrain of Irish cinema (the system and the structure). Within this discourse, the appearance of genre signifies only alienation, cultural homogenisation, and the excessive and obscene capitalist desires that were ushered in during the Celtic Tiger: something that we (filmmakers and critics) certainly 'shouldn't be getting involved with'.[13] The 'sudden' appearance of genre in national productions is seen as representative of crisis, both in national and cinematic imagination, and something that must be purged in order to return to more authentic, culturally rooted stories, stories that allegorically 'tell us who we are as a community'.[14]

Roddy Flynn's revealingly titled article 'Altered States: *Shrooms* and Irish Cinema' specifically highlights the phenomenon of the Irish horror film as a symptom of this 'crisis of imagination', placing Breathnach's film as symptomatic other to national cinema based primarily on its generic qualities: although he acknowledges that genre is 'a nasty word in any discussion of national cinema', he still positions the film as nothing more than the epitome of an insidious 'improperness' in the body of Irish cinema:

> From a textual perspective *Shrooms* offers limited possibilities for analysis. It is a genre film, and a banal one at that even if efficiently constructed [. . .] *Shrooms* seems expressly designed to evade any local references that might confuse overseas audiences.

> [It] marks the most comprehensive eschewing of all cultural
> specificity yet seen in a domestically originated project.[15]

His correlation between a (supposed) lack of cultural specificity in a
national project, and the film's generic structure in itself is significant: it cannot be read as national allegory *because* of its generic
form. Leaving aside the question of why a national project *should* be
read in terms of national allegory, the question of why a critic
should *not* refer to genre when discussing what is clearly, deliberately, and unashamedly a genre film merits further exploration.
Why is genre something of which we shouldn't speak?

The answer to this brings us right to the heart of the subject of
'Irish national cinema', to the discursive and ideological poles that
structure it. The debate about what *counts* as national cinema has
been well rehearsed, the merits of categorising by director, by producer, by funding body, by location, by theme have been deliberated
on, dismissed and discussed by many scholars in the field.[16] While
there is certainly no clear consensus on what national cinema *should*
be, there is most definitely a feeling about what it *shouldn't* be: the
borders of a 'proper' Irish cinema are predicated primarily on the
'improper' spaces. Specific dichotomies have been established as
structuring axes in the definition, legitimation and regulation of Irish
national cinema: local, not global; Europe, not Hollywood; modernist, not postmodernist; singular, not hybrid; artistic, not
commercial; and of course, specific, not generic. Within this model,
the constitution of the 'proper' body of Irish film depends upon the
(r)ejection and othering of representative strategies perceived to be
foreign, specifically those associated with mainstream American filmmaking, in order to protect that body from cultural appropriation,
assimilation or homogenisation. The universality – the popularity –
of transnational ('Hollywood') forms cannot possibly generate useful
reflections and critiques of Irish national culture, since what happens
here is utterly different from what happens *everywhere else*.[17]

Of course, this depends upon an uncritical acceptance of Irish
exceptionalism, differentiation and separatism that is blind to the
deconstructive effects of global postmodernity – increased migration, the development of the mass media, changes in economic and
political sovereignty – which has radically altered the landscape of
'the national' in the last twenty years. Fixed structures, discursive,

representative or aesthetic, have become increasingly untenable: now we speak of the hybrid and the multiple rather than the monolithic and singular. If it is problematic to speak of national identity – even to speak of the nation itself – how are we to understand or define a national cinema? 'Seen in this light,' Andrew Higson comments, 'it is difficult to see the indigenous as either pure or stable',[18] and yet understandings of Irish national cinema remain wedded to this view. While this may not be *specific* to discussions of Irish national cinema, it is *intensified* due to Ireland's enduring postcolonial anxiety around ideas of national identity, culture and territory. The commentary around Irish national cinema is clearly marked by such anxiety, with a persistent uneasiness around the definition and regulation of the terrain. This uneasiness is projected onto the 'foreign' as a neo-colonial force, as a contaminating and corrupting agent that mutates and inhibits a truly national expression, and as a homogenising impulse that empties Irishness of its cultural specificity.

The negative effects of 'foreign' influence are specifically and forcefully concentrated on the sudden 'appearance' of genre in contemporary Irish film. Kevin Rockett, for example, in an interview on the development of Irish cinema in the contemporary period, comments specifically on the difference between 'the cinema of the Celtic Tiger' and the 'very critical and indigenous cinema of the 1970s and 1980s', specifically locating this difference within the context of (non-critical and non-indigenous) generic engagement:

> [. . .] many cultures are trying to hold on to the notion of a national cinema while at the same time 'de-nationalising' that cinema through the adoption of mainstream generic conventions. This phenomenon, which has been very apparent in relation to contemporary Irish cinema, tends to neutralize political issues by inhibiting the emergence of formal innovation.[19]

Similar criticisms of genre come from many other major scholars of Irish cinema, with Martin McLoone condemning the 'rock-musical' *The Commitments* as being a 'Hollywood film in all its essential elements', and Ruth Barton discussing the majority of Irish crime films as being more interested in 'emulat[ing] the post-Tarantino Hollywood gangster cycle' than (more properly) 'addressing issues of social exclusion'.[20] Tony Tracy goes further, singling out the 'recent spate of low budget horror films' as not only representative of a

national cinema 'unsure of where to look for inspiration and engagement', but also of a crisis in Irish identity itself in a postmodern global
environment. Celtic Tiger Ireland, he notes, as a direct result of the
'alienating' force of globalisation and consumerism, is 'less sure of
being a "tightly coherent and unified community" than at any time
since its independence [. . .] Over the past decade a traumatic breach
in the national imagination has opened up.'[21]

The discourse of Irish national cinema, filtered through a postcolonial lens, reveals itself as shot through with an anxiety around
the construction not only of a 'proper' object of study but also a
proper *subject* – a legitimated and regulated discursive order, with its
own set of 'grammatical' rules about meaning. Irish national cinema
is a symbolic subject: in a Lacanian sense certainly, but also in a
Kristevan sense in that its 'proper' expression is predicated on the
abjection or repression of 'other' signifying codes that would disturb
or disrupt its established meaningful surface. For Kristeva, discourse
is split into two competing orders that work with each other to create
reified or structured forms of signification: the symbolic, which designates the referential system that orders meaning, and the semiotic,
which designates the 'non-linguistic' elements that contribute to
meaning (rhythm, tone, etc.); these two modalities work in a dialectic
to produce a discursive structure – depending on the balance of that
dialectic, the discourse will more or less be fixed in nature (symbolically or semiotically determined).[22] The subject of Irish national
cinema can be seen to be more symbolic in its outlook, its discursive
edifice determined primarily by the firm establishment of systemic
'rules' of signification (specifically, the allegorical and metaphorical
emphasis on the expression of national identity): it is not just about
representation, but about what is representable. This is predicated on
the construction of a stable, coherent identity through the abjection
of 'improper' forms of representation: genre is one such 'improper'
discourse, 'beyond the scope of the possible, the tolerable, the thinkable'. Irish cinema 'turns aside; sickened, it rejects'. [23]

If the creation of Irish cinema as subject and object of discourse is
so dependent on the rhetoric of containment, exclusion and binary
oppositions between the self and the abjected other (in whatever
modes that dichotomy is expressed: local/global, commercial/artistic,
proper/improper), then the generic functions here as a strategy
which can effect a traversing of these boundaries and the creation of

interstitial spaces within which a new sense of engagement with 'Irishness' can be facilitated: a harnessing of the abject to rearticulate the subject. Kristeva calls these spaces 'thetic' positions, a word she borrows from Husserl's phenomenological investigation of meaning. The thetic is the point at which the subject is posited, where subjectivity is enunciated; it marks the 'threshold of language',[24] a point at which heterogeneity can introduce itself, transforming and transgressing normative and normativising symbolic codes. Thetic intervention, or rupture, engenders both a crisis in representation and the potential for new forms of the representable – new modes of meaning, and thus, new modes of subjectivity. This is a necessary practice, in Kristevan terms, in order to prevent a reification of subjects and bodies: the semiotic must intervene to maintain representation as a 'practice and a productivity'.[25] The generic, due to its formal preoccupation with intertextuality and transposition, can facilitate this rupture by forcing a destabilisation of discursive and symbolic positioning: in this sense, it functions as a 'poetic language', a mode of expression that operates against the rules of signification with discourse.

While the notion of poetic language usually refers to deconstructive, experimental or non-linguistic interventions in communication, fundamentally it describes anything that 'breaks up the inertia of language-habits'.[26] Genre, ordinarily, can be seen as a primarily *symbolic* discourse, but when understood as an abjected, non-representable discourse within Irish national cinema it becomes something 'other' – a semiotic (poetic) force that undermines, and indeed energises, symbolic representability.[27] Generic language, at least insofar as it intervenes in the symbolic language of Irish cinema, inhibits discourse from 'hiding the semiotic process that produces it', and prevents the reification of the subject as a 'transcendental ego'.[28] In this sense, the dialectic that is established in Irish horror films between a disruptive, semiotic generic sensibility and an established, symbolic national sensibility works to deconstruct and rearticulate the postcolonial bias in the discourse of Irish national cinema. More than that, it actively functions through hybridity, otherness and transposition to alter the thetic space of representation and facilitate both a new subject and object of Irish cinema to emerge.

Syntax to dialect(ic)

Flynn's and Rockett's criticism of the generic impulse in contemporary Irish filmmaking is based explicitly in the belief that 'genre' and 'cultural specificity' are mutually exclusive. However, considering genre as a poetic language that operates by transposition, it is clear that this is impossible: as Kristeva argues, texts are inextricably linked to their social, cultural and indeed textual contexts: they function within a semiotic framework that contributes to their 'double-voiced' nature. Certain words, images and tropes are always already ideologically loaded, they 'retain an otherness within the text'[29] that re-produces them. Kristeva calls these moments of short-circuit 'ideologemes': transpositions between textual practice and the contextual 'historical and social coordinates' from which they are inextricable.[30] It is thus impossible, within any given signifying system, for a text to be entirely depoliticised: its every utterance is bound up with socio-cultural discourse.

This essay opened, somewhat playfully, with an example of such an ideologemic transposition: the cow's multiple semiotic coding. It is difficult to deny, however, the uncanny and uneasy 'otherness' that is brought to mind when confronted with the lingering shot of the burning carcass of the infected cow in O'Brien's *Isolation*, directly referencing the stark images of the mass culling of cows on farms across the UK in the early 1990s in the wake of the BSE outbreak, which were beamed into Irish homes throughout the crisis. The persistent focus on the borders of the farm also underlines this semiotic connection: the repeated close-ups of the fences, the chained-up gates, and the hastily erected notices warning interlopers to 'keep out' refigures the isolation of agricultural spaces and the strict border controls put in place in the UK and Ireland during that outbreak, and the outbreak of foot-and-mouth in the late 1990s. The blackly comic scenes in McMahon's *Dead Meat*, in which the surviving humans are rounded up and taken to quarantine by tranquiliser-gun-wielding government agents in white hazmat suits can also be read in this way. Terrified, wailing, slipping and pushing against the barriers erected within the transportation vans, these scenes clearly recall the footage of farm animals being transported for slaughter during the numerous agricultural crises that directly preceded the production of the film in 2002.[31]

Cultural specificity is one thing, however, critique is another – one of the charges most often levelled at genre films in an Irish context is that they are not political, indeed that they actively work to *neutralise* political or social issues.[32] Interestingly, this understanding is something seemingly unique to its Irish context: while genre films are often generally criticised as mimetic, repetitive, unoriginal, they are rarely if ever considered politically neutral. If anything, and this applies to horror films in particular, they are considered *excessively* ideological, usually conservative and reactionary. It's useful to return to Flynn's critique of *Shrooms* at this point, where, in dismissing the film as devoid of national markers and therefore limited in terms of analytic potential, he comments:

> If pressed, one could possibly construct a hypothesis on the manner in which the script mobilises the spectre of industrial schools – now universally understood (in Ireland, at any rate) – as sites of irredeemable evil for thousands of young men and women. To do so however would [. . .] merely credit the script with depths that are entirely absent.[33]

His outright dismissal of the 'spectre of industrial schools' raised in the film is curious. One does not have to be 'pressed' to appreciate this reading: the horror of the industrial school is explicit, tangible and persistent throughout, with repeated and disturbing flashbacks that focus on the experience of the child inmates at the hands of the Christian 'Black Knights' – beatings, torture and abuse. The film's refusal of overt politicisation of that representation (in the manner of Aisling Walsh's *Song for a Raggy Boy* in 2003, or Peter McMullen's *The Magdalene Sisters* in 1999) might well be problematic, but to deny it is short-sighted indeed; Breathnach's approach is formal, following the genre's tendency to filter fears and anxieties around socio-cultural events and upheavals into archaic, mythic or essentialised forms.[34] Metaphorical, allegorical or heavy-handed, the horror film's business is exploiting trauma, and in the case of *Shrooms* this trauma has specific cultural resonances that, while perhaps not explicitly rendered, cannot be evaded.

This 'cultural textuality'[35] of the horror film, drawing as it does on both generic and socio-cultural contexts, positions it as a privileged vehicle of the semiotic transposition Kristeva deems necessary to tear apart traditional structures of representation and create spaces in which new articulations of subject and meaning can emerge. This move is especially crucial, given the ideological contexts in which the Irish horror genre is 'appearing' or being produced. As mentioned, the landscape from which these films emerged is one that was, and is, contingent and undergoing rapid social and cultural change. The Celtic Tiger, and its persisting effects, has led to axiomatic transformations in the discursive structures of Irish national subjectivity – immigration, multiculturalism, globalisation and secularisation (and now, of course, the recession) all contribute to an Ireland in which the structures of citizenship, class, religion and gender have undergone significant rearticulation. In the dynamics of contemporary culture, Irishness has been thrust into its own sort of thetic rupture, and its own crisis of representation. The current crop of Irish horror films are made within that rupture, and cannot help but be shaped and reflective of it – seeing them as both ideologemic and semiotic allows for an appreciation of the manner in which these films articulate the traumas and anxieties that accompany the birth of new subjective realities and new symbolic orders.

They cannot be dismissed, then, as politically *neutral*: on the contrary, many of these films are explicitly engaging the political on both a narrative and aesthetic level. In her essay in this volume, for example, Zélie Asava considers the ideologically charged site of the mixed-race body in Irish culture, reading both *Isolation* and *Boy Eats Girl* as allegorical or connotative of uneasiness around multiculturalism and migrancy in contemporary Ireland, specifically as it is mapped onto the reproductive bodies of 'non-national' women. *Isolation* in particular foregrounds this anxiety about how (hybrid) subjects are brought forth by these m/others: that the contagion is passed on through pregnancy and reproduction, through the birth of hybrid (contaminated) offspring, is significant in that it openly taps into the cultural anxiety and unease around the very real pregnant bodies of refugee women and so-called 'citizen tourism', and what threats those bodies pose to the borders of singular and monolithic Irishness. Likewise, the film's aesthetic contributes further to its ideologemic interest in the breaching of national (geographical and subjective) borders. Preoccupied with containment and contamination, the film is marked by a heavy sense of security and surveillance: the camera frequently keeps the fences central and visible when shooting scenes, with repeated low angle and obstructed point of view shots, from beneath and behind these (broken and damaged) fences. Here, clearly, is a comment on both the literal and ideological ways in which the state works (and fails) to control access to the 'proper' space of the nation by restricting or isolating the movements of 'foreign' subjects.

Through the use of the generic form, however, the film also functions semiotically, in 'double-voice': the filtering of these thematic concerns through the codes of the horror film means that *Isolation* also foregrounds the cultural anxiety that accompanies the breaching of these borders. The film therefore neither *ignores* issues of social exclusion nor attempts to *account* for those issues: rather, it reflects the ambivalence of the thetic encounter, presenting both the semiotic and symbolic terms of its engagement. Similar ambivalences can be tracked in McMahon's *Dead Meat*, which uses the already pre-loaded trope of the zombie-as-capitalist-excess to critique the government-endorsed neo-liberalist ideology that underpinned the Tiger economy (one of the survivors, deftly dispatching the infected Cú Chulainn style with a hurley and sliotar, looks directly into the camera and delivers Fianna Fáil's 2002 election slogan: 'A lot done, more to do'). At the same time, it completely eviscerates any hint of sentimental fantasies of a return to a more 'authentic' Irishness as an alternative to the 'alienated' subjects of postmodern Ireland: the zombie outbreak is concentrated not in the typical urban environments of the shopping centre and the suburban estate but rather in the traditional repositories of bucolic, pastoral national identity – the stone cottage, the rural farm, and the nostalgic site of the ruined abbey (which one of the survivors attempts, ridiculously, to situate within its heritage discourse: 'actually,' he begins, as the zombies come over the hill, 'this is where Cromwell . . . never mind').

Semiotic landscaping

The deconstruction of the motif of Ireland as rural idyll is central to many of these films: most are set in pastoral landscape radically refigured as threatening, dangerous and suffocating. This, of course, is not new: it merely places them alongside an iconoclastic tradition in Irish cultural representation that seeks to challenge or complicate a cultural nationalist-inspired ideological trope. What is significant, however, is the way in which their engagement with these cinematic and literary codes draws attention to, rearticulates, and subverts the seductive discourse of allegory central to understandings of national cinema. The generic sensibility they deploy – their reticence to hide the 'semiotic process' of their production – intensifies their discursive intervention: by openly presenting and recodifying the thetic space from which the subject of Irish cinema has traditionally been constructed, the Irish horror genre 'enact[s] very violent transformations of the codes of representation'. Both Keating's *Wake Wood* and Walsh's *The Daisy Chain*, for example, present a radical reinterpretation of the Ireland-as-damaged-child motif that connects narratives of Irish childhood with narratives of national change, juxtaposing Irish (modern) futurity with the child-subject's oedipal struggle with an older generation:[36] in both these films, the child completely resists its symbolic function, and instead is rearticulated semiotically as threatening the very futurity it traditionally signals (a transposition, of course, of another symbolic code within horror, the evil child).

Paddy Breathnach's *Shrooms* also plays with the double-voice of representability, transposing (and through that transposition, disarticulating) the language of genre, the language of cinematic representation, and the language of postcolonial representation through the character of the English 'tour guide' Jake, signalling the 'violent' intent of its discursive strategy. Jake's presentation is a throwback to nineteenth-century Anglo-Irish culture, both in his Revival-ist interest in Celtic folklore and mysticism and his imperious attitude to the native landscape (his early encounter with Bernie and Ernie, the wild, inarticulate and simian pair of brothers who live in the woods is a clear nod to colonial-era discourse: tossing them the carcass of a dead deer, he comments 'I think that's what we call the indigenous people'). Bernie and Ernie themselves are modelled on both Punch-style representations of Irishness (savage, uncivilised, animal-like) and more cinematic forms of this trope – their characters undermine the 'simple peasant' familiar in nostalgic American films such as *The Quiet Man* (John Ford, 1952), *Darby O'Gill and the Little People* (Robert Stevenson, 1959) and *Waking Ned Devine* (Kirk Jones, 1998) by mapping this national code onto the transnational generic one of the inbred, backwards redneck. *Shrooms'* self-conscious play on the traditional 'pictorial codes' of Irish cinematic representation, specifically the 'non-indigenous' British and American forms (Ireland as threatening, atavistic and wild; Ireland as a diasporic rural idyll), can be read as a violent intervention into the discursive structures of Irish cinema, facilitated by its harnessing of a generic poetic language.

The transformation of the Irish pictorial landscape performed by these texts is a disarticulation of the subject of Irish cinema, not as a response to a 'crisis in imagination', but to a crisis in/of the representable in the wake of the more general transformation in the landscape of Irish subjectivity post-Celtic Tiger. Irish horror can thus be reimagined as a general comment both on the integrity of Irish national cinema as subject *and* the integrity of the Irish national subject as cinema. While Irish critics may lament the 'collapse of the solidarity central to the national project' – a new thetic phase indeed – the horror films that flourished over the last decade are speaking directly to the disarticulating effects and affects of that 'collapse'. A 'traumatic breach in the national imagination' can, and does, create a potential thetic space for new forms of representability. Kristeva notes that, in order to work against reification or stultification in subjectivity, to allow us to understand the subject as one that is constantly in-process, we should:

> argue in favour of an analytical theory of signifying systems and practices that would search within the signifying phenomenon for the *crisis* or the *unsettling process* of meaning and subject rather than for the coherence or identity of either *one* or a *multiplicity* of structures.[37]

When questioned by their teacher about 'what being Irish means to you', the students of zombie film *Boy Eats Girl* are largely silent: when pressed, one reels off, wearily and by rote, 'myths and legends, scholars and writers, Joyce, Beckett, Yeats'. His recourse to the symbolic narratives of Irish identity is immediately undermined by another student's dismissive retort, 'grow a brain, who reads those guys anymore?' A third student's intervention is telling. 'How does being Irish make you feel?' asks the teacher. His reply: 'suicidal'. In the zombie film, however, death means reanimation. The changed landscape of the nation requires a renewal of traditional 'dead' signifying structures through the infusion, the transposition, of new (poetic) discourses: the thetic space of Irish cinema is transformed through this 'crisis' of imagination rather than annihilated by it. Zombies, mutants, talking cows: these *are* the stories that address who 'we' are as a community.

Chapter Eight

FILM INTO NOVEL: KATE O'BRIEN'S MODERNIST USE OF FILM TECHNIQUES

Aintzane Legarreta Mentxaka

How normative are the boundaries of and between art mediums? Can we see the adaptation of film language into novels as a queer practice? The literary borrowing of filmic language questions given and static definitions of art mediums, as well as rigid understandings of clear delimitations between art forms. The term 'queer' has been used to refer to any confrontational disruption which challenges identity categories, and it can be applied in the same way to describe links between mediums (inter-medial) and between art forms (inter-art). In a novel such as Kate O'Brien's *Mary Lavelle*,[1] as we will see, there is a deliberate and complex hybridisation of artistic languages, a form of 'mixed media' which is characteristic of modernism, although it is regularly overlooked by critics. This queering of form in O'Brien's novel is linked to a queering of identity, because cinematic techniques are used to encode a more radical narrative within a more normative one. My argument is that intermediality (not to be confused with intertextuality) is a modernist feature, seeking to merge media, disciplines, art forms. In this essay I consider one type of inter-mediality, the hybridisation of cinematic and literary language, in one particular author, Kate O'Brien, looking at this strategy through the lens of queer theory.

Virginia Woolf, who was passionate about film, once described the alliance of film and the novel as 'unnatural', because the two mediums appeal to eye and brain in incompatible ways.[2] However, there is a long history of cooperation, and it is in fact well established that we can date the invention of the cinematograph, but not the cinematic.[3] There was of course a narrative and technical language specific to film, and its adaptation into literature began as soon as the new art made its appearance, in the late nineteenth- and early twentieth-century. This was a time when modernism brought about a productive identity crisis in fiction, a time when, suddenly, the novel seemed to be in transit, jolting between sculpture, film, music, photography; visiting everywhere, losing itself in everything.

This restlessness was evident in both form and content, and it is misleading to focus on one of those aspects, as commentators tend to do. For example, discussing the visual arts in a broader context, Bernard Smyth has coined the term formalesque to emphasise the modernist 'drive towards formalism', claiming that the movement 'reduced meaning to style and style to form'.[4] Yet there were also new themes, such as sexuality, which required new modes of representation in literature. In fact, it is possible that the modernist upheaval regarding mediums, grammar, words, sprang in part from a need to speak of sex in a way that was discreet yet accessible.[5] What is clear is that there is a frenzy of interconnectedness in modernism, a resolve to mix genres, re-shape or at least un-shape form, a determination to break free of linearity and compartmentalisation – an impulse exemplified by collage, a technique which caught the attention of modernists early in the twentieth century and was developed and embraced by surrealists in the 1930s.[6] This intertextuality, intermodality and intermediality can be seen as a reaction to modern alienation, and as a friendly gesture expressing the will to share, embrace, exchange.

Modernism is 'a critique of Modernity',[7] and there is an implicit political impetus behind this repudiation of one's own boundaries. This is not immediately obvious, because the most politicised years of the period are largely absent from canon and curriculum. One could think that the suffragette movement never happened, and that socialist ideas were circumscribed to the Soviet Union. Similarly, a normative bias on gender, sex and sexuality is noticeable in criticism dealing with the avant garde,[8] despite the fact that modernist art is amenable not just to a queer reading but to an analogy with the disciplinary incoherence of queer theory itself. Accounts of modernism never deem relevant the debates on representation which were so crucial for the early feminist movement.[9] Also, the modernist intermarrying of modes (such as comic-historic), genres (such as erotic fiction-fairy tale), literary forms (such as poem-play) and art mediums (such as literature-film), may be linked to the pervading internationalism among writers and artists of the period.

Modernist writers were particularly alert to experimentation in film. This is exemplified by *Close Up*, a magazine on film theory edited between 1927 and 1933 by the poet HD, the novelist Winifred Bryher and the filmmaker Kenneth MacPherson. The three collaborated in *Borderline*, an experimental film from 1930 and a rather magnificent ending to the silent era, relying on anti-realistic editing and dealing with racial and queer issues. Furthermore, Dorothy Richardson, Virginia Woolf and George Orwell, for example, wrote essays on film, while James Joyce was involved in setting up the first cinema in Dublin, the Volta. Joyce's own work was infamously described, at the Soviet Writers' Congress of 1934, as 'a heap of dung, crawling with worms, photographed by a cinema apparatus through a microscope'.[10] There is an anxiety about 'proper' distance here, an understanding of modernism as moral kinesis.

Irish modernist literature, with its interconnectedness and variation at the levels of structure, reference and mode, may be read partly as an antidote to the pressing univocality of de Valeraism, but we must not forget that modernism predated the establishment of the Irish free state. For example, W.M. Letts' collection of poems *Songs of Leinster*, first published in 1913, can be considered a modernist project in its documentation of multiple voices, offering a hive-like portrait of Irish life at that moment in time.[11] Among other Irish modernists, we find quite a few examples of hybridisation of film and literature. Blanaid Salkeld, in her poem 'Templeogue' from the 1933 collection *Hello, Eternity!*, zooms in and out of a soul landscape in a way that only film or words can do.[12] Patrick Kavanagh's novel-poem of 1942 *The Great Hunger* also borrows cinematic techniques such as zooming.[13] In Elizabeth Bowen's 1929 novel *The Last September* the page turns occasionally into a screen, for example showcasing subjective point of view shot/reverse shot camera work: 'And as the four candles went up with the ladies, drawing a tide of shadow, she and Lois had turned at a turn of the stair to see him still there, looking up from the staggering mounting dark.'[14]

In Ireland, like elsewhere, modernist artists and writers shared family ties and social circles, and there were also links by training;

Bowen, for example, went to art school before deciding to become a novelist. There were some common traits among Irish modernist artists, such as the fact that the antidogmatic, militant anti-Christianity of much international modernism was tempered in Ireland.[15] Indeed, despite the prevalent agnosticism in the avant garde, a spiritual inflection is clear in the medievalising impetus of much modernist art, from the 1913 publications of Albert Gleizes in France to the lectures of his disciple and collaborator Mainie Jellett, who believed that the revaluation of Celtic art in Ireland 'would give our art a national character'.[16] Among Irish writers, Austin Clarke and Kate O'Brien, for example, hailed a communitarian and creative Celtic monasticism as 'a kind of utopia', suggesting Romanesque style as a referent for their own twentieth-century political and aesthetic allegiances, anti-authoritarian and modernist.[17] It is nevertheless highly ironic that *Mary Lavelle*, Kate O'Brien's masterpiece of queer cinematic appropriation, was published in 1936, because it coincided with Pope Pius XI's encyclical *Vigilanti Cura*, which called for cinema 'to be put to the service of morality', directly inspiring the creation of the National Film Institute of Ireland.[18]

There has been a boom of studies tracing a 'filmic sensibility' in novels, even if the authors were active before the invention of cinema, as is the case, for example, with Jane Austen.[19] Cinematographically speaking, there is much in Kate O'Brien that is easily translated into film, including stories that revel in collective visual experiences (the bullfight, the Catholic mass, school performances, the opera), and psychological, dramatic plots that suit a certain kind of film. The librarian at the O'Brien Archive in Limerick always makes a point of mentioning to visitors that the heroine of David Lean's film *Brief Encounter* (1946) pops into the library to get 'the new Kate O'Brien' which she has reserved, a reference that the audience was expected to understand. The reference is in fact a subtle indication of the forbidden-love story about to unfold (an O'Brien staple), and it suggests that this O'Brien fan has a framework for the ethical issues she will confront in the narrative.[20]

Kate O'Brien was a keen cinema-goer since childhood, when her 'chief craze' was Pearl White, the star of the serial *The Perils of Pauline*, proto-action films where the protagonist got into various scrapes and managed to escape by the end of each instalment.[21] In O'Brien's novel *Pray for the Wanderer*, the autobiographical Tom is a novelist banned in Ireland who loves popular film (praising Stan and Ollie, and Chaplin).[22] Tom borrows cinematic terms to explain that his job is not to moralise but to show '[t]hat life is so and so on *the screen of my closed eyelids* [. . .] I give you life translated to my idiom'.[23] After her initial success as a playwright,[24] O'Brien attempted to become a scriptwriter in the 1930s. As Alison Butler has pointed out, 'women's involvement in the movies was a natural progression of their involvement in the theatre'.[25] At the level of writing, it has been claimed that 'cinema is theatre taken to wherever the author chooses', and O'Brien's scripts, dialogue-dependent and dominated by static indoor settings, often seem indebted to drama.[26]

In 1938, however, Kate O'Brien published an article on film where she showed a sharp awareness of medium limits and potentialities. The article, titled 'Why the Rage for French Films?', opens with her claim that 'we are all movie-fans now – not to be is to label oneself a museum piece'.[27] O'Brien declares that, even though film is destined to become the 'sister art' of theatre, the links between painting and the novel in fact run deeper, and cinema is a place 'where certain functions of those two arts can be united, to re-create life in a new medium'.[28] In this pseudo-evolutionary scale, film seems to be running ahead, so perhaps O'Brien's 'return' to fiction was simply a consequence of her failure to make her screenwriting financially viable.

Kate O'Brien wrote at least two film scripts, *A Broken Song* and *Mary Magdalen*, and set one of her plays, *Gloria Gish*, amidst the emerging film industry in England. They show an interest in pushing thematic and visual boundaries. *A Broken Song* is a never-produced, undated screenplay, which perhaps could be dated 1931–2.[29] The script of *A Broken Song*, which was sent to a New York agent, is set in Munich, Paris, New York and London. It is the story of a young tenor born in Australia of Irish parents,[30] who has repeated dream-like visions of a woman's face. The dream sequences are straightforward but their inclusion punctures the main narrative. It is interesting to recall that Germaine Dulac's adaptation *The Seashell and the Clergyman*, of 1926, often considered the first surrealist film, was followed by a series of films by surrealists, who cherished the possibilities of the new medium to disrupt perceptions of reality, particularly through dreams.

Kate O'Brien's *Mary Magdalen* is another never-produced, undated screenplay, possibly from the 1930s,[31] which shows a greater proficiency in film techniques. It is a political and existentialist fable, centred on Mary Magdalen from the Christian gospels as she takes the life-changing decision to follow Jesus. The script has a contemporary feel, as if it had been accidentally set 1,900 years in the past. It reads like the biography of a wealthy and well-educated flapper who pursues sexual promiscuity as a sort of ethical compulsion, out of a sense of duty to herself as a modern woman, but who is in fact living in what Jean Paul Sartre called bad faith.[32] The typescript at the National Library of Ireland is technically undemanding, but it evidences a sustained radicalism of vision, for example in the suggestion that the Virgin Mary and the whore of Magdala were in fact one and the same.

Gloria Gish is an unproduced play, possibly written in the early 1930s.[33] The story is a twentieth-century rewrite of the legend of Helen of Troy, set in London probably in the late 1920s or early 1930s. The play follows Gladys, a beauty who is charmed away from her financier husband by a film producer who promises to turn her into a star, the next 'Gloria Gish' (a composite of early film stars Gloria Swanson and Lillian Gish). In the play, Gladys is associated with Ealing – where she was born – an area famous for its film studios, and perhaps the character itself is a commentary on the alluring vacuity of many film productions of the time.

After these interesting efforts in other mediums, O'Brien returned to fiction with a sharpened sensibility. Critics regularly claim that the radical content of her novels was unmatched by form,[34] yet this is not accurate. In her most experimental work, the 1936 novel *Mary Lavelle*, she adapted the languages of architecture, bullfighting, painting, interior design and cinema. We could refer to this practice as 'mixed media', a term normally used in the visual arts. Kate O'Brien was particularly interested in experimenting with film language, but she was a novelist borrowing film techniques rather than a filmmaker manqué. In her novels she is partial to panoramic and moving shots. We find them, for example, in the description of an upper-middle-class house interior in the 1938 *Pray for the Wanderer*, with the narrator's lens surveying 'the wood fire, the Victorian sofa, pink flowers on the wall paper, the old brass cake stand'.[35] Or in a 'cinematic' scene in the 1942 *The Land of Spices*,[36] where a flashback marked by a subjective camera-like point of view structures the narrative progression as a young woman discovers her father in a homosexual embrace and runs away. By 1958, in her novel *As Music and Splendour*, a moving shot of a practise-room will seamlessly open the narrative, introducing the main theme of learning to sing/sin, and advancing the end of the book and the co-protagonist's tears after her lover, another woman, sails away in the Saint Catherine. In the scene, the narrator's camera moves from 'a glass door leading on to a dark passage', to 'an oleograph of a young woman with a palm branch in her hand', to 'a tuning fork on the shelf', and then shows how '[r]ain beat against a tall window'.[37]

Set in 1922, *Mary Lavelle* recounts the experiences of an innocent but spirited Irish girl, Mary, working as a governess in the Basque country in the north of Spain, where she falls in love with her employer's son, Juanito, a communist revolutionary and a married man. A 'governess abroad' bildungsroman, the book is also a historical and documentary novel recording a changing society in the laboratory of identities that was the city of Bilbo (Bilbao) in 1922, before the coup d'état of general Primo de Rivera. A novel dealing with identity and change, its language, like its existentialist heroine, takes risks in order to move forward. In *Mary Lavelle*, chapters and scenes are conceived in visual terms, so that consecutive settings give information about inner states. There are many close-ups (mouths, rubbish, cigarettes, cables). The chapter 'A Walk with Milagros' has the feel of a long moving shot (two women philosophise while walking by the edge of a cliff), while 'Candles at Allera' and 'San Geronimo' include the equivalent of panoramic shots (right-to-left visual movements registering city life from the vantage point of a hill and a balcony). The key scene in the 'A Corrida' chapter is, as we will see, a summation of frames recorded with the coldness of a camera in documentary style, all the best to elicit a non-mediated emotional response. If Mary's final tears are comparable to a fade out, the novel's 'Prologue' is the equivalent of a voice-over by an all-seeing all-knowing narrator. The opening and ending of the novel are marked by a visual repetition that would not have been out of place in a film: a governess's trunk opened at the border.

One of the main features of the novel is the constant, even compulsive, use of flashbacks. Remembrance, and the deliberate fixing of an *image* in a store of memories, is one of the main themes of the novel; Mary's mantra is 'I must remember this'. It may be argued that flashback is not a specifically cinematic technique, but other stylistic features in O'Brien's novel, such as zooming, moving shots and lighting, are clearly indebted to film language. For example, Mary recalls a bullfight, in a way that resembles a tightly edited documentary film:

> She apprehended [. . .] the summery sweetness of scene and hour. But a cloudy region of her mind was showing her other things: a boisterously running bull, a cape bunched up for a veronica, a blindfold horse, a drooped muleta, a matador's placating hand. Her head was full of the day's new images.[38]

Experiences are edited, creatively re-mastered, and finally projected in 'a cloudy region of her mind'. Memory does not quite work in this way – film does.

How should we approach this startling hybridisation? One way is to consider the adaptation of film techniques into literature as a queer practice. The term queer refers to 'those films and popular culture texts, spectator positions, pleasures, and readings that articulate spaces outside gender-binaries and sexuality categories',[39] in Alexander Doty's words, creating a 'cultural "queer space"' which may be occupied by anyone'.[40] As Michael Warner points out, some kinds of representation are 'inherently uncontrollable, queer by nature', although queer theory's 'focus on messy representation' in fact helps show that queerness is everywhere.[41] Taking up the eclecticism and 'refusal of disciplinary coherence' in Noreen Giffney's description of 'quare theory',[42] it is illustrative to consider novelistic mixed media in the context of Judith Butler's epistemological investigation of gender and sexuality: the claim of true gender identity may be a 'regulatory fiction', and the postulation of a true genre/medium identity may be another.[43] Kamilla Elliott has claimed that novel and film 'contain and invert the otherness of each other reciprocally, inversely, and inherently', and that their relationship is therefore comparable to a looking glass.[44] Judith Butler follows Derrida to suggest that 'the structure of gender imitation is such that the imitat*ed* is to some degree produced – or, rather, *re*produced – by imitation'; that is, '*imitation* does not copy that which is prior, but produces and *inverts* the very terms of priority and derivativeness.'[45] In the same way, the use of cinematic language in Kate O'Brien's fiction is an '*inverted* imitation', breaching the illusory coherence of novelistic boundaries.

Mary Lavelle gives structural preference to two events: Mary's going to a bullfight in Bilbo, and a sex scene between Mary and Juanito in a field in the outskirts of the city. The protagonist is a queer heterosexual woman: she is sexually non-normative because she assertively demands sex from a married man, something that goes against the social and moral regulations of the time. In the sex scene, O'Brien carefully repeats the words deployed in the narrative to describe the bullfight, so that both events merge into one another, and a brutal and painful sexual initiation is transmuted into a stylised mortal combat. This subtext empowers the woman (and queers her) even further, by giving her the ability to penetrate her male lover and fatally wound him. The novel in general, and this scene in particular, rely on intertextual references to Ernest Hemingway's 1932 essay-manual on bullfighting, *Death in the Afternoon*, to such an extent that O'Brien's book can be described as a collage.[46]

The climatic scene in *Mary Lavelle* merges words and film. Through visual clues, Mary is presented as a bull, and her reluctant lover as a bullfighter who will not survive the encounter. The text relies on a favourite technique in many silent films: double exposure. Words facilitate the duplication and juxtaposition of visual details. For example, curls drenched in sweat clinging to the forehead – we see them on a bull first, later we see them on Mary after attending a bullfight, and finally we see them on Mary in the sex scene: 'He saw her set teeth and quivering nostrils, beating eyelids, flowing, flowing tears. The curls were clammy on her forehead now.'[47] Another example is the choreographed notation, from the bullfight where '[t]he matador drew his enemy to his breast, and past it, on the gentle lure; brought him back along his thigh as if for sheer love',[48] to the love scene where '[t]he pain made her cry out and writhe in shock, but he held her hard against him and in great love compelled her to endure it'.[49]

Yet another example is the visual rhyme between a matador's cape and a blanket: the movement of the cape to persuade the bull to step out of a 'querencia'/attachment to the wooden barrier in the bullfight later metamorphoses into Juanito's throwing a blanket on the ground near the tree trunk on which Mary leans. When Mary draws her lover towards her, we read that Juanito, after some hesitation, 'took her quickly and bravely',[50] a direct reference to Hemingway's advice in such a situation (with the bull in a querencia) to 'kill [the bull] quickly, not well'.[51] Juanito's 'piercing gentleness'[52] cannot guard him from Mary, who despite her innocence is 'a fatal exception that makes splinters of everything normal'.[53] As Hemingway had pointed out, bullfighting is founded on the 'simplicity and [. . .] lack of experience' of the bull, who ideally has '[no] remembrance of previous work in the ring'.[54] The inexperienced Mary is therefore the perfect match for him; in the cinematic montage of the novel, she is the perfect nemesis.

It is possible that Kate O'Brien saw Cecil B. DeMille's silent film adaptation *Carmen*, released in 1915, where DeMille subtly linked the bullfight to the murder of the female protagonist by having the first as backdrop (happening unseen behind a wall) to the second. While DeMille is realist – the staginess notwithstanding – O'Brien is, by contrast, surrealist. Lumière cameramen had documented bullfight scenes as early as 1900, but the most relevant cinematic use of it was the 1922 *Blood and Sand*, a vehicle for star Rudolph Valentino. He played a bullfighter named Juan (his mother calls him Juanillo, or 'little John'), who is seduced away from his wife by an amoral wealthy woman looking for a thrill. It is likely that O'Brien saw this film, and she may have been inspired by the climatic death of the bullfighter after he becomes 'reckless' in the bullring, consumed by anger and guilt. While in the film the death of the bullfighter is implicitly caused by the temptress, in a predictable resolution to a story about the fall of a good man, for O'Brien there are no villains, and her bullfighting mise en scène destabilises the normativity of characterisation and plot by splitting the story. When the novel ends, at the textual level the couple part amicably, whereas at the cinematically encoded visual level the man is killed by the woman. In this way, O'Brien's montage offers a subtextual plot dealing with grief, guilt or revenge – on the part of the woman.

This is not the only visually coded subtext that distorts and displaces the 'main' narrative. Another one, for example, triplicates a character (Nieves/Mary/Agatha) through 'her' striking blue eyes, to offer a lesbian bildungsroman. The use of colour to signify a likeness has had a long use in painting; but in *Mary Lavelle* a pair of unusually bright blue eyes, 'deep blue and full of light',[55] is a code that allows the reader to link three segments of a life as they unfold. The very careful montage shows a young woman experimenting with her sexuality (Mary), the same woman in her thirties coming out as a lesbian (Agatha), and the same woman again as a transgender girl who longs to be a boy (Nieves). Like a cinema screen segmented in three, we see past, present and future selves simultaneously. With a fluidity that may have felt strained in a film, O'Brien shows the three characters interacting, giving advice to each other, arguing, and so on. She approaches this intricate project with remarkable lightness, even humour; for example, when someone remarks to Mary that '[y]our double would take a bit of finding', Agatha quickly adds '[t]hat's a fact'.[56]

Doubling and trebling characters was a stylistic technique particularly favoured by modernist artists and writers, an investigative strand of the modernist enquiry on subjectivity. *Mary Lavelle* has many striking connections, in characterisation and plot, to a film with a duplicated protagonist, Fritz Lang's *Metropolis*, of 1926, connections which I have discussed elsewhere.[57] If some features of *Mary Lavelle*, such as the idea of 'Mary as bull' or the doubling of characters, are reminiscent of surrealist film, there is one other school of filmmaking that is crucial in the novel. The recurrent use of dramatic light and shadow effects in the book is indebted to German Expressionism, a movement which enhanced certain moods by non-realistic exaggeration or 'angularity' in set designs, acting, composition, lighting and cinematography. For example, when Mary meets her employer Don Pablo, she explains: 'Shadows and lines overdramatised his face in the evening light, so that Mary felt his foreignness with exaggeration, even remotely with alarm.'[58] When she encounters Juanito, '[t]he evening sun, pouring in at the landing window, lighted each very sweetly for the other, as with a fatal halo',[59] and when they meet again, in a square:

> She leant against the tree, and looked at the figures moving in beauty through the violent depths of light. [. . .] Juanito found her under the tree. There was a white, hard light streaming in on her obliquely.[60]

At another particularly cinematic point, the novel explains that Mary 'could see Doña Consuelo's shadow reflected on the terrace from the window. And [Juanito's] passing shadow, with Nieves' as they danced.'[61] This overemphasised play between light and shadow is a recurrent stylistic thread in *Mary Lavelle*, and there is no reason, *in writing*, for this investment on striking lighting effects and the heightened contrast between black and white popularised by German Expressionist film before the advent of colour or sound. In a unique way, the tactic allows O'Brien to recreate a certain mood, as well as to emphasise the constructedness of the narrative.

Kate O'Brien did not publicly admit the debt of her 1936 novel to German filmmaking, and reserved her praise for French films produced around that year. The best place 'to learn what cinema really is', she declared in her article of 1938, is in French films; it is the French who deserve most of the credit for the creation of this new art form, after leading in other arts for over a hundred years. In the article, having discussed with admiration and a critical eye the work of filmmakers like Jean Renoir, Julien Duvivier or Jacques Feyder, O'Brien traces what today we may call 'cinematic elements' in earlier French literature and painting, and links them not to a general interest in the visual but to the new form of perception inaugurated by modernist art:

> The French mind has not so much learnt from Cezanne as accepted his announcement of the weight of significant beauty[62] which can lie in a rumpled table-napkin, and a half-empty glass; with Flaubert it recognises quite unselfconsciously the melancholy potentialities of a cab in a rainy street; with de Maupassant it smiles at a fat little feminine hand on a café-table; with Matisse it is made attentive by canaries in a café or sunlight falling across a sofa.[63]

O'Brien follows this by claiming that the French mind 'finds the screen a good meeting place for the novelist's and the painter's perceptions – and *it is interested in having them assembled,* is interested in the *artist's* flashlights on life'.[64] Assemblage was a characteristic modernist technique, and here O'Brien extends the notion of assembling objects/segments into the joining of different perceptual modes, different mediums. Further, she italicises the word 'artist', to de-emphasise the differences between painters, novelists, filmmakers.

Kate O'Brien's article on film adopts assemblage as a critical stand, rebuking any expectations the reader may have from a well-known novelist. Non-normative thinking and creativity are challenging, because they are ostensibly messy and because their thoroughness and craftsmanship are not immediately obvious. In *Mary Lavelle,* queer identity is itself produced in part by the queer practices of intertextuality and intermediality; the novel adopts a new way of reading visually, so that we 'move' with the text, are blinded by its electric lights, and are productively disconcerted by its unexpected visual analogies. O'Brien's novelistic filmic techniques facilitate a queerer and richer narrative. Yet in order to appreciate the experimental daring and accomplishment of a novel such as *Mary Lavelle*, we as critics need to address the modernists' queer vocation to challenge 'natural' boundaries.

Like other queer practices and identities, intermedial tactics within any given art form are 'running commentaries' on the 'naturalized positions' they 'repla[y] and resignif[y]'.[65] According to Judith Butler, 'a subversive or *de*-instituting repetition' is possible, by being aware of the excess inherent in any 'narrativization'.[66] When Kate O'Brien was writing *Mary Lavelle* in the 1930s, film was a minor form; to bring film techniques into her novel was not a colonial incursion nor a drag act, but rather a friendly gesture, a voluntary stepping down from a privileged position. The intermediality of modernist fiction was a political exercise in de-instituting the novel, but above all it was a way of underlying the fact that all the arts are in an inherently queer continuum.

Chapter Nine

THE FENG SHUI OF LOUGH DERG: THERAPEUTIC LANDSCAPES AND THE MARKETING OF SPIRITUALITY IN CONTEMPORARY IRELAND

Anne Mulhall

According to Will Gesler's influential formulation, a therapeutic landscape 'arises when physical and built environments, social conditions and human perceptions combine to produce an atmosphere which is conducive to healing'. Gesler uses *healing* 'to include cures in the biomedical sense (physical healing), a sense of psychological well-being (mental health) and feelings of spiritual renewal (spiritual healing)'.[1] Therapeutic landscapes are marketed and consumed as oases of escape from the pressures of modern life. The 'wellness' industry clearly intersects with the production of therapeutic landscapes: to some extent, the relation between place and the user constitutes the landscape as therapeutic and this relation is packaged, marketed and sold to the consumer. Equally, the lexicon of wellness and healing, of the holistic renewals of mind, body and spirit performed in the interactions between self and place, locates the 'wellness' industry in relation to what is loosely and problematically termed the New Age movement. These intersections attest to the apparently contradictory positioning of such therapeutic landscapes within the spaces of both 'tradition' and 'modernity', in the process troubling the false dichotomy these terms are often made to encapsulate. Such landscapes are in part constituted through their connection with the natural world, and their historical and cultural resonances with the 'non-modern', while also being, in the contemporary context, associated with the commodification of spirituality, wellness and healing in the 'spiritual marketplace'. The logic of the 'spiritual marketplace' is well illustrated by the 'rebranding' of two very different religious sites in Ireland, the pilgrimage site of Lough Derg during their 2004 marketing campaign and the marketing of Krishna Island, the Irish centre for the International Society for Krishna Consciousness (ISKCON, or the Hare Krishnas) on the island of Inis Rath in County Fermanagh, as a holistic retreat desti- nation in the early 2000s. Focusing on the visual texts used to advertise these centres – posters, fliers and websites – this essay will explore the multiple and often conflicting semiotics of authenticity and 'wellness' enlisted in the construction of these religious sites as 'therapeutic landscapes'.

Sharp distinctions between the somewhat amorphous New Age movement, alternative spiritualities, and some varieties of the new religious movements can be difficult to draw. In the Irish context clear distinctions between the committed adherent and the 'spiritu- ality shopper' can be particularly difficult to assert or maintain. In their study of the history and sociology of Buddhism in Ireland, Laurence Cox and Maria Griffin's respondents illustrate the local fuzziness of such boundaries, partly traceable to the hegemonic posi- tion of the Catholic Church whose effects continue to be felt in terms of Catholic Irish-born peoples' attitudes to religious identifi- cation and to the historically peripheral position of Ireland in global terms. Cox and Griffin describe this peripheral positioning suc- cinctly: 'If, in the last 150 years, Buddhist Asia has acted as the "central region" to the "border regions" of western Buddhism, Ireland is arguably a border region to the border regions, a second- hand recipient of developments in more powerful societies.'[2] Cox and Griffin's study is specific to Buddhism in Ireland, but given the eclecticism that marks alternative spiritualities in Ireland, their find- ings are likely to be important for other 'non-indigenous' spiritual imports as well, most particularly Hinduism and practices such as yoga, ayurveda and non-dualist philosophies (such as Advaita Vedanta) that derive from that tradition. Buddhist groups in Ireland tend to be quite informal and reliant on 'import gurus' and 'blow- ins' from abroad, particularly from the UK. Thus, institutional affiliations and networks tend to exist on a global rather than local level. Cox and Griffin conclude that 'Irish people appropriate Buddhism for themselves, within largely self-directed and informal agencies and privately', which has led to a syncretic effect whereby practitioners engage with beliefs and practices from a variety of religious systems and traditions, including the perceived indigenous practices of Catholicism and 'Celticism'.[3] For Cox and Griffin, this is both consequent upon and illustrative of the historical peripherality of Ireland in relation to Anglo-American culture, through which Buddhist practices continue to be mediated, as well as Ireland's peripherality in terms of global Buddhism, in turn a function of its historical global position.

Ireland's arguably peripheral position in relation to the global circulation of 'alternative spiritualities' in recent decades finds an important precursor in an earlier phase in the 'westernisation' of Asian systems of belief, thought and practice. The imperialist logic of 'Orientalism' has been well established since Edward Said's analysis. According to Said, Orientalism is the discursive vehicle of colonial and imperialist expropriation and racial othering, operating through a binarised West–East representational economy and constructing an image of the Orient that further embeds Western hegemony.[4] Whether that construction is overtly stigmatising and racist or romanticising, both negative and positive constructions serve Western ends and obscure the realities of non-Western existence. While Said focuses on the Middle East rather than on South and East Asia – the provenance of the Hindu, Buddhist and Taoist systems that have exerted the greatest influence on alternative spiritualities in the contemporary West – his critique is likewise applicable to these strands in the Orientalist project. However, the historical peripherality of Ireland in relation to the colonial metropole complicates the position of Ireland in Orientalist discourse. As Joseph Lennon has argued, the engagement of Orientalist discourses within the Celtic Revival in particular illustrates the complex historical relation between colonised Ireland and the 'Orient'. He observes that 'textual links between Celtic and Oriental cultures existed independently in Irish and Gaelic culture', most persistently in the legendary origin stories that imagined Scythian and Phoenician geneaologies for 'Celtic' Ireland.[5] As Lennon explains, even when such theories were disproved, their imaginative power remained available in the cultural sphere, where the 'semiotic connection between Celt and Oriental' was deployed to great effect in the construction of a mythical, mystical, romanticised version of the pre and transhistorical 'spirit' of the Irish nation.[6] Lennon notes that 'The origin legends became foundational to Irish cultural nationalism in the eighteenth century and developed into a literary and mystical connection during the Celtic Revival in the early twentieth',[7] while 'Oriental' figures and analogies were employed to speak to the Irish situation and to assert cross-colonial connections. This was a distinctly romanticising version of Eastern knowledge, and analogies with Celticism in turn confirmed the lofty nature of the Celtic spirit, associating both with the past, the premodern, the precolonial, the spiritual rather than materialist, the traditional rather than the modern.[8]

If 'Irish Orientalism' at the *fin de siècle* was both complicit with and subversive of Empire, what position does the contemporary global circulation of 'peripheral' spiritual and indigenous practices and beliefs within New Age and alternative spiritualities hold in relation to contemporary forms of cultural appropriation?[9] Charges of imperialist expropriation are frequently made, particularly in relation to the commodification of indigenous cultures and spiritual systems in the era of late capitalism for a Western market. In this view, non-Western cultures and traditions are valued primarily for their usefulness to the Western consumer; religious systems and indigenous beliefs are adapted to suit Western tastes and demands, and practices such as yoga, reiki and ayurveda are detached from the place, culture and religious systems in which they are rooted, again in response to the Western spiritual marketplace. Thus an 'exotic', distorting and ahistorical version of the East continues to circulate. However, while such a formulation does capture the amnesiac voracity of cultural commodification and its ruthless appropriation and assimilation of difference to Western 'sameness' in the contemporary era, well-illustrated by the lucrative 'mainstreaming' of previously 'alternative' and 'counter-cultural' practices, beliefs and lifestyles, it also obscures the agency of Asian and other actors in these global circulations, as well as the cross-cultural relationality that is often involved in the constitution of therapeutic place, knowledge and practice. Clarke notes that the globalisation of Asian cultures cannot be adequately represented within a model that accounts only for Western cultural hegemony. As he states, this aspect of 'orientalism' has often resulted not in 'the obliteration of indigenous Eastern cultures [. . .] but with their revivification and re-empowerment' and that, for instance, Western translations of the *Bhagavad Gita* contributed to a renewal of Hinduism in India and to indigenous nationalist resistance to imperial rule, while the

Theosophical Society in part enabled many indigenous actors, including Gandhi and Krishnamurti, to revive Hinduism as a powerful political rallying point on the local and global levels.[10] Further, Asian teachers and gurus have been instrumental in the global dissemination and adaptation of Asian spiritual belief systems and practices from the nineteenth century to the present; as Clarke concludes, 'From Vivekananda through Suzuki to the Dalai Lama there is a distinguished line of Eastern scholars who have both participated in and actively encouraged the orientalist pursuit, and who cannot simply be dismissed as victims of Western manipulation.'[11]

The recent 'rebranding' of both the ISKCON-run Lake Isle Retreats and the Lough Derg pilgrimage illustrate the 'unprecedented intensification in the pursuit of wellness in the history of tourism' and the 'mainstreaming' of the semiotics of the New Age in the Irish spiritual marketplace.[12] As a pilgrimage site, Lough Derg mobilises the binarisation of tradition and modernity. The pilgrim's journey itself enables this distinction, as the pilgrim moves from 'the profane to the sacred, from the everyday life to an encounter with the divine'.[13] Gesler notes that pilgrimage sites (which are, Ronan Foley has noted, genealogically related to modern 'wellness' and spirituality tourism) are usually found in remote, 'peripheral' areas, so that pilgrims might 'sever themselves from everyday life for a time' the better to achieve self-transformation.[14] In his study of Lourdes, he identifies how pilgrimage represents a disenchantment with 'modern lifestyles' and a temporary, restorative respite from the pressures attendant upon those lifestyles.[15]

As Peggy O'Brien has elaborated, Lough Derg has a deep symbolic significance in terms of Irish cultural history and prehistory. The tradition of legend and literature about Lough Derg has been central in constituting its reputation as a site outside of modern time, confirming it as a transhistorical repository of 'authentic' indigenous Irishness with a genealogy that stretches back to the mists of mythical, precolonial prehistory. O'Brien recounts the Fenian tale that accounts for the etymology of Lough Derg, where a maggot lodged in the corpse of Fionn's mother transforms into a monster that the Fenians slay, turning the waters red. The story mutated over time to include St Patrick in place of Fionn, and the story becomes an allegory of the defeat of a feminised paganism by the masculinist powers of Christianity.[16] The legend of Lough Derg makes it a symbol of the continuity of indigenous tradition and the spirit of Celticism and a prime site for the articulation of Irish 'Celticity' and historical colonial struggle. This 'authenticity' is inevitably part of what constitutes the site as a therapeutic landscape for pilgrims who journey there seeking a transformative, healing, restorative spiritual experience.

Discourses of Celticity, prehistorical myth and Irish colonial history intersect with the semiotics of wellness and therapeutic restoration in the descriptions of Lough Derg on the pilgrimage website, drawing from but also constituting the interconnections between affective, spiritual and 'indigenous' authenticities. However, this intersection is inseparable from the nexus between strategies of heritage, spiritual and wellness tourism, calling into question even so apparently 'authentic' a site as Lough Derg as a wellspring of a traditional 'Irishness'. The written text combines with the visual images of the island buildings, set in a landscape of stone, grass and water, emphasising the harmony of built environment and natural setting in an oasis far removed from the stress of modern living. There were some changes, however, to the visual composition of the site between 2007 and 2010. Whereas the 2007 homepage was dominated by a picture of the current monsignor, a maroon fleece covering his clerical garb, a welcoming smile for the would-be pilgrim, the 2010 website bore a different image of the monsignor; the maroon fleece is gone, the man's expression more careworn, and the written text rather than the image of the monsignor now dominates the visual field.[17] The replacement of the 2007 photograph with a more grave and formal image indicates the changed circumstances of the Catholic Church following the Murphy and Ryan Reports,[18] and reflects the changed circumstances too of the would-be pilgrim in a time of economic recession. The written text remains the same, however, in both the 2007 and 2010 versions of the website, emphasising the ancient and Celtic lineage of Lough Derg while downplaying its position as a specifically Catholic institution. Instead, the text presents the site as a place of sanctuary, a respite from the stresses of contemporary life, a place of rejuvenation and perhaps transformation:

> Part of our Celtic heritage and renowned throughout Europe and the Middle Ages, Lough Derg is a unique place of peace. In today's modern world – where everything is fast and instant – Lough Derg still manages to maintain a pace where people have

to move more slowly, where the mind can be stilled. [. . .] If you are seeking an opportunity for calm, for renewal or growth, then this ancient Sanctuary of St Patrick might well be the place. We invite you to become part of what has been an Irish tradition since the sixth century.

The welcome is extended beyond affiliative lines: 'Whatever your creed, background, social circumstances or religious practice, you are most welcome.'[19]

In 2004, the pilgrimage centre underwent a significant rebranding. The campaign can be situated within the context of the Celtic Tiger era, and is notable for the way in which the semiotics of the spiritual marketplace and a mainstreamed New Age lexicon were deployed in advertising images, in newspaper articles, and in pilgrim 'testimonials' at that time. A central aspect of the 2004 marketing strategy was the designing of two poster campaigns that ran simultaneously (Figs. 9.1 and 9.2). One arm of the campaign targeted the 'faithful', and the other a younger, secular demographic. This dual strategy was manifest in two different poster templates. One was for display in churches, and the other was posted on the Dublin public transport system, both Dublin Bus and the DART. According to Deborah Maxwell, the marketing director behind the 'Soul Survival' campaign, the second poster was designed to appeal to a young constituency, with the intention that 'the more modern images will hopefully attract the attention of the "spiritual searcher"'.[20] Two versions of the poster were displayed on Dublin transport, one featuring a young woman and the other a young man, both employing very similar compositions. The visual field is dominated by the sole of the pilgrim's foot, which is in focus; the smiling faces of the pilgrims are out of focus and they are dressed in casual, comfortable 'leisure' clothing (Fig. 9.1). In the image reproduced here, the focus on the sole of the woman's foot recalls the 'pilgrim's feet' associated with Lough Derg. It is also, obviously, a textual pun on the strap line: Soul Survival. The image of the carefree woman against a pure blue sky, and the poster's slogan, suggest that the campaign borrows not just from travel advertising but more specifically from the 'wellness' niche of that market and from the 'New Age' spiritual lexicon that informs it. The campaign avoids any distinctively Catholic or Celtic associations, but instead carries connotations of self-spirituality and the holistic milieu of mind, body

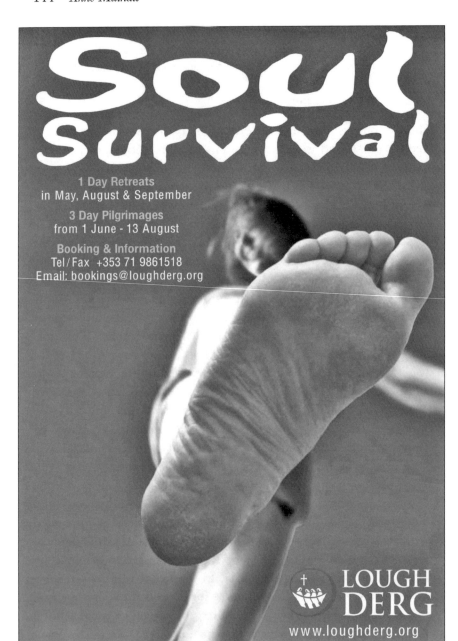

Fig. 9.1 'Soul Survival', Lough Derg marketing poster, 2004.

and spirit. This frame of reference becomes yet more evident when we compare the campaign aimed at a secular audience to the poster that was simultaneously distributed to churches, where the connection between the poster image and Lough Derg itself is

Fig. 9.2 'Re-Kindle Your Spirit', Lough Derg marketing poster, 2004.

foregrounded to a much greater extent. Whereas the Lough Derg logo is consigned unobtrusively to the corner of the first poster, here it appears embossed on the candle that dominates the composition (Fig. 9.2). The candle suggests Lough Derg as a main source of spiritual sustenance and renewal, from whose inextinguishable flame the pilgrim lights his or her meagre taper. The image gestures towards a long-standing tradition, sturdy enough to withstand time, robust enough to feed many lesser lights, represented by a group of out-of-focus candles that are evocative of human figures. The candle, foregrounding Lough Derg as a community of pilgrims, takes the place of the young woman in the first poster. Instead of the individualistic self-spiritualiser in the 'Soul Survival' campaign, with the play on 'soul/sole' emphasising singularity rather than collectivity, the church poster's imagery symbolically represents the communal tradition of the faithful, the wellspring from which the believer is invited to 'Re-Kindle Your Spirit'.

The two very distinctive campaigns appear to be marketing two quite different experiences, two distinct versions of Lough Derg as a therapeutic landscape. The pilgrimage itself is a notoriously harsh and exacting one, rooted in Catholic ritual and tradition. However, the 'secular' poster suggests nothing of this penitential aspect and, against the aspect of 'communitas' symbolised in the church poster, emphasises the individual rather than the collective, constituting Lough Derg as a holistic retreat from the stresses and pressures of the frenetic materialism and pace of Celtic Tiger Ireland. The testimonials of some pilgrims underline this distinctive construction of Lough Derg as holistic New Age retreat, with descriptions of the pilgrimage as 'feng shui for the head', 'a detox for soul and body'.[21] In an article on the rebranded Lough Derg in the London *Independent*, one returned visitor explains his motivation: 'I feel I want to get out of the world, away from the rat race. Apart from the spiritual end of it, it's to escape the pressure of this commercialised world.'[22] For the committed Catholic pilgrim, the place represents something different, a community of faith that is imagined as stretching back to St Patrick himself, however mythical that association might be.

The meaning of place changes, then, according to its relational constitution in collaboration with the individual user and the discursive field through which the landscape is made to bear particular meanings. An apparently singular landscape can thus be articulated through distinct and apparently antithetical discursive fields so that its constitution is shown to be contingent rather than essential. While Lough Derg is emblematic of tradition and the indigenous, the 'Soul Survival' campaign suggests its malleability, so that the authenticity of its indigenous 'Celticity' and vernacular Catholicism is displaced by a different register of the authentic that foregrounds self-realisation as opposed to transhistorical communitas, situating the landscape within the globalised discourse of the 'New Age' spiritual marketplace and the holistic milieu.

Writing about 'emotional geographies', Joyce Davidson and Christine Milligan underline the intersection between 'heritage and spiritual tourism', which acts in tandem with the state to 'commodify the rural landscape through a deliberate appeal to our sense of the romantic, the mystical and the spiritual'.[23] The borders between heritage and spiritual tourism are particularly indeterminate in relation to the marketing of Ireland, at least in part because the 'Celticity' that is a staple of the Irish tourist industry constitutes Ireland as a therapeutic landscape so that the appeal to the 'mystical and the spiritual' is fundamental to Ireland as global brand. As the case of Lough Derg demonstrates, this global branding can then be used in turn to 'sell' this emblematic site of putatively anti-materialist vernacular Catholicism. Moya Kneafsey observes that the semiotics of Celticity are especially associated with Ireland and Irishness in the global tourist industry, and foreground peripherality, nature, spirituality, the premodern and archaic as intrinsic to the Irish landscape, symbolically metonymic with 'Irishness' itself.[24] In her analysis of Bord Fáilte advertising, Kneafsey notes that Ireland continued to be represented as an oasis of tranquillity and peace even as the economic boom was in the ascendance, 'a refuge from modernity, a place of spirituality and authenticity which presents an opportunity to restore one's self through a return to nature', with advertisements and brochures frequently depicting a lone holidayer in contemplative stance amidst the tranquil beauty of the Irish landscape.[25]

These semiotic markers of the putatively essential, indigenous, 'non-modern' 'spirit' of Irishness are also deployed in the marketing of the Hare Krishna-run 'Lake Isle Retreats' in County Fermanagh, underlining the mobility and commercial efficacy of the key signifiers of 'Brand Ireland' in all its guises. Further, the mutually distinct ways in which one space is represented and constituted in this case is suggestive, in ways yet more marked than Lough Derg, of the strategies employed in the spirituality and wellness industries within contemporary processes of cultural globalisation. ISKCON, the International Society for Krishna Consciousness, otherwise known as the Hare

Krishnas, was established in 1965 in New York by an Indian man, Prabhupada. He moved to Haight-Ashbury in San Francisco and the first ISKCON commune was established in West Virginia in 1968. While the Hare Krishnas have been popularly perceived in the West as a cult, ISKCON is regarded in India as a legitimate Hindu movement, and its membership contains both Indian Hindus and Hindus from other parts of the world and other ethnic backgrounds. The organisation in fact has several temples in India, with its international headquarters situated in Mayapur in West Bengal.

As with other global Hindu movements, ISKCON raises the issue of whether or not Hindu spiritual systems are in fact viable outside of India itself. Many argue that 'Hinduism' is 'an ethnic religion, a religion of a particular people, and associated with their land or place'. Such an argument holds that a person is Hindu by birth, and is then governed by the dharma or rules and customs of his or her community. Further, 'the realm of dharma, the Hindu universe, was known by the bharat, the land ritually purified by the Brahmin and surrounded by kalai pani, the black waters, which the Hindu is not supposed to cross.'[26] The authentic is, in this formulation, coterminous with the 'originating' landscape itself, and religious authenticity tied to indigenous and territorial belonging. However, the history of a movement such as ISKCON contradicts this perspective on Hinduism: founded in the US by an 'import guru' and attracting both Indian and Western membership, ISKCON is a good example of the globalisation of indigenous culture and religion in the contemporary era, and of the circulations and feedback loops between 'East' and 'West' in the twentieth-century history of Asian belief systems.

The ISKCON centre on Inis Rath on Lough Erne in County Fermanagh was bought by the Hare Krishnas in 1984 and opened as a temple in 1986. The centre had always established set hours for non-ISKCON visitors to come to the centre free of charge, but in 2005 Krishna Island began to offer a range of paying retreat breaks in the centre. This is related to the exposure of the terrible and endemic abuse of children in the organisation's 'gurukulus' or boarding schools during the 1970s and '80s. Payments to people who had been victims of abuse meant that the organisation was in financial crisis by the early 2000s, in turn necessitating this commercialisation of resources. Apart from the histories of abuse underwriting this commercialisation, it also speaks to the relations between the local and the global, between 'authenticity' and commodification, as the centre and its surrounds caters for two distinct kinds of user: fellow Hare Krishna devotees and paying spiritual 'tourists'. The multiple names of the site point towards the relational constitution of the island as a palimpsest of interrelated yet distinct therapeutic landscapes: as Inis Rath, the island announces its emplacement within traditional, indigenous Irish history and culture; as Krishna Island or Govindadwipa its position within the international ISKCON network is foregrounded; and finally, as Lake Isle Retreats, the site is located within the contemporary 'spiritual marketplace' and the 'wellness' and spiritual tourist industries, with more than a nod towards 'Celticity'. This latter 'landscape' is dependent upon the legitimation provided by the other sites that simultaneously inscribe and reinscribe this 'space' – the 'Celticity' of its indigenous origins and the spiritual 'authenticity' of its use as a religious community. Analysing the reproduction of the Indian yogic place in a different landscape, Anne Cécile Hoyez emphasises the role of visual and textual representation in thus constituting and authenticating the transplanted yogic space, focusing on the semantic markers deployed in the advertising of spiritual retreat holidays. Most interesting for the Hare Krishna centre on Inis Rath is the example of Dhanakosa in Scotland that Hoyez discusses. A 'Buddhist, Meditation and Yoga retreat centre' located in a former hotel, this site accommodates Eastern practices to the lakes, mountains and forests of the Scottish, 'Celtic' landscape. The Celtic landscape is resignified through the use of a 'yogic rhetoric'[27] so that a hybrid landscape is produced, illustrating the way in which local specificities interact with global and globalised processes in the 'glocal' production of therapeutic place. In the case of Lake Isle Retreats and Krishna Island, however, the 'place' thus constituted is not merely hybridised, but plural, and these multiple resignifications reveal again the contingency of what is constituted as essential and authentic.

'Lake Isle Retreats' has been advertised primarily via the internet, as well as in Hare Krishna outlets that a non-devotee might frequent. For instance, the retreats first came to my attention in 2005 when a friend passed on a flier she had picked up in the popular Hare Krishna-run restaurant in Dublin, Govinda's.[28] The images and text of the flier demonstrate a hybridisation of Celtic and Hindu symbolic 'authenticity' that situates the retreat centre at the intersection of heritage, wellness and spiritual tourism, recalling Hoyez's observations as well as the lexicon of heritage tourism and its constitution of the landscape as alchemical agent of authentic experience. The viewer's attention is drawn to the photograph of a smiling Indian woman in a saffron sari, arms outstretched and palms open in welcome. The woman is framed by the surrounding landscape and the house in the background – which was built by Lord Erne's son-in-law in the mid-nineteenth century and used as a summer house – suggests the 'glocal' interface between the Irish context and Hindu tradition. 'Lake Isle Retreats' is presented in a typeface suggestive of old Irish script, and the hybridisation performed by the advertisement is reinforced by the accompanying images of the natural landscape: one, an aerial photo of the islands on Lough Erne, the other, of a spectacular sunset – a sunset that exoticises the landscape, transforming it to a spectacular golden glow. The text makes no reference to the Hare Krishnas, but instead uses the lexicon of New Age holism and spiritual tourism: 'For a short holistic break come and experience a lake isle retreat on Inis Rath . . . workshops in yoga, naturopathy, story tales, meditations, veg cooking, martial arts and more . . .' The text again recalls Hoyez's description of the therapeutic landscape as a process whereby imported practices are accommodated to preexisting landscapes:

> Inis Rath is a beautiful wooded island which is owned by the Hare Krishna community in Ireland. Peacock, heron, swan and deer wander freely in the peaceful Lakeland atmosphere. Monks practice meditation from the early hours, whilst an elaborate golden shrine – an exotic introduction from India – is a new feature to the island's 19th-century Victorian house.

The Hare Krishna centre fulfils different simultaneous functions. The authenticity of Krishna Island within the global ISKCON network is held quite distinct from Lake Isle Retreats as tourist destination for the unaffiliated spiritual seeker. This is illustrated by the links between the various websites. The link to Inis Rath on the homepage of the UK and Ireland ISKCON website leads to the homepage for Krishna Island, but there is no link to Lake Isle Retreats, further inscribing the distinction (and the felt need for such a distinction) between these two 'places'.[29] The Lake Isle Retreat site emphasises the services provided to the paying visitor; the range of activities and the semiotics of 'wellness' constitute this version of the landscape as a retreat from the stress of modern living. Resonating with the 'wellness' lexicon deployed in the 2004 Lough Derg 'Soul Survival' campaign, the consumer is encouraged to 'Take time for yourself', 'Rejuvenate and relax', 'Break free from stress', and 'Enjoy a weekend away'. Retreats include a yoga summer school, a women's relax and restore retreat, 'Tastes of the Orient' – a vegetarian cookery course, 'Mind Body Spirit Rejuvenation Adventure' and 'ABCs of Success'. The range of activities recalls Possamai and York's analysis of the 'spiritual markeplace': yoga, meditation, classes in eastern philosophy and vegetarian cookery, with holistic therapies such as reiki, reflexology, Indian head massage, and aromatherapy available at additional cost. While there are several images of the natural landscape of the island, reinforcing the therapeutic and holistic services on offer, there is surprisingly little information about the history of the island itself.[30] The visual lexicon of the homepage, however, renders literal Hoyez's description of the hybridisations involved in the configuration of 'yogic space', with the image of the smiling Indian woman superimposed on images of the 'natural' landscape, thus bringing into relation the dual 'authenticities' and 'origins' of the Hindu 'homeland' and the presumptively intrinsic spiritual Celticity of the land itself. The website for Krishna Island is substantially different. The home page foregrounds the island as a sacred religious space, with images of Krishna and his consort Radma and little visual referencing of the Inis Rath landscape. Links on the main page offer information about the ashram itself and a detailed description of the temple, as well as a short history of the island. The antiquity of the Hindu tradition is emphasised, as is the prehistoric origin of the island. Upcoming festivals and religious events are listed and aspects of the temple and of the landscape that have been constituted so as to assert the connection to the central region in India are foregrounded.[31]

While Inis Rath appears to be a singular place, then, it is constituted as several distinct places at once with divergent meanings and functions according to the discourse through which it is constructed, roughly bifurcated into the religious and the commercial, with both the putatively 'traditional' and 'modern' symbiotically and constitutively dependent upon each other. The bifurcation between committed adherent and 'spiritual seeker' (or secular consumer) is thus maintained by a plural signification of the landscape itself and a certain sanitary distinction between these two 'places' in the virtual life of Inis Rath. This distinction is much more marked than is the case with the Lough Derg 'Soul Survival' campaign, and perhaps plays into the romanticising tendencies which have marked Western interactions with Hindu and Buddhist belief systems and their derivations since the nineteenth century. This romanticism bears the traces of Said's ascription of Orientalism, but also serves to cover over the sometimes scandalous realities of religious institutions, underlined by the 'hidden history' of abuse of children in the Hare Krishna gurukulus that necessitated, at least in part, the commercialising of the Inis Rath community's resources – a covering over that gives another slant to the commodity fetishism that impels the production of spiritual 'authenticity' no less than any other object for sale in the late capitalist marketplace.

For Slavoj Žižek, the consumer in the spiritual marketplace is complicit with the logic of contemporary global capitalism, and indeed this industry as he sees it is the perfect realisation of the workings of commodity fetishism and alienation. He believes that 'although "Western Buddhism" presents itself as the remedy against the stressful tension of the capitalist dynamic, allowing us to uncouple and retain inner peace and *Gelassenheit*, it actually functions as its perfect ideological supplement [. . .] which definitely works better than the desperate escape into old traditions'.[32] In this essay, I have attempted to point towards some ways in which this distinction between the 'new' forms of what Žižek calls 'the 'Western Buddhist meditative stance' and the 'old traditions' no longer obtains within the logic of late capitalism. However, such a diagnosis positions the 'user' as merely an unconscious agent of such global economic forces, and problematically excises what exceeds that system. The quest for critical impermeability does not leave much room for the messiness of human need and desire, and neither does the orthodox position of religion and the spiritual within the Irish variant of post-colonial critique, with its ideological suturing of the spiritual and the tradition or the non-modern, provide many coordinates for considering these messy realms of experience and need otherwise.

IDENTITY

Chapter Ten

'INDEBTED FOR THEIR EXISTENCE TO THE INESSENTIAL': ON THREE IRISH ARTISTS

Colin Graham

In Joe Duggan's exhibition *Family Man*, which was shown in Limerick in 2007,[1] there is a photograph that is, at first sight, one of a happy, even banal, normality (Fig. 10.1) It is an image of paternal contentedness, and of a father's symbolic connection with his son as a younger version of himself. The father and son are dressed similarly, the son is looking up to the father, they are connected by the string on the kite that they are about to fly, and they look to be about to attain the freedom symbolised by the kite. So positive and wholesome, indeed, is this image that it seems to barely qualify as art at all, other than through its size and its placement in an exhibition space. Of course, all is not as it appears, and Duggan's 'family man' is struggling with more than a kite on a windy day. His son, and the rest of his family, are fictions. They are stage-managed falsehoods, devoid of any identity because his 'family' (including the son here) are posed shop-window dummies. And he himself, the family man, is lost in the midst of them. Of the millions of photographs taken every day the family is surely, in some form or other, the most popular and universal subject. The images in Joe Duggan's *Family Man* take this common occurrence and turn it into pure artifice. A father figure, by turns bemused, pathetic, happy, thoughtful and tender, tries to make a real family out of a family of mannequins, as if they were a projection of the clichés by which he imagines and knows what a family is. Both the photograph and the very idea of family are turned into something awkward, unreal, and even, frankly, bizarre. Duggan's photographs are decentred by pure, self-induced dislocation in the midst of the signs of a meaningful and fulfilled life.

Fig. 10.1 Joe Duggan, 'Like Father, Like Son (Kite)', 2007.

'Second Harvest'

In Section 72 of his loosely autobiographical book *Minima Moralia*, a section entitled 'Second Harvest', Theodor Adorno contemplates creativity, melancholy and the nature of the modern, fractured self, and does so, in one instance, in familial terms:

> To a child returning from a holiday, home seems new, fresh, festive [. . .]. No differently will the world appear, almost unchanged in its constant feast-day light, when it stands no longer under the law of labour, and when for homecomers duty has the lightness of holiday play.[2]

Joe Duggan's images might be said to participate in a disappointed version of Adorno's childhood freshness of vision and to look, vainly but valiantly, for that 'Second Harvest'. Adorno does not often look towards a world 'no longer under the law of labour', and his negative dialectics rarely admit such unbridled and unlikely utopianism. Our current state of 'unhappiness' may come from living under the rule of work, but for Adorno that state of being is not simply a misery set dichotomously against the potentialities of an unrealised future. The 'Second Harvest' section of *Minima Moralia* is remarkable for its poetic contemplation of gestures, moments and modes of being which register unhappiness, and which find that unhappiness caught in a precise, paradoxical and repetitive vice grip in which identity is a ruling and fraudulent concept. Adorno talks, for instance, of waking from even the worst of dreams to feel 'disappointed, cheated of the best of life',[3] while even 'the loveliest dream bears like a blemish its difference from reality, the awareness that what it grants is mere illusion'.[4] And it is the structure of this illusion which Adorno circles around in this section of *Minima Moralia* – a knowledge, with a twisted logic that is frustratingly never broken, that we are estranged from a full knowledge of ourselves, that we live in a state of self-alienation, and that this passes for a meaningful system of living. Adorno's touching example is of his own unguarded use of a syntactically incorrect dialect phrase from his childhood: 'Language sent back to me like an echo the humiliation which unhappiness had inflicted on me in forgetting what I am.'[5]

Forgetting, or never fully knowing, 'what I am' is our state of being, a state which is one of profound non-identity, in which we can never fully equate ourselves, our individuality, with the categories by which our world is governed and which thus constantly return us to 'identity' as a marker of who we are. The self is then alienated, not only in terms of the rupture of its own labour, as an integral part of itself enters the marketplace, but more profoundly the self as an idea, as an aspirational whole, is in a continual state of inflicted humiliation for never being able to fully recall what he or she is. Adorno's existential crisis is, of course, written into the very form of *Minima Moralia*, subtitled *Reflections on a Damaged Life*, as it tries to find a way in which to capture its continually disappearing, disappointing subject, which is the 'subject' itself, and Adorno in particular. *Minima Moralia* plays with aphorisms that then collapse. It grasps at certainties, experiences and texts which only hint at the endpoint which the book knows it will never arrive at. Adorno's fractured self-portrait, in its form and its ideas, outlines a particular notion of a kind of tyranny of identity in late capitalism, seeing identity (primarily in the philosophical sense) as an equation of two things in which one side is never completed, but in which the illusion of true identity is continually peddled. If identity is thus to be

understood as a continually broken promise, then the forms of identity which are used as categories in cultural criticism may play out
the same illusion. In the work of three Irish artists discussed in this
essay – Joe Duggan, Hannah Starkey, and John Gerrard – the examination of 'identity' is signalled primarily through the differing forms
of portraiture that they deploy – a form which, of course, immediately directs us to think about the self, the subject and the history of
its self-knowledge. But more than this, all three find different ways
in which to engage in an examination of the self in the contemporary world, to understand the individual in a state of alienation from
herself or himself, and to place in their work a crisis of identification
in which the co-ordinates of identity, cultural and metaphysical, are
conceptually unreliable.

Joe Duggan

In Joe Duggan's 'Family Man' and 'Like Father, Like Son' series a
paternal identity is undermined, its authority is quickly collapsed
and made uncanny, while the father's fictional corporeality echoes
back to him his own emptiness. In every image, and through a range
of scenarios, he wants to be included. At times he looks gently
pleading, suggesting that he imagines himself as being always just
outside the bonds of this family. And why wouldn't he? He is trying
not to be overcome by the weirdness of his 'family' and their environments. And when he is part of them it is primarily because they
are a reflection of his uneasiness in his role, which he learns to play
better as the images progress.

Duggan's photographs parallel the artificer and the father, the
maker of the family and its image. The family of dummies is turned
partly, but not self-indulgently, into a self-consciousness about photography in 'Family Man, No. 5' in which the father figure takes a
snap inside the photograph (Fig. 10.2). When we add to this the
photograph which constitutes the fake backdrop, the family of
dummies are enclosed on both sides by photographs and caught in
another one at the moment at which we see them. The father is then
all around them, making them visual from every angle. They are his
(photographic) fantasy, but he too is of this fantasy.

The strangeness which the father visibly struggles not to be overcome by is equally unsettling for the viewer of the images. When, in

Fig. 10.2 Joe Duggan, 'Family Man, No. 5', 2007.

'Family Man, No. 1', the mother of the family throws her head back to catch the sun we are thrown off balance by the carefree casualness that is imitated. The constant artificiality means we are alerted to every ordinary detail as a strange and significant one (the repeated reminders of boyhood versions of manliness, for example – the boy dressed as Batman in 'Family Man, No. 1', or the military outfit and the toy gun which the 'same' boy totes elsewhere). And we then begin to notice the artifice involved everywhere; we think about how long it must have taken to set up this scene and how the leaves which are out of focus in the foreground falsify depth. There is an artistry, an aesthetic at work in these photographs, which is often very beautiful to look at. In 'Like Father, Like Son (Kite)' the vapour trail which gently marks the sky echoes the taut line of the kite. In 'Like Father, Like Son (Ball)' the ball thrown upwards by the father hangs in the air like a sun (a pun that is picked up again in another image in which father and son watch a setting sun). In the lazy outdoor arrangement of figures in 'Family Man' there are reminders of Impressionist bathings and picnics. In 'Like Father, Like Son (Kitchen)' even the banality of the domestic space is given shape by the converging lines of the cupboards in the centre of the image. The aesthetic rage for order is appropriately in tandem with the mania which bubbles under the surface of these images, demanding a happy family.

The 'Like Father, Like Son' series extends Duggan's range, obviously becoming more specific in terms of paternal relationships but also delving more deeply into the psychology of the family man and the unsettled balance of identity which exists between father and son. The nonchalance of the father figure merrily throwing the ball in 'Like Father, Like Son (Ball)' is a joke at his own expense. Here Duggan imagines the father–son relationship in frank terms, all the time drawing us up on ourselves with the simple reminder that the son is not real and that the father we are seeing is playing at fatherhood, in a melancholy yet comic way. Despite all that we quickly know about the pretences and staginess of these photographs, we cannot but empathise with the moments that are imagined in each image and almost believe the authenticity of the tenderness which is effectively mimicked here. Collectively the images in *Family Man* rise above the cynicism of their apparent deracination of the idea of family. In this, Joe Duggan's photographs provoke us to think about the way in which we each play out our roles in a family. They also make strange the photograph or snapshot as a way of confirming family. Like 'theoretical criticism', as Adorno says, it is easy to show the 'sham character' by which we live, but for 'countless individuals [. . .] the thin, ephemeral veil is the basis of their entire existence'.[6] Duggan's photographs show this sham, and display the thinness of the veil which barely masks the fact that we are 'indebted for [our] existence to the inessential, illusion'.[7] In the fact of their self-conscious, constructed and staged loss, and 'sham character', they find a way in which to photograph the rupture underlying the everyday deployment of identity and what Adorno calls its 'abomination';[8] this abomination is played out in Duggan's work in the father's endless and hopeless pursuit of his identity.

Hannah Starkey

Duggan's paternal relationship ends nervously at the edge of a catas-trophe of failed identity. Hannah Starkey's best-known works are polished, atmospheric and equally staged, their central figures studies in cosmopolitan loneliness and femininity. Both Starkey's and Duggan's work can be understood as part of a mode of staged photography which registers the influence of Cindy Sherman and Jeff Wall, and has similarities with some of the early 1990s photog-raphy of Philip-Lorca diCorcia, in Starkey's case, and perhaps the surreal domesticity found in Charlie White's *Understanding Joshua* in the instance of Duggan's *Family Man*.

The isolation of identity into its singularity has more ambiguous, and less immediately cataclysmic, effects in Starkey's work than in Duggan's, yet the elevation of the photograph as a form, allowing and encouraging a study of the concept of individuality, is common to both. Starkey's work, or at least one strand of it, is typified by 'Untitled – March 2002', an image of a solitary woman caught at a still moment in a narrative, with no explication offered of the events before the image or the events which are anticipated by the moment. As in much of her work, the blankness of individuality as a vacuum, filled with the accoutrement of modern life, is an essential part of the images, and an interest in a minimalist, architectural, almost designer interiority develops in Starkey's work in parallel with her contempla-tions of individuality and isolation, so that an aesthetics of contemporary urbanity comes to frame and often enclose the image's contemplation of the self in suspension. It is as if a designed life is emptied of its content and tends towards stillness, while her images occasionally veer close to fashion photography and her individual women come close to draper's models. Where there are signs that point more persuasively to material and worldly pain they are laced with ennui rather than agony. 'Untitled – June 2007' shows a young mother with an infant child in front of a wall map (Fig. 10.3). There is a dignity yet disengagement (which hovers on falling into disen-franchisement) in the woman's face and in her stare, directed out of the frame and angled away from the viewer. The map itself and the framing of the subject hint at, while refusing to fulfil, a photography of social documentary suggesting antecedents such as Dorothea Lange's images of American migrancy or David Seymour's famous

'Air Raid Over Barcelona, 1938'. But whereas those arc images from the political 1930s, here the possibility of mobility is viewed with less pathos, and perhaps even in a way that questions the photographer's capacity for empathy, in order to create an uncertainty as to whether this mother is homeless, migrant or simply waiting. The image sits between a concerned and engaged socio-documentary mode and a consideration of placelessness as tragedy or opportunity, necessity or choice, and as such it exists at one end of the spectrum of work that Starkey has produced, with a less materially troubled yet interrogated bourgeois cosmopolitanism at the other end.

Starkey's concern with the contemporary female self, its development and the sense of breached wholeness which pervades the artifices of the self, is perhaps most dramatically captured in 'Untitled – May 1997', an image which doubles the self as illusion and implies a pure, maybe even naïve, narcissism set against the weariness of the older woman who looks on as a younger woman touches her own reflection in the mirror (Fig. 10.4). Such painterly tableaux signal that we should read significance rather than specificity into Starkey's work, and that if her photographs are moments in a narrative, then their stillness is indicative of epiphanies about to come, or in the case of this image, just unfolding. Starkey's work is manifestly set against the spontaneity of the 'decisive moment'.[9] The irony of her work is that it carefully, thoughtfully and artificially stages decision and deliberation by the photographer and inaction in the subject. In this the artist is empowered creator, only for the artist's agency to be undercut by the stasis of the subject and its motionless lack of physical and intellectual agency. The real drama in Starkey's work then is the knowing frustration of female agency as the photographer's artistry engages itself with the unengaged female self.

Adorno begins 'Second Harvest' with exactly this conundrum – the energy of creativity and the containment of its resulting art: 'Talent is perhaps nothing other than successfully sublimated rage, the capacity to convert energies once intensified beyond measure to destroy recalcitrant objects.'[10] This fury is a desire to be free of confinement. But Adorno suggests that art is more likely to reiterate that confinement when he asks: 'Might not the very conciliatoriness of art have been only bullied out of its destructiveness?'[11] So the work of art becomes what Adorno calls 'an uncommitted crime',[12] a contained rage, a gesture, akin, in Adorno's example, to the disdain

Top: Fig. 10.3 Hannah Starkey, 'Untitled – June 2007'.
Below: Fig. 10.4 Hannah Starkey, 'Untitled – May 1997'.

which teenagers show the world when they put their hands in their pockets and their elbows out, ready to meet the world.

For Adorno, art is always in danger of subsiding into the patterns of mass culture and its 'liquidation of conflict'.[13] As always with Adorno it is form, and experimentation at the limits of form, which can save high art from the repetitive dullness of mass culture (an experimentation of which *Minima Moralia* is, of course, an example). 'The improvisatory displacement of things' is one way in which Adorno characterises this experimentation and for him such practice will necessarily 'leave the road of the always-identical'.[14] Thus it is not just the mere repetition of form inherent in mass culture that Adorno is allergic to but the deeper insistence on the 'always-identical' that is both formal and philosophical, which leads not just to boredom but the normalisation of the failed self which does not know itself.

John Gerrard

Adorno's stringent modernism invests formal experimentation with the capacity to be the last refuge of metaphysical knowledge and political change, since, in late capitalism, according to Adorno, it is only in form and not in content that conflict can be treated.[15] And within and as part of that form 'nonchalant gestures' of rage and containment signal the desire to kick against the pricks of the 'always-identical'.[16] Small gestures in a contained world may, according to Adorno, be futile, but they do signify that 'sublimated rage' which he attributes to the artwork, and after modernism this may be a more meaningful gesture than it was in modernism. The saturation of high culture by mass culture and the blurring of hierarchical cultural boundaries, which Adorno fretted about, means that the 'Second Harvest' is further away than ever, and that art's ways of seeing are more soundly contained, so that containment itself is expressed formally and aesthetically. The portrait, as a form that superficially registers the presence of the human subject, then becomes an ironic container for the question of presence, a consideration of the possibility of non-identity, or the exposure of the fading 'reality' of a notion of being which has become intertwined with the classified, repetitive annunciation of identities.[17] The small, nearly invisible gestures which occur in the midst of a general stasis and 'formality' in the work of Duggan and Starkey can be imagined as yet quieter versions of the 'indexical marks' which Hal Foster, discussing Rosalind Krauss, describes as characteristic of 1970s art and a pervasive desire to confront the '"trauma of signification"'.[18] The codification of the politics of identity to the point at which they become a cultural and personal form of aspic underlies the aesthetics of stillness in these photographic works – within that stillness each finds a mechanism through which to stir, question and reform a possibility of individuality.

John Gerrard's work in computer-generated media is indicative of the way in which an immersion in new forms, in this case the technology of gaming, can create hybrid rather than oppositional art, forms in which sublimation is entirely dominant over rage, but which as a result pinpoint a resistance to quietude. Gerrard's portraits, and other works, draw on traditional painting and photography, and their unflashy use of technology at reduced speeds takes on the ontological traumas which interactive computing might be thought to lead to, turning them with slow deliberation back to existential questions more familiar from late modernism. So in the combination of technology and subject matter Gerrard's work looks for and questions the existence of the remnants of individuality in the contemporary, and does so through portraits which strip away many of the referents which allow identity politics to pervade all forms of knowledge and self-knowledge.

Typical is 'Portrait to Smile Once a Year (Mary)', a computer image and screen that does exactly what it says – once every year it smiles. The animation of this portrait is minimal, slowing down a speeding world, in the same way that 'Saddening Portrait' changes over one hundred years or that the sun will eventually rise in 'One Thousand Year Dawn (Marcel)'. If the gesture, the futile gesture, is the sign of fury at containment, and, for Adorno, the evidence of a recognition that identity is a failed concept, then Gerrard's various portraits encapsulate that tiny gesture as their only contemplative, internalised action, while often offering the viewer the chance to move virtually around the image, circling its near non-action. The selves, the individual subjects of these portraits, inhabit the same suspended state of 'longing [. . .] for the fullness of [a] manifestation'[19] of themselves as Duggan's father and his dummies and Starkey's women who wait or contemplate. If their time of waiting for agency and action is stretched in a virtual world, Gerrard's set of relatively traditional photographs, entitled 'Dark Portraits', come as close as possible to the instantaneous capturing of the unaware self. 'Dark Portraits' are photographs of adolescents, sitting in an utterly dark room and unsure of when their photograph will be taken. Gerrard takes a technique used in public by Philip-Lorca diCorcia in New York, around the year 2000, into the intimacy of the studio. It is as if Gerrard were checking, and asking us to check, whether there might still be an uncomplicated way of 'approach[ing] ourselves purely',[20] a reality of the self, found in the pre-adult world, which is without rupture, which inhabits itself fully.

Does it make any sense, then, to view these artists as Irish? The only solid basis for doing so seems to be a biographical one. The impetus to do so perhaps comes from having Irishness, Irish culture, or Irish art as a pre-existing category with a pre-existing investment underwriting it. A weak argument could be made about a foundational Irishness to the work of Starkey, Gerrard and Duggan. Starkey's 'The Butterfly Collectors' is the best-known example of her early work in Belfast (best known, perhaps, because it is in the Saatchi Collection). Like her later work it is a staged image with female subjects. Its mixing of urban realism with a pathetic fantasy prefigures the poles which converge more assuredly in some of her later, more urbane and cosmopolitan images, and it could be said that her later work could be understood in the context of this early piece, both in terms of her aesthetics and in her examination of urban femininity. John Gerrard's recent series 'Smoke Trees' uses trees from near his childhood home in Tipperary as the basis for a commentary on, amongst other things, environmental change, and when seen in relation to his work 'Dust Storm' or 'Animated Scene (Oil Field)' can be thought of as constituting a question about localism and its connection to the global politics of oil and Iraq. Equally the virtual landscapes that Gerrard used as part of his *New Work in New Media* exhibition in Dublin in 2003 might be thought of as a nod to an Irish pictorial tradition, both in art and popular culture, but their virtuality seems, again, unyielding to a specificity of place. Joe Duggan's *Family Man*, like the work of Starkey and Gerrard, is careful to eschew visual markers of specific place, yet in one image the licence plates on the cars, deliberately or otherwise, give some sign of where this happens, or who the story in *Family Man* happens to. These small signs and ways of reading Irishness into these artworks and these bodies of work are, though, unconvincing in the face of images that are at pains to minimise the signs of identity that they include in order to isolate the very concept of identity.

The variations on the portrait form that reappear in these three sets of work might also offer a way in which to conjugate some mode of Irishness with which to understand them. The portrait's tendency towards contemplation of the self can tip over into the forms of isolation, loneliness and melancholy which run through the work of Gerrard, Starkey and Duggan, and, rather sentimentally, or with a belief in the power of exilic imaginations, we might see these images as being underscored by the migrancy of artists who have left Ireland behind. But again this would be to, in every sense, mis-identify and particularise what is formal, generic and general. The forms of portraiture undertaken in these works is, to borrow a phrase which Vilém Flusser uses about all photography, 'an image of concepts'.[21] These portraits, especially as portraits, variously engage in (what Baudrillard calls) the 'obsessive, temperamental, ecstatic and narcissistic' nature of photography as 'a solitary activity'.[22] That solitariness is a stripping away of specificity in order to scrutinise the 'image of a concept' rather than to record its representation.

Adorno writes in the last section of 'Second Harvest' that the individual has become 'null and void'[23] – by its own logic, according to Adorno, the concept of individuality (and, we might say, the logic inherent in the portrait image) has collapsed, and left behind only contingency, a partial version of the individual which is a constant reminder of the failure of the concept. Adorno notes the paradox that 'absolute contingency [. . .] is itself the essential'.[24] The individual is left pining for the broken promise of fulfilment (conscious that she can say 'I was happy' but never 'I am happy').[25] The work of Duggan, Starkey and Gerrard recognises the world, in Adorno's terms, as 'abomination', 'its appearance [. . .] a stand-in for truth', 'its unifying principle [. . .] division'.[26] These selves divided internally can never express wholeness, yet they can yearn for it, yearn, that is, for self-identity – by staring in the mirror, in Starkey's work; by longing for family in Duggan; by the creation of virtual selves in Gerrard. If each can be shown to have a resonance of locale within their work, it is a resonance that cannot be limited to that locale, nor does it seek restitution in locale. If we want to read these artists' works as 'Irish' we need to recognise that term, that declension of identity, as failing to equate with itself, as being one unifying division amongst many, as what Flusser terms a 'posthistorical image'.[27] For Flusser the photograph and its ubiquity are one of the first signs of the control of the individual by the apparatus, signalling a loss of agency and subjectivity – Duggan, Gerrard and Starkey create works which each carry within them a recognition and interrogation of this very loss of individuality, as it is made strange, cosmopolitan, even virtual. The 'concept' that they photograph is in the process of disappearing, it is 'absolutely contingency, permitted to persist as a seemingly abnormal state'.[28] It is not identity but the illusion of identity that is their subject.

Chapter Eleven

POST-FEMINISM AND THE CELTIC TIGER: DEIRDRE O'KANE'S TELEVISION ROLES

Claire Bracken

Created by Ian Fitzgibbon and Michael McElhatton, the television series *Paths to Freedom* and *Fergus's Wedding* were screened by Irish state broadcaster RTÉ in 2000 and 2002 respectively. Produced in the Celtic Tiger period (circa 1996–2008), which was a time of unprecedented economic growth in Ireland, these shows – both comic dramas of six episodes – take an ironic and sardonic look at turn-of-the-twenty-first-century Dublin. *Paths to Freedom* is a mock-documentary that tells the story of Raymond ('Rats') and Jeremy, two recently released convicts from Mountjoy Prison in Dublin. The series is set over a year period, following the men as they readjust to their lives on 'the outside'. A polarised class division is set up between Rats and Jeremy, in that the former, convicted of burglary, is from a working-class community, while the latter, a consultant gynaecologist convicted of a drink driving hit and run, lives in the middle-class suburb of Blackrock and operates in the upper echelons of Celtic Tiger wealth and privilege. It is Rats, however, who emerges as the stronger character at the end of the series: he successfully launches a rap band, while Jeremy suffers a nervous breakdown and is re-incarcerated, this time in hospital.[1] Less 'naturalistic' and more 'heightened drama',[2] *Fergus's Wedding* is, as its title suggests, about a wedding: Fergus Walsh, proprietor of 'Ferguccinos' coffee shop, is marrying Penny, an English woman who lives and works in Ireland. The series takes us through the trials and tribulations of their wedding planning, which include the death of the best man, the loss of €90,000, disputes with a headstrong and

169

determined wedding planner, and repeated family in-fighting.
Thrown into the mix is the fact that Penny and Fergus are members
of a Dublin swinging club, which is mockingly constructed in the
show as both uninteresting and unerotic.[3] Ultimately, the series presents a satirical take on Celtic Tiger excess, represented in the
hyper-consumerism that surrounds contemporary wedding productions and the exorbitant performances of supposed liberal sexuality.

Deirdre O'Kane, well known for her stand-up comedy as well as
acting parts in Celtic Tiger films *Intermission* (John Crowley, 2003)
and *Boy Eats Girl* (Stephen Bradley, 2005), plays a role in both
series,[4] skilfully (and hilariously) portraying Helen, Jeremy's wife, in
Paths To Freedom and Lorraine, the wedding planner, in *Fergus's
Wedding*. In an interview with O'Kane, Mick Heaney identifies similarities between the two, noting:

> The hectoring tone, the power dressing, the disdain for the
> lower orders: when Deirdre O'Kane turned on the catty attitude
> as Lorraine, the snobbish wedding planner in *Fergus's Wedding*, it
> seemed a tad familiar. The Drogheda comic had sealed her
> already formidable reputation with her bitchy turn as Helen, the
> ghastly bourgeois harpy in RTÉ's *Paths to Freedom*, now here she
> was doing a bitchy turn as the ghastly harpy in the follow-up
> series.[5]

Both characters epitomise post-feminist womanhood in late capitalism, a cultural construction which, as Angela McRobbie notes,
exercises supposed female agency and independence through consumerism, particularly relating to women's grooming and
self-fashioning.[6] Lorraine owns and manages a wedding-planning
business, and her role in *Fergus's Wedding* is entirely concerned with
consumption, while in *Paths to Freedom* Helen's energies are spent on
spending, in a paradoxical attempt to undercut a passive position as
upper-middle-class wife. O'Kane's performances, lauded by audiences
for both shows, capture a caricature of middle-class Irish womanhood
in the contemporary period as materialistic, self-absorbed and
shallow. Tapping into popular constructions such as the 'yummy
mummy' and 'Celtic kitten', popular feminine tags to characterise a
nation perceived to be trivial and overly consumptive, the post-feminist characters of Lorraine and Helen function with respect to the
series' more general critique of late capitalist Celtic Tiger Ireland.

An analysis of O'Kane's roles facilitates reflection on two important gender issues relevant to contemporary Irish culture: the
deployment of post-feminist identity categories in the service of capitalist ideology, and the cultural tendency in Ireland to use the figure
of woman as symbol of national meaning. Drawing on the theories
of psychoanalyst and philosopher Luce Irigaray, I chart the identification of post-feminism as product of phallogocentric capitalism,
focused on deploying the feminine as object of support for a neoliberal economy that continues to value masculinity as the dominant
marker of power.[7] Helen and Lorraine are both parodic examples of
a post-feminist womanhood sanctioned by the patriarchal symbolic
of late capitalism (what Irigaray would term a 'father's daughter'),
thus providing an important, and very necessary, gendered critique
of a dominant figuration of femininity in contemporary Irish
culture. Moreover, an analysis of O'Kane's two characters also
reveals the continuation of a well-established representational system
in Irish culture, which uses the feminine in the service of meaning
and signification. Both *Paths to Freedom* and *Fergus's Wedding* end with
the removal of the post-feminist figure (Helen moves to Paris, while
Lorraine's business, 'Perfect Day Productions', goes bankrupt), and
conclude with images of motherhood in the frame. The exclusion of
the post-feminist character reflects the desire to destabilise the capitalist condition more generally; by the same token, it repeats a
process whereby woman works as a carrier of cultural meaning, as
the (post-feminist) feminine is deployed to *represent* Celtic Tiger
Ireland in pejorative terms. While the concluding images of motherhood suggest a more positive, different and 'authentic' future to the
artificiality and excess of the Tiger years, the difference established
between post-feminist woman and mother is diffused in a 'scene of
representation'[8] whereby inclusion of the feminine depends upon
her ability to reflect and support the dominant ideologies of the
current symbolic system.

Celtic tigresses: capitalism, consumption and post-feminism

As a discourse, post-feminism became more prevalent in Ireland
during the Celtic Tiger period. Debbie Ging notes that 'free-market
economics have conspired with a broadly post-feminist culture to

support a distinctly neoliberal political agenda on gender which, beneath its liberal rhetoric, is both deeply regressive and potentially highly coercive'.[9] Postfeminist discourse centres on configurations of femininity as upper-middle class, white, young, and hetero-normative. Thus, as Diane Negra and Yvonne Tasker have suggested, popular post-feminism is fundamentally exclusionary in terms of class, race, and age – a list to which I would also add sex-uality.[10] The hyper-consumerist and commodity-driven market of the 'Tiger' was one in which the 'beauty myth'[11] reigned, engen-dering an hysterical policing and regulating of the female body, evidenced in an increased focus on women's purchasing power centred on the beauty and fashion industries. As Wanda Balzano and Moynagh Sullivan note in the editorial of the 2007 *Irish Review* special issue 'Irish Feminisms':

> If the use of the term 'post-feminist' reveals in its 'consumers' a desire to be at all costs modern, and post-modern, in other words progressive and trendy [. . .] then this dangerously mirrors the more alarming aspects of a winning Celtic-Tiger mentality. One cannot but remain unconvinced of this kind of entrepreneurial, self-congratulatory, *à la mode* feminism that follows the capitalistic model closely and is an indulgent form of bourgeois individu-alism, encoding a contradiction in terms that pits the group (women) against the self (woman).[12]

The circulation of post-feminist ideas in contemporary Irish culture is processed by the machineries of free market ideology, which priv-ileges the self over community, the individual over the group. The rhetoric of choice, via consumption, is promoted so that women are encouraged to think not of 'women' but 'woman', their own self (rather than others) that is always (and only) a body that can be groomed, shaped and dressed in the currency exchanges of Ireland's new-found wealth.

Establishing a connection between Celtic Tiger capitalism and post-feminism is a focus of *Paths to Freedom* and *Fergus's Wedding*, chan-nelled through the two characters played by Deirdre O'Kane – Helen and Lorraine – who are both (parodically) configured as con-sumer subjects. In *The Aftermath of Feminism*, Angela McRobbie argues that post-feminism operates according to a paradigm of positivity, a 'you go girl' sensibility, focusing on what women *can* do rather than what they cannot.[13] In general, such post-feminist 'doings' take the form of consumer-related activities, a configuration presented in the character of Helen, Jeremy's wife, in *Paths to Freedom*, who renegotiates the pre-feminist, self-sacrificing condition of that traditional role by considering her needs and desires just as important as that of her husband. However, the refusal of feminine passivity does not equate to a feminist transformation in this case. Rather, Helen's desire is entirely focused on material consumption, something made particularly clear when she goes to Paris with her friend Gwen to take a break from life with Jeremy, who is becoming increasingly mentally unstable after his release from prison. In a scene shot in Dublin airport's Duty Free, as Helen browses the beauty product counters, her body framed by the brand logos of Lancôme and Estée Lauder, she says to the camera crew, 'I'm exhausted trying to get through to Jeremy, I'm practically hoarse trying to communicate with him', followed by 'Do you know I haven't had a holiday since Puerto Banus six months ago?'

The consumerist specifics of the Duty Free *mise en scène*, with its variety of products on display, contributes to a configuration of Helen as a 'choosing' subject (she decides to go to Paris for herself), with that choice very specifically linked to money and class. Wedding planner Lorraine, of 'Perfect Day Productions', is a slightly different post-feminist construction. Rather than operating, like Helen, as a Celtic Tiger heiress – a lady of leisure and lunches – she works for a living. She can thus be characterised as, in McRobbie's terms, the 'working girl' who prioritises 'earning a living as a means of acquiring status, ensuring an independent livelihood, and gaining access to the world of feminine goods and services'.[14] Lorraine's line of business emphasises this all the more, in that it is fundamentally about the purchasing of female-coded objects: dresses, flowers, menus. In a scene that takes place in a flower shop, Lorraine gives Penny advice on which flowers to choose for the wedding day. Fergus is located outside the shop (flowers the source of one of his many allergies) in the background. The shallow depth of field renders him out of focus; he is literally on the margins looking in, a spectator to the action of the scene. In alignment with dominant post-feminist constructions, Lorraine is presented as domineering and authoritative. When Fergus refuses her suggestion of roses (Penny shouts suggestions through the window's glass), she marches outside and tells him, 'Fergus, you cannot be allergic to every flower in the shop.' Her refusal to acquiesce to Fergus and his desires can be likened to Helen's character in *Paths to Freedom*, whose sub-servience to masculine authority is ultimately re-channelled into a post-feminist investment in the authority of material products. In the case of *Fergus's Wedding*, consumer trends and fashions constitute the altar upon which Lorraine works and worships – she knows her products and is committed to *making* Penny *make* the right choices so that her wedding day is 'perfect', the 'aim' of 'Perfect Day Productions'.

Shaping bodies = active subjects?

Critics of post-feminism argue that it is not just connected with cap-italist ideology, but is actually produced by it, in the service of its own ends,[15] with contemporary womanhood operating as emblem of the successes of Western neo-liberalism, 'an attractive harbinger of social change'.[16] Thus post-feminism, while ostensibly being about women-for-themselves, actually functions to replicate a traditional gendered arrangement, whereby women and women's bodies are deployed in the interests of patriarchal capitalism. This observation can be fruitfully explored alongside Luce Irigaray's critique of phal-logocentrism and the symbolic order as outlined in early works *Speculum*[17] and *This Sex Which is Not One*. Irigaray's argument is that Western systems of meaning are predicated on an 'opaque matter',[18] a 'hidden foundation'.[19] This 'opaque matter', a materiality that cannot be seen, shrouded in darkness and impenetrable to light, is the mother's body, which, according to classical psychoanalysis, the self separates from so as to gain access to subjectivity and language, a process that constitutes and enables the operations of a system of meaning governed by the phallus – the symbolic order. The power of the mother's body to (re)produce and birth the self is rendered 'opaque' as the symbolic order appropriates this function and the subject is birthed and re-birthed through meaning and representa-tion, with a concurrent repression of the maternal feminine.[20] In a double gesture, as the symbolic represses, it also *incorporates* into its realm 'woman' in terms of masquerade, sexual difference covered over in the garb of patriarchal sameness, as the feminine is con-structed as the 'other of the same', an exchange object who operates as support for the order that denies her difference and subjectivity. In 'Veiled Lips', a section of *Amante Marine*, Irigaray makes an analogy between the myth of Athena, who was born out of her father Zeus's head, and the symbolically sanctioned feminine.[21] Irigaray claims that appearance is the dominant term of the incorporated feminine – a father's daughter who is dressed up in the garments of patriarchy.[22] This feminine space of appearance, of masquerade, works to shore up and mirror the operations of the symbolic order. Concealed is the artificial nature of this configuration, the fact that this is a remodelled feminine, 'which reveals nothing of its construction, allows nothing to be suspected of its technique, nothing to be guessed of its artifices'.[23]

Irigaray's conceptualisation of the feminine as father's daughter, the incorporated feminine of masquerade,[24] can be read in terms of the post-feminist subject working for (and produced by) a capitalist system that is not fundamentally interested in women's sexual difference or desire. For example, in *Fergus's Wedding*, Lorraine, as wedding planner, is in the service of a late capitalist symbolic order, employee of a system that reproduces the patriarchal institution of marriage, albeit in a more commodified form. The expensive intensification and proliferation of the wedding industry in the Celtic Tiger period ultimately functioned to reproduce the woman-as-exchange paradigm, with an abundance of expensive consumer goods of which the bride is principal object. Lorraine manages and organises these events, clearly demonstrating the post-feminist subject as a type of feminine facilitator, making sure it all goes right on the night. Furthermore, her appearance also signals post-feminism as capitalist product. She is very much a dressed-up feminine body, a 'woman' of masquerade, as evidenced in the first episode when she holds an initial meeting with Penny at 'Perfect Day Productions' (Fig 11.1). The contrast between the two is striking. Penny is dressed in bland pastel colours, with no make-up, while Lorraine's face is (overly) made up, her hair is dyed and she is wearing a loud pink and navy check jacket and short black skirt. Her dressed body makes an interesting complement to the equally loud surroundings of the office (emphasised by the high-key lighting of the scene), which has wine cushions on the chairs and a large colourful photographic backdrop. This is similar to the *mise en scène* of *Paths to Freedom*, in which Helen is regularly constructed as matching the scenery of Celtic Tiger capital: her impeccably

Fig. 11.1 Deirdre O'Kane as Lorraine in *Fergus's Wedding*
(Grand Pictures, 2002).

decorated home matching the attention paid to her manicured and groomed body. This merging of body and background, character and scene, points towards a connection between post-feminist identities and consumer objects. They are both *products* of a larger (re)producing system that is late capitalism – objects of exchange in an economy that prioritises masculine concerns and vantage points.

Following Irigaray, then, post-feminist identity categories can be interpreted as *products* of late capitalism, which models and dresses the feminine in specific discursive (and material) garments, hence constituting the '[d]issimulation of woman in the thought of the father. Where she is created fully-clothed and armed.'[25] However, the paternal role of capitalism is subtly manoeuvred. While the female body continues to be shaped in the interest of a phallogocentric symbolic, this shaping or moulding is not hidden or naturalised. Rather, the activity of the female subject in post-feminism is fundamentally based on the dressing and beauty-managing of the body. Subjective choice is always already connected with consumer choice.[26] The explosion, throughout the Celtic Tiger period, of available products and services related to female grooming speaks to this post-feminist shaping. 'SSIA Breast Augmentation Deals' were regularly advertised throughout 2006 and 2007, as plastic surgery clinics capitalised on the matured funds of Irish women's SSIA accounts (a government-sponsored special savings incentive). Thus, in this updated 'de-centred symbolic'[27] the feminine is consistently presented in the process of (self) making and shaping, whereby the appearance of the feminine is not naturalised (as per Irigaray), but rather the construction of appearance, the enactment of the masquerade, becomes a hallmark of the post-feminist condition itself. Furthermore, shaping processes are continuously presented as being connected with female agency. It is seemingly women's *choice* to manicure, groom and dress their bodies; the mechanisms of patriarchal capitalism – Irigaray's phallic father – are not visibly in the picture. As McRobbie notes, 'The Symbolic is faced with the problem of how to retain the dominance of phallocentrism when the logic of global capitalism is to loosen women from their prescribed roles and grant them degrees of economic independence.'[28] It does so by delegating 'its duties to the commercial domain (beauty, fashion, magazines, body culture, etc.) which becomes the source of authority and judgement for young women', ensuring that traditional 'gender relations are guaranteed'.[29]

The relationship between capitalism and phallogocentrism is suggested in *Paths to Freedom* in a key scene where Helen is in a spa getting treatments (Fig 11.2). She speaks to the documentary camera crew about the need for bodily upkeep: 'There are women out there who haven't set foot inside a salon. And they expect to keep hold of their men [. . .] think of all the treatments you can have now: pedicures and manicures and waxing, reflexology, ah it's endless – liposuction for god's sake.'[30] In 'Veiled Lips', Irigaray's argument is that the incorporated feminine operates as a mirror for male desire.[31] The scene in the salon illustrates this idea, revealing that while in a post-feminist climate women are doing the self-shaping, it is still fundamentally about male desire, overtly stated in Helen's comments about women keeping 'their men'. The whiteness of the set (Helen and the beautician are both in white, as is the wall, the spa bed and the equipment) suggests Irigaray's idea of a 'blank canvas',[32] while a mirror and reflective beauty inspection light located in the background reinforce the sense of reproductive imaging and the female body. Laura Mulvey's arguments regarding the male gaze and how

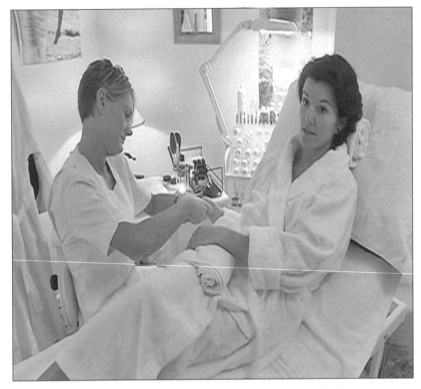

Fig. 11.2 Deirdre O'Kane as Helen in *Paths to Freedom*
(Grand Pictures, 2000).

it 'projects its fantasy onto the female figure, which is styled accordingly' are relevant here.[33] While Helen ostensibly seems to be in
control of her own desires and choices, her self-positioning as
embodied 'canvas' locates her as support to phallogocentric structures, and demonstrates how powerfully patriarchal desire has been
internalised.[34] From this we can see how Irigaray's feminist analyses
are still pertinent in a post-feminist climate, as the updated symbolic
insidiously re-works the previous operations of phallogocentrism,
presenting, rather than concealing, the shaping of the feminine, so as
to give the *appearance* of feminine choice, agency and subjectivity.

Authentic maternity/post-feminist artificiality

Paths to Freedom, in its class-critique of Celtic Tiger excess and greed,
provides an ethical reconsideration of late capitalism in Ireland, perceptively identifying the ways in which post-feminist discourses are a

product of patriarchal economies. In *Fergus's Wedding*, Lorraine and 'Perfect Day Productions' operate in similar terms, as post-feminist employees of the symbolic order of twenty-first-century Ireland. However, even though *Paths to Freedom* and *Fergus's Wedding* both critique a capitalist symbolic order in which the division between producer and product, lively agent and passive support, can be easily confused in a system whereby the body of support *appears* active in its supporting role, they can also be read as continuing the fundamental gendering of this operation. Helen and Lorraine, post-feminist products and symbols of capitalism, are 'extras' that are removed at the end of both series; as instances of Irigaray's incorporated femininity, they are ejected in the shows' bid to reconfigure the cultural and social meanings of Celtic Tiger Ireland. For example, in *Fergus's Wedding*, Fergus specifically refers to Lorraine as an excessive extra early on in the series, when he states his resistance to hiring her:

> FERGUS: Wedding organiser – what type of a makey-uppy job is
> that?
> PENNY: She has already come up with a wonderful cupid motif
> . . .
> FERGUS: What is a motif? What is a motif and how much is it
> going to cost me?

As the show progresses, Lorraine herself becomes a 'motif' for all the excesses and extras of the Celtic Tiger period – the post-feminist working girl as a caricature of wasteful times. As a wedding planner, she is continuously associated with objects constructed as non-necessary (flowers, dresses, menus), an association that works to frame her body in similarly excessive terms.

Fergus's Wedding concludes the day after the wedding. It also ends with the bankruptcy of 'Perfect Day Productions'. The final scene is a montage, composed of shots that begin and end with Penny and Fergus in the airport bar before going on honeymoon. In the first shot, they sing the lyrics of the Joe Cocker and Jennifer Warnes love song 'Up Where We Belong' (1982), which then becomes the background score of the sequence, which pictures guests of the wedding still lingering at the hotel in various (mainly hungover) conditions. In one of these shots, Lorraine answers her phone and says: 'Perfect Day Productions went bankrupt. Yes, just this minute actually. No, no, you can't speak to Lorraine, she died. Yes very sad, tragic. Yeah. I've a load of calls to make, thanking you.' There is then a cut to a shot of the best man in a comically comatose state, before returning to a close-up of Penny and Fergus at the airport:

FERGUS: I love you babes.
PENNY: Ah, I love you babes.

They kiss and this image is frozen on screen in the still of a photograph, with the lyrics 'love lift us up where we belong' sounding loudly for the concluding shot.

What is important here is the way in which the inauthentic Lorraine is proclaimed 'bankrupt' and 'dead', survived by an authentic and sustainable 'love'. Her symbolic death can be read as a suggested eradication of capitalist values and modes of living, as the 'motif' of consumerism is constructed as defunct. She will have no relevance in the future lives of Penny and Fergus. The post-feminist woman is, quite literally, sent out of the picture. What remains *in* the picture, suggested by the closing score and image, is love, as it is traditionally constructed in the frame of marriage. Furthermore, Penny is pregnant. The fact that it is not Fergus's child (Fergus is infertile, thus they conjecture that the father is a member of the swinging club)[35] does somewhat trouble the conservative nature of the ending, given that it was Penny who introduced Fergus to the practice of swinging. Thus, the pregnancy points towards her own non-normative sexuality and desire.[36] However, ultimately, the troubling potentialities of this gesture are not maximised; Penny's S&M room is being changed into a nursery and her days of sexual promiscuity are at an end. Ultimately then, this is not a return of Irigaray's repressed and powerful maternal, which brings forth an embodied female subject of desire, but rather a different version of incorporated femininity: the traditional nurturing mother.

Paths to Freedom enacts a similar conclusion to that of *Fergus's Wedding*. Throughout the series, Helen is consistently shot in conjunction with 'extra' products such as candles and flowers. In the final episode of the series, she packs up to leave the home she shares with Jeremy, which they have to sell because of their financial difficulties (as a result of his unemployment and the legal costs related to his case). In the kitchen, Helen's flowers are wilting and dying, pointing towards the demise of their privilege and wealth. At the episode's conclusion, the audience is told that Helen has filed for divorce and moved to Paris, and Jeremy has been hospitalised after having a nervous breakdown. The end of their marriage, status and wealth can be read through the lens of the series' broader critique of Celtic Tiger Ireland. Jeremy functioned as the subject of this Ireland, while Helen operated as post-feminist object of support. His breakdown is symbolic of the series' wishful look towards a future in which capitalist power and inequities are renegotiated. On a representational level, then, the object that supports such a system, in this case Helen, is no longer necessary without that subject, as she exists only in relation *to* her male counterpart, rather than in and for herself: 'she is not the "other of the other" [. . .] but the "other of the same", the world of appearances which is supposed to be transcended in the final vision of truth.'[37]

Just as in *Fergus's Wedding*, there is a replacement of the post-feminist woman with the mother in *Paths to Freedom*, as what constitutes the incorporated feminine is transformed at the conclusion of the series, when 'Spermdotcom' perform at 'Brief Encounters', 'a small gay club in the heart of Dublin's inner-city'. Highlighting his central subjective position, Rats is dressed in white onstage, emphasised all the more by placing his body within the key light of the shot. In the dark shadows of the scene, the club's crowd is made up entirely of men – that is, apart from Rats' mother who gushes 'Oh, I am so proud of him' as he prepares to sing his opening song, 'Celtic Tiger Rap': 'Celtic Tiger is a funny type of cat. Why am I skinny, when everybody's fat?' The mother has been reinstated as the object of support for the masculine subject and his authentic phallic message: she gets 'spermdotcom' t-shirts made for them; she is their number one fan. It is significant that, in addition to the mother, gay men function as support representatives for Rats' critique of capitalism. This points towards the nature of the critique itself, which does not aim to disassemble the capitalist system (Rats wants to sell records after all), but rather redistribute the wealth, unsettle class division and make society a more equitable place: male queer culture, which like post-feminist identity has been co-opted by capitalism as symbol of 'progress',[38] is redeployed here by the discourse of critique. One possible reason for this could be an interpretation of this culture as fundamentally queering the capitalism in which it participates, its disruption of norms presenting it as a suitable object of support for a critique that has similar aims. In this way, then, the queer male body is used in the same way as that of the woman, as supportive facilitator.

As previously argued, the post-feminist configuration does not challenge phallogocentrism, but rather (as incorporated feminine) supports it in the updated global capitalist symbolic. Nonetheless, critiques of this system need to interrogate not just its contents (post-feminist discourse) but also the fundamental structure through and by which it operates (deployment of the feminine as support). Failure to do so ultimately results in the rehearsal of the same gendering processes, with the feminine again being deployed as symbol. In *Paths to Freedom* and *Fergus's Wedding* the ejection of Lorraine and Helen, as (negative) motifs of inauthentic Celtic Tiger Ireland, from the representative frame at both series' end is matched with the inclusion of a mother figure, symbolising a better, more hopeful, and 'authentic' future for Irish society. Thus we can see a continuation of the representational paradigm that Irigaray critiques in her work, whereby the feminine is shaped by symbolic structures so as to aid in the production of meaning. The post-feminist woman is (re)replaced with another example of incorporated femininity – that of Mother Ireland, the 'iconographic figure [. . .] who has popularly birthed the modern state', as the feminine continues to be used in the interests of national self-representation.[39]

Conclusion

In *The Aftermath of Feminism*, McRobbie makes the point that in post-feminism 'the whole question of left-wing politics and the impact its current state of crisis, or indeed its demise, has had for feminism, was left to the side'.[40] Ultimately, she claims that it is imperative that discourses related to feminism and gender, be they post, pre or otherwise, stay attentive to the left as a structural and generative framework. Such attentiveness is very obviously lacking in the dominant discourses of post-feminism, something which needs to be consistently and routinely addressed in Irish feminism(s) given that, as in most Western cultures, post-feminism has become the primary paradigm through which women in Ireland are encouraged to identify themselves. In this essay, I have attempted to address the troublesome connection between Irish capitalist culture and the production of post-feminist identity categories, in order to interrogate popular celebratory configurations of contemporary womanhood. *Paths to Freedom* and *Fergus's Wedding* are two texts that enable an exploration of this kind, due to the nature of their gendered critiques of Celtic Tiger excess. However, while I agree with McRobbie that new discourses of feminism need to stay close to a leftist vision, an analysis of the two television series reveal that the reverse is also the case. Critiques of capitalism in Ireland need to give thoughtful consideration to feminism, gender and the structures of representation. Failure to do so will ultimately sustain a scene of representation that has structured Irish national discourse from the colonial to the Celtic Tiger period – woman as symbol-support of the nation. It is urgent then that we begin to think otherwise and, as Patricia Coughlan notes, to 'imagine Ireland newly, reconceive the nation without that feminine personification'.[41] In the context of the recent economic recession very necessary interrogations of the Irish capitalist system are now forming in public discourse and debate. As we work through these critiques and think about ways of 'renewing the republic',[42] it is crucial to be committed to difference at the most fundamental and structural level. In doing so, the hope will be to change the scene (and future) of post-Tiger representations.

Chapter Twelve

NEW IDENTITIES IN THE
IRISH HORROR FILM:
ISOLATION AND *BOY EATS GIRL*

Zélie Asava

Mixed monsters

In October 2007, the *Sunday Times* Culture supplement opened its 'Film Special' with a look at what the feature writer Pavel Barter called an explosion in Irish horror films: 'From Stephen Bradley's *Boy Eats Girl* (2005) [. . .] to Billy O'Brien's *Isolation* (2006) [. . .] indigenous cinema has a new-found appetite to shock.'[1] In what follows, I analyse racial mixing and gender in these multicultural Irish horror films in order to explore the position of the mixed-race subject in Irish cinema and consider the representation of diversity within contemporary Irish culture. Both *Isolation* and *Boy Eats Girl* feature mixed-race female protagonists: Mary, played by Irish-Ethiopian actress Ruth Negga, and Jessica played by Irish-Zambian popstar/actress/model Samantha Mumba. These films are a unique part of Irish cinema in that they use horror conventions to privilege mixed-race issues and so reflect the changing face of the Irish nation, as well as raising issues concerning Irish identity and tradition. The essay will begin by exploring the socio-political representational schemas of each film, as well as the effects of multiculturalism in Ireland. It will go on to consider the history of Irish horror and the key thematic figure, the monster, with which will be paralleled in the historically perceived monstrosity of racial mixing. Finally, it will interrogate the Irish tropes contained within the films and consider the larger question of the position of mixed figures on screen.

Isolation and *Boy Eats Girl* are both distinctly *Irish* horror films, particularly in terms of theme, setting and language. They move

184

away from traditional Irish cinematic representations: of the nation; of Ireland as rural idyll; of the white, two-parent family unit as the model of the state; of religion; of gender; of race. They reposition the female figure in horror as active agent rather than object of the gaze,[2] and likewise reposition the mixed-race female as heroine rather than 'tragic mulatta'.[3] The 'tragic mulatto/a' is categorised as black according to the 'one-drop' rule.[4] For example, in *The Nephew* (Eugene Brady, 1998) the mixed-race Irish-African-American male is consistently framed as black and foreign by being referred to as the 'Yank', the 'African' or the 'nigger', and depicted as a dreadlocked baggily dressed American. *Isolation* and *Boy Eats Girl* are far more subtle in their exploration of race relations and represent their mixed-race female protagonists as not black *or* white but *both*. Yet while *Boy Eats Girl* and *Isolation* challenge traditional representations of race and gender, and subvert Irish cinematic representations of the nation, ultimately they fail to move away fully from cultural stereotypes, and *Isolation* in particular utilises fears of interracial reproduction as monstrous to reinforce its traditional horror themes.

The horror film plays on the terror of the unimaginable, on revulsion, fears, insecurities and uncertainties. It blurs normal with abnormal and challenges the dominant ideologies of the hegemony. For example, in *Boy Eats Girl* the 'final girl' motif challenges patriarchal models in its privileging of the heroine, and non-white culture is made visible as an ideal, while in *Isolation* (non-white) women again trump (white) men as survivors and the advancements of science come under scrutiny, as the mixing of human and animal cells becomes monstrous. The concept of amalgamation at the centre of the horror film is also a key element of the discourse of racial integration and the hysteria regarding immigration in Ireland. The increase in numbers of racial Others in Ireland, prompted by the economic boom of the late 1990s,[5] has been perceived to disturb the security of Irish identity. These themes of marginalisation, loss and exclusion are also central concerns of the horror genre, which centres on the return of the repressed, the crossing of boundaries, the death of old certainties, and the breaking of social taboos. The horror aesthetic permeates various aspects of Irish storytelling culture. However, until this decade there was no established Irish horror film genre. Likewise, until this decade, black racial issues were virtually absent in Irish cinema. I would like to argue here that there are clear parallels between the growth of the horror genre and racial issues in Irish culture. Both emerged during Ireland's economic boom and both question established certainties, challenging ideas of the nation and ideas of gender, which have been central to Ireland's cultural history.

Mixed-race issues, gender and nationalism

If non-nationals have been utilised to further nationalist aims and raise debates over the importance of safeguarding Irish identity then where does that leave those who, like Mumba and Negga, are 'impure' by nature of being of dual ethnicity, cannot lay claim to full Irishness and physically resemble the Other. According to Ronit Lentin, 'non-national women were made central to the racial configuration of twenty-first-century Ireland, illustrating not only orchestrated moral panics about "floods of refugees", but also the positioning of sexually active women as a "danger to the state and the nation".[6] Thus, these actresses and their protagonists represent Irish identity, but also symbolise foreign corruption and invasion – particularly in the case of pregnant Mary in *Isolation*. Lentin's evaluation illuminates Irish public discourse as predicated on the binary of *us* and *them*, pure and hybrid, the nation-state and its established values, versus over-sexualised foreigners and particularly over-sexualised foreign women, implying the continued need for a policing of the internal national border constituted by women's bodies. The issue of non-white pregnancy in Ireland led to a new law restricting citizenship entitlements for babies born in Ireland without Irish ancestry and revealed the issue of racism in Ireland. The 2004 Citizenship Act requires children born in Ireland to non-Irish parents (not including asylum seekers/students) to be resident for three years before being entitled to apply for citizenship. It was preceded by a referendum to establish its terms at which there was a higher than normal turnout (62 per cent), and an overwhelming response in favour of amending the Act (almost 80 per cent), propelled by media hysteria regarding 'citizenship tourism' (where women were said to have babies in Ireland to gain citizenship). As Gerardine Meaney observes:

> [T]he work of national scape-goat has simply been outsourced
> [. . .] onto immigrant women. The ease with which popular
> hysteria about pregnant migrants 'flooding' Irish maternity

hospitals with their non-national babies could be translated into 80% electoral support for a constitutional amendment limiting Irish citizenship on the basis of ethnicity and affiliations of kinship and blood indicates that racism was never a marginal factor in Irish political life nor a specific historical response to the numbers of actual migrants arriving in Ireland in the late 1990s.[7]

The tendency in Irish cinema to cast Negga in illegal immigrant/single mother roles[8] recalls the stereotypes to which Meaney and Lentin refer as she is positioned as a pregnant threat to morality and the nation-state. Mumba came to fame in the midst of these discourses and remains a key figure at which point race, gender and ideas of the nation intersect.

Isolation and *Boy Eats Girl* consider various aspects of the 'new Irish' and modern Ireland, where mixed-race characters are ambiguous agents – at once heroes and villains, alien and familiar, migrant and citizen, Irish and not-Irish. These films raise extra-diegetic questions regarding the nation which have hitherto been silent, for example regarding the representation of Irish Others and the social issues which they face (e.g. *Isolation* exposes the segregation of Travellers). They make visible that which has been made 'absent'. The mixed-race leads of *Isolation* and *Boy Eats Girl* embody a new multiculturalism while also revealing a history of interracial mixing in Irish families.[9] In *Boy Eats Girl*, a love story between Jessica (Mumba) and Nathan (David Leon) is placed at the heart of a zombie attack, thus centralising and paralleling fears of invasion, alien/human amalgamation and miscegenation. As is typical of the 'tragic mulatta' genre, Jessica is the white man's downfall, i.e. when Nathan sees her with another boy, he suspects his unrequited love for her will never be fulfilled and kills himself. After discovering her dead son, Nathan's desperate mother happens upon an old pagan text buried beneath her local church and uses voodoo to bring him back to life. However, Nathan is reborn as the undead and becomes a cannibal, whose victims turn into zombies and attack the town. Finally, Jessica finds a way to kill the zombies, redeem Nathan's humanity, save the world and end the film as a heroine in his arms.

Isolation is thematically hybrid and mixes spatial and temporal verisimilitude with the fantastic and the surreal in its consideration of amalgamation. It tends towards realism in its cinematography and refuses stylisation, but employs clearly artificial monsters that both destroy the notion of the cinema screen as a real mirror to society and yet appear in such a real setting that they seem almost plausible. Young couple Mary (Negga) and Jamie (Sean Harris) run away together after her family reject him – he is a Traveller, another of the marginalised Irish.[10] The couple escape in his caravan and end up staying on a desolate farm. Dan (John Lynch), the farmer, is a victim of the economic shifts produced by the Celtic Tiger: cheaper foreign imports, changes in subsidisation practices required by the EU, and farm pandemics such as bovine spongiform encephalopathy (BSE, more colloquially known as mad cow disease) and foot-and-mouth disease, have led to a downturn in local agriculture. Due to a dwindling income Dan has been forced to turn over some of his livestock to John (Marcel Lures), a German-accented scientist whose company, Bovine Genetics Technology, focuses on embryo transfer, cellular mixing and reproduction. His experiments are designed to produce more fertile calves that grow faster and give birth earlier, with unexpected results: the genetically enhanced calves begin to gestate spontaneously while still in the womb. The experiments lead to the production of calves with overgrown organs and vampire-like teeth, as well as a new species of bloodthirsty genetic mutations living within them – malformed exo-skeletal foetuses that kill the animals from which they emerge and all other life they encounter. Here the abject invades and contaminates the rural, the body and thus society, mimicking national fears regarding racial mixing. *Isolation*'s realist aesthetic confirms its relation to real events, including the main focus of its horror, abnormal fusions.[11]

In both films, cultural fears regarding immigration and racial mixing are manifested in narratives that consider cultural and genetic hybridity. The issue of amalgamation, which is at the centre of racial hysteria and the horror genre, is rooted, as LeiLani Nishime notes, in 'Western culture's long history of equating human with white European',[12] and non-white Others with non-human Others. Racial mixing was thus long associated with perversion, degeneracy and monstrosity.[13] Mixed bodies were, like monsters, traditionally associated with disease, degenerate morality, high mortality rates, infertility, neurological defects, an aversion to light (like vampires) and other ills, due to the assumption that they were an unnatural amalgamation. Donna Haraway describes miscegenation as 'the bloodsucking monster at the heart of racist and misogynistic terror'.[14] Racial mixing can still be read as the ultimate taboo as so few mainstream films tackle the subject head on, and even those with an interracial love story avoid representing mixed marriages or births, which can be said to reflect or promote an idea of racial mixing as impossible.[15] In *Boy Eats Girl* and *Isolation*, racial mixing is ambiguously represented; the films both centralise the mixed-race hero and tap into the horror traditions rooted in fears of mixed-race as monstrous.

The mixed cinematic body, being both white and black, disrupts ideas of humanity in the same way that the cinematic monster creates fear through the threat it poses to our established order and fixed categories.[16] Both are by nature hybrid, and it is the perceived impossibility of this amalgamation which makes the mixed figure monstrous,[17] as Julia Kristeva observes: 'it disturbs identity, system and order [and] does not respect borders, positions, rules.'[18] In its anti-homogeneity and hybridity the mixed body mirrors the monster, an interstitial subject which defies categorisation and crosses boundaries of cultural schemas, making it both physically and cognitively threatening to fixed social 'norms' and categories.

In *Isolation* and *Boy Eats Girl* the mixed-race character is the instigator of the disorder which leads to the ultimate horror, and yet also the only character with the hybrid cultural competence to restore order. As the embodiment of the in-between, she is both monstrous and heroic in her heterogeneity. This contradiction has its roots in the mythology of miscegenation, which posited that mixture would lead to an extreme, whether negative or positive; ideas of hybrid vigour, popular from 1864 to 1926, posited 'mixeds' as stronger, smarter and more attractive than 'pures'.[19] As Mary Beltràn notes, the traditionally perceived monstrosity of the mixed-race body, along with the recent shifts towards celebrating mixed beauty and mixed heritage (stimulated by the political movement which established 'mixed-race' as a racial category on the US and UK censuses in 2000 and 2001 respectively), make the screen character a contradictory figure: 'while subtly reinforcing notions of white centrism [. . .] the new ethnically ambiguous protagonist embodies concerns regarding ethnicity and race-relations with respect to the nation's burgeoning cultural creolization and multiethnic population.'[20] The contemporary mixed-race character both symbolises the ills of (multicultural) society – lawlessness, the breakdown of the normative family unit, alienation – and exhibits a 'cultural mastery' over all 'racialised' worlds, as Beltràn puts it. Their mixed identity is still somewhat tragic but it is their hybridity that allows them to negotiate difficulties with ease, sometimes making them more valuable than the white hero. This ambiguity is central to the representation of the mixed-race protagonist in both *Isolation* and *Boy Eats Girl*.

Positioning the mixed figure

Boy Eats Girl posits Irish youth against the cultural backdrop of glamorous, wealthy west coast America, and plays on dominant American genres. The film's location in the exclusive D4 area of Dublin's southside fulfils expectations of Celtic Tiger Ireland. *Boy Eats Girl* presents its mixed-race lead as a normative aspect of the capital, which is imagined to be just as multicultural a space as any other rich Western city. This ethnic diversity is not only a fantasy in an Irish society that remains largely divided, but also in Irish film, which remains largely mono-racial.[21] Yet it does signal the wave of immigration which accompanied the economic boom and which could be said to have fuelled interest in Mumba as a pop sensation and symbol of Irish diversity. After her initial success in the music industry, Mumba's image was changed to make her appear more like African-American stars Aaliyah, Destiny's Child and (mixed-race) Mariah Carey in an attempt to break America with a black (rather than Irish) act. Although this was unsuccessful, she became known as a black star and within this context her characterisation as Jessica seems to posit her as a signifier of success in the 'new Ireland' of multiculturalism and opportunity.

Yet, given her Eurocentric appearance, white family (her father, with whom she lives, is white, her (presumably) black mother is dead) and privileged economic status, *Boy Eats Girl*'s Jessica could be read as contextually white. As Ruth Barton notes, she is the bearer of the film's most excessive display of wealth, and although she is a signifier of the 'new Ireland', it is 'more the new Ireland of Louis Walsh and global pop stardom than of racial dispossession'.[22] As the child of a low-income single-parent household, Mumba could be read as a signifier of racial dispossession, yet she shot to fame and wealth as a teenage popstar (with media mogul Walsh as her manager). Like her on-screen character Jessica (and Negga), she grew up with a white parent, a mixed-race reality often overlooked in film. Mumba is thus closer to Jessica's wealthy, white contextualised character than *Isolation*'s Mary. Although both actresses are proud of their heritage, they do not differentiate themselves by discussing racism in Ireland, just as neither film explores it overtly by absenting black parents – as Meaney mentioned earlier and Steve Garner has noted extensively, there has been an extraordinary level of official denial of the existence of racism in Ireland.[23]

Boy Eats Girl challenges stereotypes and asserts difference in its presentation of Irish tropes. The popular stereotype of the Irish mother as the moral authority of Catholic, sexually regulated Ireland[24] is destroyed early on when Nathan's mother Grace (played by comedian Deirdre O'Kane) encourages Nathan to date Jessica and uses voodoo to resurrect him after he commits suicide. The handling of this topic is also unusual as suicide is rarely discussed openly in Irish culture, and indeed the censor attempted to cut the suicide scene.[25] Grace's representation thus disrupts the traditional representation of Irish mothers (as O'Kane has done in her own stand-up routines), and does so without making her into an abjected site of fear or distrust. The trope of Irish father as keeper and ruler of the nation[26] is defined by Jessica's father, a man who manipulates his power to keep her from Nathan. However, his position is undermined in an extended scene where he is shown attempting to seduce girls from her class in a bar (and she herself sneaks out to meet Nathan). As with many Irish films, one parent is dead (Jessica's mother, Nathan's father), symbolising the historically dysfunctional and decimated nature of the nation-state. This familial breakdown is also a key element of mixed-race representations and traditionally symbolises the impossibility of interracial unions, although Jessica's close relationship to her white father and boyfriend signifies an alternative model.

Following classical Hollywood narrative formulae, *Boy Eats Girl* concludes with the restoration of order and the heterosexual family unit (Fig. 12.1), but it is a new kind of unit which privileges feminine leadership and justifies racial mixing as positive, legitimate and hegemonic. This ending both marks and erases difference. Nathan and Jessica's future will be hybrid. However, if their union produces children, they will be white and economically privileged, the inheritors of Jessica's vast family estate. The erasure of difference this implies (reinforced by Jessica's Eurocentric depiction) could be read as undermining the film's legitimisation of interracial love, but it also represents the reality of assimilation (proving the illogic of the 'one-drop' rule). Ultimately however, the visual nature of the medium does not allow Jessica's difference to be erased so the final (and first) interracial kiss is indeed revolutionary in its idealisation. Jessica's black family may be absent, but the racial otherness her dark skin colour signifies is submerged in the text and paralleled in the zombies and foreign fashions of her friends. She is idealised as a love interest and as an Irish woman (she is the only young woman left alive at the end of the film, and it is she who saves humanity), in contrast to the dominant presentation in Irish culture of sex symbols and heroines as white. Jessica as protagonist thus provides a powerful visual message, ending the film as an active agent and a symbolic ideal of social progress. Here she challenges the underlying fear of miscegenation at the centre of the film, embodied by the zombies, by proving the worth of her hybridity.

Like *Boy Eats Girl*, *Isolation* depicts mixed-race Mary as someone accepted unequivocally as Irish. She is never identified as racially different (however her framing beyond the settled community and identification with a Traveller suggests her underlying difference). The film is aesthetically and thematically darker than *Boy Eats Girl* and in contrast to much of Celtic Tiger cinema it strives to show the underbelly of the boom. It uses the concept of the 'black pastoral'[27] – the idea of the rural as threatening – to deconstruct the dominant cinematic trope of rural Ireland as idyllic; for example, when Mary and Jamie arrive at the farm they are met by a sign that warns them to 'KEEP OUT'. The film follows a tight narrative and stylistic line with a highly voyeuristic tone, the camera peeking through fences and gates throughout. It bears formal and tonal similarities to horror filmmaker George Romero's work from its opening credit sequence on and evokes the feelings of classic horror; the palpable horror of the unseen and unknown, that is, the Other, as represented in this case by racial and social Others, foreign maternity and hybrid genetic mutations.

Haraway's theories on racial mixing are key to *Isolation*'s core themes: 'miscegenation is still a racist synonym for infection,

Fig. 12.1 Racial mixing and hybrid futures in Stephen Bradley's
Boy Eats Girl, 2005.

counterfeit issue unfit to carry the name of the father, and a spoiled
future.'[28] Mary tells Dan that she is from a close family of six
children, yet she has given that family up for Jamie and so it is
absent from the screen. The narrative disturbs and destabilises the
family she will produce – associating it with infection and paternal
absence. John tells Jamie that the greatest threat the monsters pose is
that they mix human and animal cells thereby infecting humans
whose children will be 'mutated, deformed' and could wipe out an
entire generation. By the end of the film Mary has become pregnant
with a baby that is corrupted by this potentially deadly genetic
mutation and her lover – its father – is dead. Midway through the
film, Jamie is contaminated by the mutant creature and it begins to
consume his consciousness, hybridising and eventually erasing his
humanity, to the extent that he forces himself on her one night,
resulting in her pregnancy. This behaviour is out of character and
can be assumed to be driven by the desire of the monster within him
that is motivated to reproduce and conquer, which parallels the use

of rape as a weapon in war[29] or as a commercial enterprise in slavery (to produce more slaves), and, more generally, sex as a method of colonisation/assimilation.[30]

The act is mirrored by a later mutant attempt to impregnate Mary, a scene which plays with ideas related to Laura Mulvey's arguments on the 'male gaze' and bell hooks' arguments on the abuse of black/mixed women by this 'phallocular' gaze.[31] As Mary sleeps, a mutant creeps into the bed and up her body, seen by spectators as a lump moving towards her under the blanket. The monster clearly embodies the voyeuristic desire of spectators seduced by Mary's innocent beauty. The use of the virgin's name for her – as well as the mimetic blue and red colours of her costume – further heightens the perverse desire to demystify and violate her privacy, to see the passion behind her demure surface (Fig. 12.2). Shifting from object of the penetrative gaze to self-determined agent, she awakens and pulls back the covers to reveal the bloodied monster at her crotch trying to get in – a shot which summarises the desire for and horror of the female form in cinema. The monster itself resembles a mutated, castrated, disembodied phallus, devoid of power without a female nest, and thus recalls feminist arguments on the positioning of the female body as a locus of power for male nationalism – and the foundation for the hierarchy of power amongst men. If, as Anne McClintock argues, 'all nationalisms are gendered',[32] this moment very clearly outlines Irish nationalism as defined by, to quote Shelley Feldman, 'colonised space as feminine, colonial power as masculine'.[33] The monster aims at the suppression of the human, just as popular protectionist politics pushes for cultural assimilation and the suppression of the non-national identity. But the monster is a hybrid body and seeks hybrid mothers, male and female, human and animal, black and white, dead and alive. It is this interstitiality that makes it so terrifying and unpredictable, and yet it is Mary's interstitiality with which we identify.

In one of the concluding scenes, Mary kills the remaining hybrid foetuses and then penetrates the body of the primary monster. Her rage is reminiscent of a rape-revenge scene as she continues beating the stick down upon its body long after it is immobile, screaming in a primal fashion and releasing all the tensions of one who has been silenced, erased, overlooked, denigrated and abused. She literally smashes to pieces the impositions placed upon her by this monster and society, breaking open the unsaid to reveal the marginalised Irish heroine. In doing so she destroys a signifier of the phallus which controlled and debased her, challenging the misogynism of the spectator's voyeuristic desire for her sex and parallel desire for her destruction, embodied by this monstrous-masculine. The monster, however, lives on within her, and in line with traditionally religious and maternal ideas of Irish womanhood, she does not consider aborting the terrifying foetus. Her pregnancy takes on an uncanny element as she is inhabited by a mixed-race baby that is also mixed-species. The fears evoked by this hybrid mirror those regarding ethnic hybrids in Irish culture, and in particular the fear of racial mixing.

Fig. 12.2 Mary's (Ruth Negga) appearance is visually connected to the iconography of the Virgin in Billy O'Brien's *Isolation*, 2005.

The concatenation of *Isolation*'s key themes is realised in the final scenes when spectators witness a birth scan of the abject foetus that threatens the death of humanity (just as anti-mixed-race debates have argued that a mixed future signals the end of whiteness, and possibly of humanity). This compounds racial mixing with monstrosity, recalling the idea of the mixed figure as a fusion of incompatible elements. The scan image evokes Freud's 1919 piece on the *unheimlich* (the uncanny), being that which is homely and familiar and yet strange and alien at the same time.[34] It is hard to make out any clear shape in the digital blur and so the image recalls a kind of abyss, frightening and unknowable, yet the doctor identifies the baby's head and assures Mary that it is a healthy girl. As we study the baby's body, the mutant inside becomes clearly present. Through its portrayal of that which is beyond control (the 'bloodsucking monster' of miscegenation, as Haraway puts it), *Isolation* reaches the sublimity of terror. The film's ambiguous approach to mixing is again emphasised as the monster both reflects Mary's hybridity and terrifies even her with its horrific mixture.

Framing and final girls

As fantastical stories, *Boy Eats Girl* and *Isolation* allow for the dominant social politic to be decentred, and for marginalised voices to be heard. Their framing of mixed-race women alongside zombies and monsters is representative of the fear of mixing, which Mary and Jessica attempt to overcome. Thus, they move away from the idea of the mixed cinematic body as monstrous and replace the traditional white male hero with mixed-race heroines. As Beltràn puts it, mixed-race characters now benefit from the hybridity which was formerly seen as divisive; both Mary and Jessica have '[the] ability to thrive in environments defined by cultural border crossings and pastiche'; 'nonwhite ancestry now has cachet'.[35] By foregrounding mixed women and multiplicity, these films privilege a politics of difference; *Boy Eats Girl* explores class, sexual and religious difference, while *Isolation* explores different forms of citizenship, class and cultural capital. In contrast to the phallocentric gaze that Mulvey identified in cinema, neither film attempts to fetishise or objectify its female protagonist. In fact in *Isolation*, Mary is always dressed conservatively and even remains clothed during the sex scene (an ambiguous image which conflates the stereo-typically sexual non-white foreigner with the non-sexual white Irish woman in the mixed figure).

Isolation and *Boy Eats Girl* avoid overt political issues but they can be found embedded within the text. Both Mary and Jessica are idealised and are the sole surviving women to emerge from their horror stories. Mary fulfils the trope of the 'final girl',[36] and as a pregnant woman she holds within her the future of her (Irish) mixed-race – although this is problematised by the demonisation of her mixed race daughter as a mutant. This problematic recalls fears of reproductive futurity associated with heterosexual interracial sex which Mia Mask describes as threatening to 'the hegemony of whiteness because it breaks the biological assumptions implicit in definitions of race'.[37] Both films ambiguously suggest that mixed subjects are normative within Irish culture whilst also promoting cultural stereotypes of the mixed-race woman as isolated, tragic, beautiful and sexual, thus endorsing and challenging hegemonic positions. Their mixed protagonists serve as metaphors for the rapid modernisation and multiculturalism of Ireland, while also signifying the fears these issues raise, in the discourse of racial mixing and gender shifts.

The narratives of *Isolation* and *Boy Eats Girl* link hybridity to a range of threats: paganism, impurity, invasion, white death and amorality. As both leads are the only non-white characters in the films, they symbolise and negate their position as part of any wave of immigration. Their isolation may not necessarily be linked to a racialised gaze, but rather may reflect the class segregation of Irish society; for example, wealth separates Jessica from other non-whites, while poverty separates Mary, Jamie and Dan from the rest of Ireland. Their representations are problematic if taken to signify Irish integration. But they can be read as feminist explorations of cultural divisions which excavate that which is unsaid – the figure of the (non-white/white) Irish woman/(m)other. By exploring the body, maternity and the danger of the foreign, they produce the possibility of countering racist discourses through feminism that Meaney has theorised as central to the integration of Irish society and culture.[38] Irish culture has been historically resistant to that which is different, associating the foreign with danger. These horror films examine cultural fears within generic conventions and prove the positivity of fluid and multiply identitied subjects. In their representation of Irish society and its fears they play an important cultural role. *Isolation* and *Boy Eats Girl* show the possibility that discourses of race and gender may reconfigure the fields of Irish studies and Irish cinema and thus create space for Meaney's vision of a newly visualised Ireland: 'the cultural maps that the new immigrants will produce, the possibility of a very differenced Ireland in the world'.[39]

Chapter Thirteen

BECOMING-WOMAN: TRANSFORMATIONS IN THE INTERSTICE IN THE CINEMA OF NEIL JORDAN

Jenny O'Connor

Introduction: new perspectives on Jordan

Traditionally, academics have focused upon thematic, historical or stylistic considerations of Neil Jordan's work (nationhood; male adolescence; Gothic fantasy; and the conflict between tradition and modernity)[1] but there is an absence of analysis on the philosophical nature of his cinema. Perhaps there are those who believe that a philosophical approach to Jordan's cinema (or Irish cinema in general) has little to offer the film critic. This essay argues to the contrary. Philosophy and cinema are natural bedfellows; each offers us a new way to think about the other. Moving images are not merely representations or icons of things in the 'real' world that make us re-examine that world; rather, cinema itself is an immediate force that can enable us to feel and think differently by offering entirely new ways to connect our bodies and brains to the screen.

Thus, cinema offers us new philosophies. However, philosophy also offers us altogether new images of cinema, as I will demonstrate through the subsequent analyses of this essay. Specifically, the theories of Deleuze and Guattari have not been taken up in the many interpretations of Neil Jordan's cinematic output, although there are a number of overlapping philosophical concerns that are central to both that cinema and those theories. Deleuze's work, of course (along with his collaborations with Guattari) is currently highly popular among scholars in cultural studies, film studies and feminist theory.[2] Operating within what could be termed a materialist, post-semiotic turn, it asks us to reject the idea that there is some firm ground from which we can explain the world; instead, we form images of ourselves and of the world that are in continual flux.[3] The great potential that is generated by Deleuzoguattarian theory is the revitalisation of ideas and concepts of other philosophies and other theories (such as psychoanalysis). While Jordan challenges the psychoanalytic roots of everyday life in his films, Deleuze and Guattari challenge the psychoanalytic roots of contemporary (film) theory. For Deleuze and Guattari, the only way to understand the subject and the world, the only way to '*really think*', is to eschew phallocentric structures and to understand life as a continual becoming in a time that flows in all directions.[4] In this context, film theory is merely another attempt to ground cinema in genre, language or history and, just as Deleuze queries the nature of philosophy and of life, we must explode film theory from within.

The aim of this essay is to look at two of Jordan's films – *Breakfast on Pluto* (2006) and *The Crying Game* (1992) – in order to examine the ways in which Jordan operates within a philosophical space. In particular, what does Deleuzoguattarian theory reveal about his cinema that other theories do not? I would argue that it focuses discussion on the possibilities and potentialities of mixtures, hybrids and in-between spaces, as they attempt to move beyond phallogocentrism. As such, this emphasises transformation as a key philosophical concept in his cinema and marks it as a theoretical touchstone. The two films examined here will ask fundamental questions about the nature of becoming in each case. Does a Deleuzoguattarian reading of Jordan allow us access to those interstices of meaning that are otherwise obscured or invisible to those focused on familiar Jordanian tropes of identity or nationhood? Do Jordan's films enable a new reading of Deleuze and Guattari's theory of becoming-woman? And finally, do these films really allow for an exploration of alternative modes of becoming or do they instead continually resist the disruptive potential of enfleshed female subjectivities? To the first two questions, this essay will claim a resounding 'yes'. Examining *Breakfast on Pluto* and *The Crying Game* through this particular lens allows us access to the specificity of intermediate spaces that many other theoretical and interpretative positions fail to acknowledge. Furthermore, these hybrid spaces play a crucial role in the disruption of phallogocentric structures in Jordan's cinema. In this way,

Jordan's work constructs a very specific and unique deployment of Deleuze and Guattari's becoming-woman theory; questions relating to the potentiality of Jordan's films and Deleuze and Guattari's theory for feminism, however, reveal a subliminal phallogocentrism which perhaps works against this potentiality.

Becoming and hybridity

The terms 'homosocial' and 'heterosocial' are key to Deleuze and Guattari's concept of 'becoming-woman'. 'Homosocial' refers to the dominant patriarchal structure of society in which men form (heterosexual) alliances with one another and women are sidelined or exchanged as tokens between men. The ultimate signifier of such a society is the nuclear family. 'Heterosocial' unions are formed by those outside, or on the margins, of such dominant structures and in these unions alliances are created between (predominantly) gay men and women. Becoming-woman, as it is articulated in *A Thousand Plateaus*, is not related to gender or sexuality, but is a move away from patriarchal, homosocial man and hierarchical constructs – it is an ungendered alternative to phallocentric structures. To become-woman, then, is to engage in a very real process of undoing, disassembling, rebuilding. It is a means by which to shed the skin of gender ideologies, and reveal new surfaces beneath. This process has no ending. The shedding is continuous, is integral to the becoming itself. However, there is no essence to becoming, no central truth to be gleaned at the heart of it. It is simply another way to live, an alternative practice of existence that does not privilege patriarchy, or matriarchy, or any gendered system of organisation at all. It is an unfolding and a refolding of identity, until that identity is no longer restricted by fixed terms. With such a shifting collective identity, those who actively become automatically place themselves outside the dominant phallogocentric nexus. With patriarchy superseded in this way, and not replaced with an alternative arboreal system, becoming is the new alternative to binary logic; not antithetical, not opposite, but rhizomatic.[5]

Becoming-woman takes place on risky bodies, on in-between bodies, on bodies that are willing to enter into an alliance with others. In Neil Jordan's cinema, the figure of the in-between wo/man is undoubtedly risky, in that it resides on the borders between gender definitions. The character of Patrick 'Kitten' Braden, for example, in *Breakfast on Pluto* inhabits a multiplicity of subject positions and has a unique ability to form alliances with marginalised 'others'. She is an interstice of potential, existing simultaneously in the troubled era of 1970s Ireland and in an alternative universe and period. While violence erupts in her hometown, she occupies a space of peace. Her innocence allows her to make positive connections with the people she encounters and territory is irrelevant to the establishment of her identity. In England, she is described as a 'Paddy', but in Ireland she is seen to be a creature from another world altogether – not masculine or feminine, not Irish or British (or Indian squaw). It is upon the feminised male body of Kitten that discourses of identity (about nationhood, sexuality and gender) emerge.

Kitten's enfleshed body – the masculine swathed in femininity – is that of Cillian Murphy, the pellucid-eyed masculine 'gamine' (Fig. 13.1).[6] Murphy is entirely aware of his ability to portray beauty, to perform femininity:

> I kind of knew very early on that I could do the looking pretty, looking beautiful stuff; it was to back that up with the soul of the character, that was the challenge [. . .] But it was a joy, I loved doing all of that – that's what we do, we put on clothes and we put on funny voices. You get into looking pretty and beautiful very easily. The only thing I did that was sore was shaving the legs, and chaffing, but you know nothing that was unbearable. There were a lot of hours in make-up; you have to commit to it 100%, so I did.[7]

By exploring the role of clothing in the manufacture of gender signifiers, gender can be deterritorialised and the process of becoming can begin. In this role, Murphy challenges laws of gender that are paradoxically reinforced by clothing, undoing 'the straitjacket of phallocentrism'.[8] The result is the creation of a multiple and univocal being that is unfettered by the binary logic of gender difference.

For Deleuze and Guattari, the process of becoming-woman is not only concerned with transgressing the boundaries of gender but the boundaries of any label that attempts to fix identity. Kitten, like Murphy, temporarily challenges phallocentric laws through her feminine clothing, but her becoming-woman takes place when she moves to London and puts her body at risk. The escape from her

Fig. 13.1 Cillian Murphy as Patrick 'Kitten' Braden in Neil Jordan's
Breakfast on Pluto, 2005.

home town is both a fantastical and real line of flight from Kitten's
everyday existence. In London, she can indulge the fluidity of her
multiple identities: film-star, peep-show girl, Womble, magician's
assistant, Tory prime minister. Kitten insists on becoming as a
means of escape from phallocentric laws; for example, she finds
herself a suspect in a terrorist nightclub bombing, but when questioned about her role in the bombings, she loses herself in a fantasy
in which she fends off IRA conspirators with her Chanel No. 5
perfume and her raw sexuality. She becomes by forming alliances
with both real and fantasy figures and by refusing to settle on one
identity. Jordan's film enables Kitten to cast off the shackles of
nation, of gender and of sexuality, and to exist in a utopian model of
kinship provided through the formation of a heterosocial family:
transvestite (Kitten), black, pregnant IRA widow (Charlie) and

priest (Fr Liam). Becoming occurs not by filiation, but by contagion:[9] Kitten does not have to possess the feminine ability to procreate in order to become-woman or form a family, but instead she continually engages in the rabid process of becoming that will never end. Her family is not connected through blood, but through affiliation. The Oedipal model of desire is overthrown, and is replaced with a productive heterosocial network that collectively becomes-woman, and is not afraid to evolve beyond itself (Charlie and Kitten eventually move back to London, without Fr Liam).

A similar negation of homosociality, and an apparent choosing of the heterosocial that is enabled through a becoming-woman, takes place in Jordan's *The Crying Game*. Here is where we first encounter the persistent and troubling paradox in these films, of course: the most challenging female roles are in fact played by men. The heterosocial, thus, can sometimes appear as an inversion of (rather than an alternative to) the homosocial. Crucially, the only biological woman in the film, Jude, is a monstrous 'ice lady', and the audience is encouraged to vilify this feminine atrocity. Once again, the transvestite figure Dil passes for female, and much attention has been given in studies of this film to a 'lack of castration' anxiety, an inversion of Freud's original theory. Žižek notes, for example, that Fergus' disgust at seeing Dil's penis is caused by the fact that he sees something where he expected to see nothing.[10] However, in the film's 'money shot', when it is revealed to Fergus (and the audience), the phallus is resignified. It is no longer merely a potent symbol of masculine power, but also the barrier to sexual fulfilment and the gateway for Fergus to begin a process of becoming-woman. In facing his fear of what the phallus represents, Fergus must reassess the system of hegemonic fear and violence that he has thus far operated within. Dil's penis is, on the one hand, the phallic order, yet on the other it represents a type of physical philosophical nomadism by reinscribing the phallus with an inherent ability to subvert itself. The enfleshed appendage thus has a dual function: to remind us of the ever-present phallic order and to draw our attention to the necessity of deterritorialising it. Dil becomes-woman, her risky body visible for all to see, but she also enables Fergus to continue the process of becoming-woman that he begins when he forms an alliance with Jody, the British soldier that Fergus' unit capture and hold hostage.

This relationship with Jody is the starting point of Fergus' journey through the phallogocentric matrix. The intimacy that is nurtured between them (they quickly develop terms of endearment for each other, for example, and Fergus even takes out Jody's penis when he wants to urinate and holds his hands to enable him to lean forward) is Fergus' first step towards becoming-woman. Jody shares stories about Dil, who was his girlfriend in London, telling Fergus that, unlike other women, she is 'no trouble at all'. Instead, she is (like Eily, Kitten's biological mother) the 'Lady as inaccessible Object',[11] the perfect Ideal that only exists (in the first half hour of the film) as a photographic reproduction of the original. The homo-erotic support network that develops between Fergus and Jody is cemented through this discussion of Dil, and she at first appears to be the object of exchange within a homosocial framework. However, we discover later that Jody's love for Dil is a heterosocial celebration of the Other rather than the homosocial fear/ fetishisation of it. The constant oscillation between homo- and hetero-social networks is another example of thinking the spaces in between binaries. If, as Deleuze and Guattari state, 'the self is only a door, a becoming between two multiplicities',[12] then Fergus is a gateway between his hetero- and homo-social selves.

Through the catalyst of Jody, the multiplicity of the self is triggered and rhizomatic lines of flight emerge. These lines of flight escape from Fergus-as-molar-entity[13] (who is caught within the patriarchal system) and settle on a plane of possibility where gender and sexuality exist in the intermezzo, between binaries.[14] When he travels to London, Fergus' very body is under the threat of retaliation and violence. His body-under-threat seeks out Dil's risky body and together they grapple with the practicalities and sexual etiquette of life in the interstice. Dil, under the impression that Fergus already understands the nature of her body, reveals all to him and forces him to confront the possibility that the feminine may not be as transparent as Jody assured him. Instead, the feminine here is drawn as an enfleshed contradiction.

Despite the fact that Dil is biologically male, she is the most challenging example of femininity in the film. She questions patriarchy by embodying the Other, by creating a gap between appearance and reality. The paradox remains, however, that a feminist-enfleshed subject (an embodied, multiple subject who challenges patriarchal structures) is not enough to challenge Fergus' dedication to homosociality, despite the fact that becoming-woman is a way of dismantling the very principles on which it is based. For Deleuze and Guattari, '[t]he question is not, or not only, that of the organism, history and subject of enunciation that oppose masculine to feminine in the great dualism machines. The question is fundamentally that of the body – the body they steal from us in order to fabricate opposable organisms.'[15] Dil does not allow her body to be stolen from her in this way, but her body *as a feminine one* is stolen from Fergus' idealised version of her. Violence is the instant reaction to the revelation of the penis when Fergus realises this 'crime'; he hits Dil in the face, knocking her over. The distinction between hitting a woman and hitting a man is implicit here: once Fergus is shocked into seeing things as they 'really' are, the recourse to violence is seen to be a natural consequence of the re-establishment of the homosocial order. He vomits and leaves.

On his next visit to The Metro bar, Fergus notices that men in drag adorn the place; he is unsettled at the thought that he knew all along, that his 'safe' homosocial vision of transgressive social spaces has proved unreliable. His desire is as yet molar, not molecular: he is governed by psychoanalytic consciousness, by moral rationality. Until Fergus extracts himself from the restraints of psychoanalysis, where guilt and fear reign, and explores the psychoanalytic drives in a schizo way, he is forced to repeat this reaction; to regurgitate again and again his masculine molarity. Deleuze and Guattari privilege schizoanalysis, which they view as a rhizomatic system, over psychoanalysis: an arborescent, or tree-root system. Psychoanalysis, they argue, dictates to the unconscious, limits possibilities and restricts flows. While they regard as positive the focus of psychoanalysis on the 'drives', they argue that, as Braidotti articulates, 'psychoanalytic theory and practice end up closing the very door they had initially opened'.[16]

The molecular line of flight towards a becoming-woman, Deleuze and Guattari argue, is not a libidinised one. On the contrary, Fergus' initial reaction to Dil's hybridity demonstrates that in psychoanalysis, 'the libido suffuses everything'.[17] Deleuze and Guattari redefine love in schizoanalytical terms:

> What does it mean to love somebody? It is always to seize that person in a mass, extract him or her from a group [. . .] then to find that person's own packs, the multiplicities he or she encloses

within himself or herself which may be of an entirely different nature. To join them to mine, to make them penetrate mine, and for me to penetrate the other person's.[18]

The subsequent relationship between Fergus and Dil after the 'discovery' is ultimately molecular, in that they enter into an interactive relationship based on mutual, transformative care. This is a deterritorialising relationship, in which one is altered, as is the other, through their rhizomatic connections. The final scene in prison is symptomatic of this, as Fergus, now the prisoner, recites Jody's story of the scorpion and the frog crossing the river (in which the scorpion, on the frog's back, stings it, killing them both – because it's in its 'nature' to do so) in response to Dil's question about why he is doing time for her. Fergus, the passive frog, and Dil, the dangerous scorpion, are not bound to their roles as the fable suggests. Instead, they are each reterritorialised through their love of the other: Dil becomes a nurturing, patient girlfriend, bringing Jimmy vitamins and telling him she will wait for him, while Jimmy divorces himself from such phallocentric notions of 'nature' that restrict heterosocial unions and proves that he will put himself on the line for his love of the hybrid Other.

In the deconstruction of binaries, the unsettling of patriarchy and the schizoanalytical approach to desire, an interstice of possibility is created; yet it is an interstice in which there are, once again, only patriarchal concerns at the core. It would seem, from an analysis of the characters in the two films, that the concept of woman is merely a device through which the male characters can escape the chains of gender-binding systems. So I would like to now turn to a consideration of the female characters in these two films, so as to examine their position in relation to becoming. According to Deleuze and Guattari, girls and women do not belong to any sex, grouping or order. They are, from a young age, diverted away from male behaviour and encouraged to be the idealised Other; therefore, they have the potential to slip through the net, defy dualisms and embody and define themselves.[19] This begs the pertinent question: within the deterritorialised system in which Deleuze and Guattari, and Jordan, operate, is there any room for feminist identity politics at all, or must feminism literally leave behind the female protagonist in order to 'get over' itself?

Deleuzoguattarian theory and the problematic question of 'woman'

In *Breakfast on Pluto*, Mr Feely tells Patrick early in the film that his mother was 'swalleyed up' by the city of London many years ago and calls her 'the most beautiful girl in the town'. Later, Kitten elaborates on this tale, telling the police to look for Eily Bergin in the house that vanished. The oral ingestion of the maternal by the urban and the disappearance of the feminine recalls feminist critic Luce Irigaray's discussion of the 'elsewhere' of female pleasure. As Irigaray states, '[t]hat *"elsewhere" of female pleasure* might rather be sought first in the place where it sustains ek-stacy in the transcendental. The place where it serves as security for a narcissism extrapolated into the "God" of men.'[20] For Kitten, the 'God' of man is her biological father, and her mother is the simulacrum of a film star – not the same, not a copy, but a version of the original (and already multiple). A version of Mitzi Gaynor is 'played' by Eily Bergin and the 'plot' of this narrative involves escaping from the dull and dreary border town. In this case, however, Eily is neither actress nor star; she turns out instead to be somebody else's wife, somebody else's mother.

With the two ideologies at odds here – the search for the female elsewhere (where Eily can find a god that is not phallocratic) and the preoccupation with the idealised lady (that Žižek describes as a 'narcissistic projection whose function is to render invisible the traumatic, intolerable dimension')[21] – Kitten fantasises a rape sequence in her school essay, 'Breakfast on Pluto', that is both comical and speaks of such repressed desire.[22] In this fantasy, her mother occupies the no-nonsense role of moral and virtuous abstract Ideal, who comments on the awakening of Fr Liam's sexual desire thus: 'Whoops! My skirt and housecoat are riding up. Better abort this task at once or we could have an exploding clergyman filling the air with pent-up sexual energy.' She soon realises that 'it wasn't Fairy Liquid he'd been playing with down there', which concludes Kitten's story about her conception. This tale of Freudian forbidden love and the repression of Oedipal desires is predictably met with dismay by the Christian Brothers. The language of naked and inappropriate desire between a woman and a man made in the image and likeness of God (the ultimate phallocrat) is not permitted.

Irigaray goes on to say that the expression of female pleasure is forbidden within the patriarchal structure, in which the God of man and the God of woman are irreconcilable. The God of man calls for women to offer up their sexuality and pleasure, and the language of both, to ensure the smooth running of androcentric concerns. The God of woman comes into being when woman crosses 'through the mirror' of binary division, into that elsewhere of self-affection, where feminine pleasure will not be ingurgitated by the phallic order. Eily's character embodies the paradox between a feminine Other that defies classification and ventures through the mirror into a realm of feminist self-affection, and the conduit for apprehending knowledge of the father, a 'spiritual guide into the higher sphere of religious ecstasy'.[23] The image of her on the red bus marks her becoming-woman: she travels away from the God of man, away from the father and the son, towards a beyond of possibility. Her becoming takes place on a risky body: a body that refutes the expectation of maternal love in favour of a self-affection. This fascinates Kitten, rather than disappointing her, creating an obsession that is focused on discovering the ingested (m)other.

When Kitten finally meets Eily, she dresses as Margaret Thatcher, and attempts to embody the 'English . . . Conservative . . . powerful' woman (as she describes herself in the film). She plays a British Telecom employee and asks questions about the telephone habits of the household, gleaning information about Eily's marital status and family along the way. The discovery that Kitten makes when she finally tracks her down in London is that Eily has reverted to the mother of a nuclear family, a position that Kitten herself cannot reconcile with the 'swalleyed' 'Phantom Lady' of her imagination. She has regressed back to the family, that which Deleuze and Guattari accuse of thwarting the schizophrenic endeavour, of 'distorting and disfiguring social desiring-production, leading it into an impasse'.[24] In this way, Eily embodies a central challenge presented by the becoming process: it appears to be more easily accessible to men than it is to women. Her line of flight to London, as becoming, has been thwarted and she has been re-instated as woman-as-other to phallogocentric man. It seems Jordan here cannot envision a becoming specific to the female body.

In Rosi Braidotti's view, Deleuze is 'stuck on a fundamental ambivalence about the position of sexual difference within his own project of "becoming-woman"'.[25] Braidotti is reluctant to offer up the feminist subject to the 'becoming-woman' framework, and to deny in the process the validity of the sexually differentiated female subject position. However, she views the process of becoming as coterminous with the Deleuzoguattarian concept of nomadism. In Braidotti's words, 'The nomadic or intensive horizon is a subjectivity "beyond gender" in the sense of being dispersed, not binary, multiple, not dualistic, interconnected, not dialectical and in a constant flux, not fixed.'[26] Therefore, as already noted, the process of becoming-woman is not only about gender, but about identity in general. Yet the kernel of the problematic term 'becoming-*woman*' remains.

The process of becoming-woman does essentially negate the materialism of the feminist subject, and so could be said to negate feminism itself. However, if becoming-woman is a process that undoes patriarchy, then surely it is a feminist process. Rosi Braidotti notes that becoming-woman offers us new possibilities out of the deadlock of Woman as the Other of the Same.[27] However, she does repeatedly claim that we need to be more attentive to the differences of gendered becomings, as sexed bodies experience the process differently. While the work of Jordan and the theories of Deleuze and Guattari may suggest 'a new kind of masculine style of philosophy [. . .] which has learned to undo the straight-jacket of phallocentrism',[28] it still remains focused on a masculine starting point. The figure of Jude exemplifies this (Fig. 13.2). A monstrous, inhuman character, she is akin to the 'traumatic Woman-Thing' of Žižek's courtly love trope, a femme fatale who attempts to 'bring ruin to the hard-boiled hero'.[29] However, this is not a 'straight' film noir in any sense, and Jude's inhumanity can be seen to be monstrous. Jude becomes-mad before she becomes-woman, which inevitably results in psychosis instead of schizosis.

At the beginning of *The Crying Game*, Jude engages in a gender performativity rather than a becoming-woman: dressed in a denim mini-skirt, she constructs herself as an object of desire for the male gaze to apprehend. Once she has engineered the capture of Jody, her make-up and high heels are removed and she is revealed to be a phallic woman. When Jody attacks her, she shudders and tells Fergus that it was not easy to have him 'all over' her, but suggestively admits that 'one of you made me want it'. Moving within and without the male expectation of female desire, Jude lures Fergus into an embrace.

However, shortly thereafter, she abandons any semblance of compassion for Fergus or Jody and begins her journey through becoming-monster (her monstrosity deriving from a psychotic determination to maintain the patriarchal order) before death. Eily's becoming could not be imagined in *Breakfast on Pluto*, while Jude's becoming in *The Crying Game* is configured in terms of the negative. It is impossible because it is made to move in the wrong direction; it is not rhizomatic and productive, but molar and reductive. It moves forward towards a goal of power instead of in all directions, with the process as the prize.

The much-maligned character of Jude has been discussed broadly as a 'femme fatale' figure in Emer Rockett and Kevin Rockett's book on Jordan,[30] as well as in Žižek's essay on courtly love. Yet this interpretation does not reach the core of the process of becoming (or

Fig. 13.2 Miranda Richardson as Jude in Neil Jordan's
The Crying Game, 1992.

reversal thereof) on which Jude destructively embarks. Rather than simply operating as one who brings about the downfall of the male hero, she exists independently as an in-between of feminine masculinity, or masculine femininity, the most heinous of creatures imaginable. Jude cannot be female Other outside the Pale of andro-centric society and virtual male inside the border of phallogocentric dominance and power. Therefore, she must choose. By becoming-monster, she embraces the contradiction, yet she also attempts to become-man, which can never be successful: 'there is no becoming-man because man is the molar entity par excellence, whereas becomings are molecular.'[31] Jude's endeavour is misconceived, and her desire to be at the centre of the patriarchal circle is not subversive or challenging, but regressive and limiting. She is a woman who fails to see the disruptive power of the feminine. Like Dil, her clothes define the social perception of her, yet underneath, her biology betrays her. Dil is female with a penis; Jude is male with a vagina.

This is the crux of the problem for feminists: why is it that the male body can evolve beyond itself, while the female body cannot truly become? Why does the female figure function, once again, as the negative other through which the male self-defines? Why are Eily and Jude destined only to embody this anti-becoming? Although becoming-woman is the first step in the process, we find the female subject position immediately displaced and presented as a stepping-stone to other, more desirable becomings. For Deleuze and Guattari, this is not to supersede the importance of the role of the feminine, but rather to highlight it as a disruptive, schizophrenic force in itself. In *A Thousand Plateaus*, they tell us that while women must continue a feminist practice in order to reclaim their history and subjectivity, they must be careful not to confine that subjectivity to molar manifestations.[32] The power of the feminine is in its molecular, disruptive possibilities. It should be 'capable of crossing and impregnating an entire social field, and of contaminating men, of sweeping them up in that becoming'. However, they also state that woman 'as a molar entity has to become-woman in order that the man also becomes- or can become-woman'.[33] Thus, the problem lies in their indecision regarding whether or not the enfleshed subjects of 'girl' and 'woman' are important to, or embedded in, the becoming process itself. On the one hand, Deleuze and Guattari (and Jordan) privilege the female subject as one who can destabilise the phallogocentric regime; on the other, she merely enables man to free himself from his own shackles.

This problem is very clearly played out in Jordan's films, with the resultant contradictions regarding the role of the feminine in processes of phallogocentric destabilisation. In *The Crying Game*, while Dil's refutation of social convention is a positive statement of difference, Jude's desire (and Jordan's depiction of her desire) to be other than female Other is a disappointing return to the Same. Jude's dying desire is revealed in her last comment to Dil. By proclaiming 'you sick bitch', Jude accepts that Dil will be what she never will – a successful hybrid, a wo/man. In this depiction, the very contradictions at work in the Deleuzoguattarian theory of becoming are revealed. Thus, while Jordan's work can definitively be seen as limiting the potential of the enfleshed woman to truly become, from a more positive viewpoint his work does enable a philosophical consideration of the feminine that highlights the complexities and paradoxes inherent in the philosophical process of becoming itself.

Although it appears that Jordan's cinema can be 'read' according to Deleuzian tropes, classifications and concepts, it is his films themselves that *elicit* this reading. To ignore the multiplicity inherent in Jordan's films is to consign his oeuvre to the application of theories that prove or disprove his interest in themes such as nationality, the Gothic and male adolescence, all of which tend to focus on an identity model that ultimately fails to give a proper account of the mixtures and hybridities so crucial to his work. This is not to suggest that such interpretative readings of Jordan's films are invalid or irrelevant. The great potential that is generated by Deleuzoguattarian theory is the revitalisation of ideas and concepts of other philosophies and other theories and the forming of alliances and connections. For Deleuze and Guattari, a philosophy is a question or problem, not a solution, and their theories rework what has gone before and problematise it from a whole new perspective.

Therefore, the identification of the *processes* involved in becoming is a move away from the *application* of a theory or philosophy. Jordan's cinema aims to do what Deleuzoguattarian philosophies also attempt – to envisage the possibilities for disruption that emerge between categories, between binaries, between theories. Jordan's cinema, for all its alleged flaws (androcentrism, political bias, the need for narrative 'closure', etc.) is infused with a desire to go beyond boundaries – not to cross them, but to find oneself between genders, in the gap between sanity and madness, on the borderline between nationalities. It is from here that both Deleuze and Guattari, and Jordan, create their most interesting works – this cleft in the rock, this gap between territories. Therefore, it is only fitting to examine these diagnosticians of schizophrenic becomings in tandem with one another. While Jordan may be accused of instating the wo/man (rather than the woman) as the true figure of destabilisation of patriarchy, he nonetheless advocates the power of the hybrid, the possibility of the rhizome, the potential of the multiple to unsettle the binary rationality by which we live.

Chapter Fourteen

Mourning Sex: The Aesthetics of Queer Relationality in Contemporary Film

Fintan Walsh

[T]he subject's dispersal will come about, principally, through unexpected couplings – connections both to the human and the non-human . . .[1]

In a special issue of *Film Ireland* dedicated to exploring sex and sexuality in Irish film, guest editor Mark O'Halloran (writer and actor) recalls attending a conference at which he claimed that the Irish film industry was, relatively speaking, still in its infancy. Despite certain achievements, he suggested at the time that there were many avenues yet to be explored. Taking a prime example, O'Halloran pointed out that there had never been 'a great Irish erotic film', and that this was something he was hoping to create himself.[2] Relaying the occasion, O'Halloran remembers how the audience and panel started to laugh before another topic was briskly rolled out for discussion. Nonetheless, in the time that followed, he was prompted to think further about 'how sex, sexuality, and the erotic are dealt with by Irish artists in the film industry and also the reactions of Irish audiences'.[3] Conceding in his editorial preamble that sexual subjects are not strictly ignored within Irish film, O'Halloran concludes that they invariably appear as troublesome, and the erotic is generally sacrificed in the production of the distinctly Irish 'Sex Catastrophe Movie'. At the end of the foreword, O'Halloran asks timely questions that still concern Irish film and culture more broadly, and which reverberate to a certain degree throughout this essay: 'Is there room here for an Irish Almodóvar? Someone who will penetrate deep into the fun and frolics of our sexual identities?'[4]

215

I contributed an article to the same publication that rehearsed some ideas on representations of homosexuality and queerness in Irish film that I would like to develop further in this essay. What concerned me then, and now, is how sexuality has often been deployed in Irish film, and indeed many films about Ireland, to comment upon Mother Ireland and Father State, in a manner that stifles the erotic and forecloses its thematic and stylistic potential.[5] Within a largely narrativising film culture, sexuality has usually figured as an instrument of national reflection, rather than as a complex web of identifications, desires and affects, which I understand the term more accurately to index. Viewed against the outputs of our European neighbours, for example, there is little in Irish film to match the easy sexiness of Federico Fellini's work, the latent carnality of Luis Buñuel's, or the libidinous charge of Catherine Breillat's. Even in the films of Neil Jordan that are regularly lauded for their attentiveness to the subject, sexuality as a mobile charge that might flit between actors, spectators and their associated worlds is more often than not contained by rigid narrative and extensive allegory. This failure to explore sexuality as a discrete theme or intensity, rather than as national symbol or symptom, has certainly resulted in a slowness to represent a range of marginal subjectivities and practices, but it has arguably also yielded a relatively limited visual aesthetic. If one accepts that the cinematic and the sexual are affectively interrelated – that is to say, that the cinematic canvas operates both as an object and a subject of our desires – then the problem of erotic foreclosure, with which O'Halloran was concerned, might also be seen to reflect, if not exacerbate, a crisis of aesthetic invention.

One precedent to the emergence of the erotic in Irish film might be the queering of its aesthetic and cultural conventions. In a bid to consider this notion further, this essay aims to discern and describe a strand of what I'm framing as a queer representational aesthetic in Irish film, where desire and its excesses are cinematically animated through the collapse of difference and distinction. To an extent, I attempt to respond to O'Halloran's call in a small way, by examining a selection of his own collaborations with director Lenny Abrahamson. Focusing on A*dam and Paul* (2004) and *Garage* (2007), the essay strives to illuminate how these films might be seen to actually mourn the absence of the queer in Irish film and culture, and charts how this process operates on thematic, relational, ecological and aesthetic domains. Significantly produced and released at the height of the Celtic Tiger, these films focus our attention on lives lived on the margins of economic privilege, social mobility and cultural centrality.[6] The essay maintains that although the queer is only subtly implied in these works – in the odd couplings, frustrated desires and complex intimacies – in a timely fashion the films go some way to register the excluded place and space of queerness in Irish film and culture.[7]

Screening sexuality

Lance Pettitt has observed that film activity and homosexuality have shared 'a fractious, officially suspect existence in Ireland since before the state's formal inception in 1922'. In an essay entitled 'Pigs and Provos, Prostitutes and Prejudice: Gay Representation in Irish Film, 1984–1995', Pettitt focuses on the representation of homosexuality in films 'which represent gay male desire, narratives featuring men who choose men'. Pettitt understands gay representation in two related senses:

> Firstly, I use it to imply the experience of being subjected to a process of image-making in a society where, to misquote Jarman, 'heterosexuality is just common, not normal.' Secondly, I use it in the sense of gay men being active, productive agents, reading and making films in Irish society.[8]

Pettitt is correct to underscore how male homosexuality has been negatively imagined in Irish film and media, in addition to noting how female homosexuality has been rendered virtually invisible. The truth is that when homosexuality has historically appeared in Irish film or other modes of cultural representation, it has typically been linked to trauma, perversion, paedophilia, and a range of social and political tensions.[9] More recently still, the figure of the homosexual has stood in as a symbol of Irish cosmopolitanism. In both Liz Gill's *Goldfish Memory* (2003) and David Gleeson's *Cowboys & Angels* (2003), for example, gay and bisexual characters appear as pseudo-prophets of both sexual freedom and urban excitement. However, both films shy away from exploring the complexity of gay lives or homosexuality's history of representation in Ireland, in favour of exploiting the figure of the homosexual as a sparkly emblem of neo-liberalism. In this, queer sexuality can be seen to fulfil a highly symbolic role in Irish film, insofar as it marks the outermost limits of social degradation (usually associated with a past Ireland that we are trying to forget) and future possibility (the ideal Ireland we imagine, and attempt to purchase into being.) As a consequence of this complex, contradictory history of representation, the queer subject has been oddly evacuated of agency in the present, torn between his/her function as a symbol of national dystopia and utopia.

While some knowledge of this pattern of representation is useful for identifying oppressive mobilisations of power in Irish culture, I think it is also necessary to extend our understanding of what the term 'queer' might be taken to signify, in a way that allows us to account for a range of non-normative identities and relationalities which, although not expressly homosexual, are queerly unfixed and unsettling. One of my main conjectures is that the collaborations of Abrahamson and O'Halloran are among the closest examples of queer art cinema that Ireland has produced, likely escaping such an analysis so far because of the subtlety of their queer articulations.[10] In particular, *Adam & Paul* and *Garage* can be seen to counter the trend of negatively imagining sexuality on screen, either as national trauma or economic success, by situating their central subjects within a complex, unresolved domain of desire and otherness, which I understand to be a crucial strategy of queer figuration.[11] In both films, non-normative relationships between men negotiate hostile social milieus, and queerness saturates the cinematic landscape as a mark of loss and exclusion, but also as a force of possibility in the face of a precarious present and an uncertain future. Perhaps rather surprisingly, none of the main characters in these films openly declare their sexual desires, let alone engage in sex with other people. But this ambivalence only adds to the films' compelling queer resonances.

Thematics

Both *Adam & Paul* and *Garage* take disenfranchised men in contemporary Ireland as their focus subjects. The eponymous protagonists of the first film are working-class Dublin men who largely spend their time searching for drugs, or the means to acquire them. Events unfold over the course of a day during which the dejected characters, fondly drawn in the likeness of Laurel and Hardy or Vladimir and Estragon, set off from the urban wasteland in which they have spent the night. While the core action takes place in economically deprived pockets of inner-city Dublin, the film never lets the viewer dwell too much on material poverty. Nor does it indulge us with some of the opulent images of economic success that proliferated the Celtic Tiger imaginary. Rather, our eyes are always drawn to other dimensions of the film's core characters and their experience of the world: the palpable intimacy between Adam and Paul, the natural world which shimmers through the destitution, and moments of intensity between humans and their environments that emphasise the phenomenological charge of being. Although Adam and Paul ostensibly seek out drugs, they do so within the context of a more complex filmic journey, which might be defined as the desire to find meaning in an ostensibly hopeless situation. Unable to forge or effectively sustain links to their immediate community or the wider culture, the men are pitted into social and ultimately real death. So, in addition to the film's homosocial coupling, the desire for encounters beyond those immediately available to them marks the film as particularly queer.

On a thematic level, *Garage* presents something similar. The main character in this film is Josie, a man who lives and works alone in an isolated rural garage. Josie's desires are not directed towards material gains. Even though new apartments are being built all around the locality, and whispers maintain that the garage is to be sold to property developers, Josie neither has nor wishes for access to this wealth. Rather, he is primarily concerned with reaching out to others, even though he struggles desperately to do so, and despite the fact that many people resist him: the already-spoken-for Carmel; his teenage co-worker David and his group of friends; and a work-horse that occupies a nearby field. Rejected by Carmel, who can be seen to represent normative relationality, Josie is primarily drawn to David and his friends. When the law condemns this relationship after Josie shows the teenager pornography, the former returns to his favoured horse, before finally retreating to a river, in which he drowns himself. Josie and the non-normative model of relationality that develops around him are unsustainable in this world, and so he commits suicide.

Relations

While the notion of the male outsider connects these films on a thematic level, they are not simply narrative driven. Certainly an arc of development can be discerned, but the films are striking insofar as the dialogue is significantly reduced and restrained compared to mainstream commercial film at least, in a manner that angles our attention to other cinematic properties and aesthetic devices. On the issue of queer relationality in film, the work of Leo Bersani and Ulysse Dutoit is especially enlightening. In *Forms of Being: Cinema, Aesthetics, Subjectivity* (2004) Bersani and Dutoit consider unexpected couplings in Jean-Luc Godard's *Le Mépris* (1963), Pedro Almodóvar's *All About my Mother* (1999), and Terrence Malick's *The Thin Red Line* (1998). Taking each film in turn, the authors reveal how non-normative relationships between humans and non-humans are engendered when linguistic meaning fails or when individuals are failed by logocentric registers of knowledge. Such instances excite a dispersal of subjectivity that redirects *jouissance* as destruction, and leads the subject to encounter as 'allness' the impossible luminescence of being and becoming:[12]

> Immanent in every subject is its similitudes with other subjects (and other objects) – similitudes that are illuminate, that 'shine' into visibility when those others intersect with the subject's spatial or temporal trajectories. Traumatised perception shatters the security of realized psychic and social identities; it makes visible traces of everybody's limitless extensibility in both space and time. The connections are universally immanent.[13]

This interpretation of the relationship between aesthetics and sexuality is typical of Bersani's project in particular, which has long been concerned with the self-effacing capacities of both aesthetic and sexual experience. The self, Bersani asserts, is 'a practical convenience; promoted to the status of an ethical ideal, it is a sanction for violence'.[14] One might avoid 'the tyranny of the self',[15] he speculates, via the experience of *ébranlement* or self-shattering. Writing on Bersani and Beckett, Calvin Thomas describes this *ébranlement* as 'a beneficent crisis in selfhood [that] may be said to depend upon a specific moment of sexual practice or erotic exuberance'.[16] It is only through losing 'our selves' – that is, our egos – through our worldly engagements that we might find ourselves anew.

Adam & Paul and *Garage* also document queer couplings which, although constituted through social deprivation, ultimately become the occasion for precipitating, or at least signalling, other relational modes. To a certain extent, both films begin at a point of self-divesture insofar as the main characters are already undone through their social exclusion. Nonetheless, without being sentimentalised, as so many other contemporary films tend to do,[17] this primary exclusion is followed by other encounters that eroticise loss and mobilise an ethics of queer relationality quite unique in Irish film. For Bersani and Dutoit, the fragmentation of a stable sense of selfhood through contact with others or art provides the opportunity for reconfiguring our worldly relations: 'To open ourselves to these correspondences requires a relational discipline capable of yielding an ascetic pleasure that may, at least intermittently, supersede the *jouissance* of "the blindest fury of destructiveness."'[18] Revealing a similar logic, in both films in question, subjective crises provoke the search for other relational configurations.

Adam and Paul are clearly at odds with their wider social milieu. But further to their shared history of crime and drug-taking which is mapped out in the film, the men also recently lost their best friend, Matthew. Although the film does not foreground this as a consciously recognised loss, the deceased's family constantly remind the pair of how close they once were, and how they should appropriately mark his death, by remaining clean, sober, and observing traditional mourning rituals.

A number of scenes explicitly highlight the queerness of Adam and Paul's relationship next to those around them. The first occurs when they amble through St Stephen's Green where they meet their recently deceased friend's family and friends – Marion, Orla, Wayne and Georgie. Matthew's sister Marion is the spokesperson for the group, and she rages against the pair for being so disorganised and dishevelled. Although she claims to be having a picnic for the children, it is clear that her main intention is to drink in the park while the youngsters are left to fend for themselves. And even though Paul tries to engage one of the children, he is told by Wayne to stop frightening him, which he clearly is not doing. In foregrounding this tension, the film makes very clear that the normative family unit is far more dysfunctional than the loose, lyrical relationship between Adam and Paul.

Another scene develops this idea further. Shortly after leaving the park, Adam and Paul walk into the flat of Matthew's partner, Janine. Their plan to steal a television is spoiled when they hear a baby cry. Entering one of the bedrooms, the men find the infant unattended, and cradle it together. During this scene, the film switches from witty, poetic realism towards something altogether more earnest and dream-like. The sounds of the immediate environment are blocked out while soft music picks out the atmosphere, and warm close-ups screen the men lovingly embracing the child. Janine joins in, as if to complete the unlikely configuration of melancholic lovers. (At another stage, she tells her baby 'Say day-day to your daddies.') Here, a number of losses appear to be mourned: the loss of a friend, lover and father, and the loss of Adam and Paul's (re)productive futures, in terms of children but also social opportunity. But supplementary to this negativity, the rich affective power of the scene exposes a queer intimacy independent of the normative family unit, where loss might be overcome through an alternative configuration of bodies and desires. Here, this potentiality registers as four bodies melting into one. However, at this stage, this is only a possibility, and no sooner has the soft sequence played out than it is repeated in real time with Janine interrupting the scenario to aggressively interrogate the men as to what they are doing in her apartment.

This scenario can be read to both deftly critique heteronormative constructions of the family, while also suggesting that the same world can neither support nor provide for couplings like Adam and Paul. Although Janine was once an addict too, she is currently sober, and brother Wayne rewards her by buying furnishings for her flat. But Adam and Paul have no interest in the building blocks of heteronormative life, or the material excesses in which the Ireland of the film's setting gorged upon. As Paul comically puts it, the material world is always already lost: 'Crazy, spending all your money on your flat [. . .] only gets robbed in the end.'

Another scene crystallises this resistance to normative imaginaries. Wallowing after a long day of meandering, Adam and Paul sit outside an apartment that is being raided by the police for drugs. Suddenly, a bag of heroin lands at their feet, and they immediately shoot up. The bright lights of the city sharpen, and music takes over as they loll about in slow motion. As the couple loop across James Joyce Bridge, with an image of Joyce in the background, the scene is framed as a kind of contemporary Dublin Odyssey.[19] But if it is the experience of drugs that allows the men to rehearse liberating dissolution, it is the occasion's aesthetic mediation which affords the spectator access to a similar phenomenon. The camera pans closely over the men's bodies and faces, no longer separate beings but part-objects circulating in a greater ecosphere of human and non-human intensities. For Bersani and Dutoit, this kind of doubling and dispersal of forms might be seen 'to propose an ontology of universal immanence: the surfaces of all things "quiver" from the presence within them of all the other things to which they relate'. [20] Albeit through the stimulus of drugs, the scene manages to quite movingly convey something of the characters' participation in a vast spectrum of being, as they ecstatically conjoin the world around them.

Although we are given a ready-made couple in *Adam & Paul*, the central protagonist of *Garage* must negotiate a range of relationships by himself. Josie lives alone, and most of his daily interactions are passing exchanges that take place around the buying and selling of goods: with his boss, who employs him; with the lorry driver to whom he supplies diesel (and who in return brings him pornography from Amsterdam); and with Carmel, the local shopkeeper. Out of these, Josie's relationship to Carmel is most interesting. She has been jilted by Breffni, a boorish man who gets great pleasure from ridiculing Josie whenever he can. In their inability to relate, the couple paints a picture of heteronormative relationality as unyielding and violent. Even Carmel, the ostensibly spurned lover, while initially kind to Josie, eventually humiliates him in public when he touches her back while dancing. What is most curious about this moment is that Josie says or does little to suggest that he is actually interested in Carmel sexually. In fact, he is just as likely seeking friendship. Rather, it is Carmel's paranoiac insistence on categorising him as a sexual aggressor, because he is unlike other men and does not declare his desire, that produces the tension. This is the first of a number of rejections that Josie endures which work to undermine normative relationality, while prompting him to seek intimacy elsewhere.

Carmel aside, Josie seems to be most obviously drawn towards David, a teenage Goth who takes on a part-time job in the garage. At first, it seems that Josie is being used to supply David and his friends with drink, but later it appears as though the pair have developed a genuine friendship that rarely expresses itself in words, but in moments of silent companionship. Unlike other characters in the film, Josie's attachments are not rigidly defined, and he seems oblivious to the codings of gender, sex, age, and indeed respectability that are so important to others. In his relationship with David, this blindness becomes his downfall. Josie shows the teenager sexually explicit material, not to pressure or seduce him into a sexual scenario but out of the pursuit of titillation, a confused desire for shared experiences, or some preconceived notion of what the boy would like to see. Nonetheless, Josie's relationship with David is the most significant of his human encounters. Ultimately, it is pathologised and criminalised in the eyes of those around him, and he is violently disenfranchised.

Josie's most steadfast relationship, however, is with the horse he regularly visits. He first notices the animal while returning from Carmel's shop, where she gives him free apples to take home. Carmel encourages him to take the fruit, underscoring the biblical resonance by saying that they are 'half-rotten like the rest of us'. In the next scene, Josie feeds the apples to the horse, in a gesture that transfers the rotten objects of desire between human and animal worlds, and anticipates the trajectory of Josie's desire. Following on, the horse becomes Josie's closest friend, and he regularly stops off to feed it. Although others destroy human life (in the way Josie is rejected), and the lives of other animals (local man Sully drowns a litter of puppies), Josie's truest expressions of affection are with the horse. Although he naïvely advises David that 'the town looks out for its own', this is certainly not the case for him.

Ecologies

Even though both *Adam & Paul* and *Garage* screen socially disenfranchised men who find intimacy in non-normative relationships, these disparate connections extend beyond human and animal worlds to include the natural world and the potential it seemingly emanates. Luciana Parisi's writing on 'hypernature' offers us one way of thinking about sexual ecologies in the space of technology as processes of becoming involving a multiplicity of elements. For Parisi, the term hypernature is diagrammatic of the 'destratification of sex [. . .] intersecting the biological, biocultural and bio-digital organizations of a body-sex'.[21] Parisi writes, 'Hypernature unfolds an ecosystem of micro-relations between bodies that defines the potential of a body-sex to become.'[22] I also see something of a destratification at play in the films in question, by which sexuality not only becomes desexed, degendered, and even decorporealised, but redistributed among human and non-human worlds – even between the screen and the spectator. While the films narratively document bleak social circumstances, they are shot in a way that highlights the exchange of energy and influence between human and non-human forces, or what Jane Bennett refers to in *Vibrant Matter: A Political Ecology of Things* (2010) as the 'vibrant materiality' of all objects.[23]

The exacting opening shots of *Adam & Paul* are of flowers and water, and these eventually give way to Adam and Paul sleeping together on a mattress, in a grim urban outpost. Following the men's confrontation with the family in the park, the camera takes a number of seconds to register the extraordinary oak tree under which the group sits. Adam and Paul are posited in a triangulated relationship with the society from which they are excluded, and the natural world which seems ripe with promise. The pair appear most at home in the world when they take drugs, and suddenly everything becomes fluid and vibrant, border free and care free. Nonetheless, when Adam dies on the beach at the end of the film – now underneath one Poolbeg tower, rather than two as in the opening sequence – this ecological significance is reinforced. When Paul realises that his friend has passed away on the strand, he turns from the city that lies behind them, and faces the ocean. During the prolonged shot we wonder if he might even kill himself. However, he chooses to continue his precarious existence and, taking the necessaries from Adam's coat, walks on.

Garage similarly opens with a series of shots of the natural world that establish an important association between Josie and the environment in which he finds himself: a grassy bridge – peat – trees. Josie walks through this evocative terrain in the opening sequence: the colours almost seem to bleed into him, or from him. His relationship with the horse is always expressed in terms that visually impress the necessity of sharing natural resources and space: around the fields, progress is afoot, and the natural world is under pressure. When Josie kills himself at the end of the film, the scene is performed without any morbid anticipation. His actual death is not shown, and his passing is framed as an obvious return to nature: river – darkness – bog – birds – trees – horse.

By a lakeside Mr Skerrit confides in Josie about having his son taken away from him by his wife many years previously. Breaking down in tears, to Josie's embarrassment, he confesses, 'You think it's going to stop – it never stops.' When Josie turns the conversation to the building developments in the town, he retorts, 'Ah to hell with the town Josie. No such things as towns anymore.' For Skerrit and Josie, socio-economic change has led to alienation. The striking closing shot of the film, in which the horse defiantly walks along the tracks that Josie once walked, directly towards the screen, is the only sign that the film world offers to mark Josie's passing. It is a gesture that both mourns his death and admonishes the community (which includes us) for allowing it to happen.

Queer aesthetics and Irish film culture

Critical responses to Irish film have traditionally drawn upon socio-logical paradigms inherited from Irish literary and cultural studies. As a result, vocabularies that might best respond to changes in visual practice are still evolving. While this essay has proposed some of the ways in which *Adam & Paul* and *Garage* can be seen to envisage particular kinds of queer subjects, experiences and relationships to the world, the work of Patricia MacCormack allows us to consider the notion of queer spectatorship in a broader sense. For if we are to seriously consider the significance of queerness in Irish film and culture, then a deeper understanding of the link between represen-tation and spectatorship is required.

In her book *Cinesexuality* (2008), MacCormack draws upon Gilles Deleuze's writing on immanence to imagine proliferative circuits of desire linking humans and non-humans in the cinematic space: 'Desire is the undifferentiated flow connecting bodies, power, society and ecosophical territories, within the folds and between all rela-tions.'[24] Further to this, MacCormack emphasises the fused aesthetic and sexual appeal of the cinematic image, and its potential effect on the spectator: 'The image is as capable of materially transforming and affecting its disciple as is the flesh of the lover, albeit perhaps through different configurations of libidinal plateaus.'[25] In particular, she argues that imagistic elements compel the viewer above all else: 'Colour saturation, gesture, angular and corporeal inflection, timbre, camera velocity and trajectory, the familiar become unfamiliar.'[26]

Perhaps most important to this essay, MacCormack foregrounds the filmic image's invite to think desire beyond dialectics, in a way that complements Bersani's and Dutoit's writing on the self-displacing effects of art, and in a manner which endeavours to dodge the deadlocks of narrative film and its criticism. To think about aesthetics and sexuality in dialectical terms, MacCormack maintains, is also to reify the normative and foreclose other forms of co-mergence:

> Desire beyond dialectics is the vertiginous nothing that is fully present through us and we through it. Reifying cinema as part of repetitive systems of heterosexuality, homosexuality, male, female and the many other binaries which are the paradigmatic spine of the social corpus not only preserves those systems but allows the very idea of the human to emerge via the way the spectator inserts themselves into the possibilities of the self an image offers [. . .] Images do not represent or describe entities but make their possibility in the world. [27]

Although MacCormack focuses mainly on Baroque film, her work underscores the queer attributes of aesthetics, and their role in the queering of the spectatorial experience and, by extension, maybe even our way of queerly viewing and making the world. While there is nothing in Abrahamson's and O'Halloran's oeuvre that approximates the visual feast of the Gothic, their collaborations stand out for offering a subtle queer perspective on Irish urban and rural life during a period of unprecedented monetary mythologising and prosperity for some. In his preface to MacCormack's book, series editor Michael O'Rourke develops Jacques Rancière's ideas on the 'distribution of the sensible', which appraise the socio-political implications of sensory apprehension and action.[28] In coming to images, O'Rourke suggests, we may be able 'to remap the territories of the visible, thinkable, sayable, doable, knowable [. . .] In this way *coming to* images anticipates what Rancière calls a "community to-come", the becoming-queer of *all* viewers.'[29] Despite the erotic dearth in Irish film, which I mentioned at the outset of this essay with reference to O'Halloran's concerns, his own creative coupling with Abrahamson has resulted in films that can be seen to mourn this cultural absence while signalling ways in which a queer tendency might extend our relational and aesthetic possibilities. At best their work creates an aesthetic breach in the Irish cultural imaginary that both returns something of what has been repressed or refused recognition, and resists foreclosure in the present.

NOTES AND REFERENCES

INTRODUCTION (Bracken and Radley)

1 See 'The Fun Starts Here' (Red Rage Films, 2010), http://www.youtube.com/watch?v=F-cwJXvBG7k [accessed 19 August 2010].

2 In the visual arts, two notable examples are Fintan Cullen's *Visual Politics: Representation of Ireland 1750–1950* (Cork: Cork University Press, 1995) and Fintan Cullen and John Morrison (eds), *A Shared Legacy: Essays on Irish and Scottish Art and Visual Culture* (Aldershot: Ashgate, 2005), while prominent film studies publications include Kevin Rockett, John Hill and Martin McLoone (eds), *Cinema and Ireland* (Syracuse, NY: Syracuse University Press, 1987); Martin McLoone's *Irish Film: The Emergence of a National Cinema* (London: British Film Institute, 2000); Lance Pettitt's *Screening Ireland: Film and Television Representation* (Manchester: Manchester University Press, 2000); Ruth Barton's *Irish National Cinema* (London: Routledge, 2004); and Michael Gillespie's *The Myth of an Irish Cinema: Approaching Irish-Themed Films* (Syracuse, NY: Syracuse University Press, 2008).

3 Linda King and Elaine Sisson (eds), *Ireland, Design and Visual Culture: Negotiating Modernity, 1922–1992* (Cork: Cork University Press, 2011); Eóin Flannery and Michael Griffin (eds), *Ireland in Focus: Film, Photography, and Popular Culture* (Syracuse, NY: Syracuse University Press, 2009).

4 Patricia Coughlan, '"Bog Queens": The Representation of Women in the Poetry of John Montague and Seamus Heaney', in Toni O'Brien Johnson and David Cairns (eds), *Gender and Irish Writing* (Maidenhead: Open University Press, 1991), pp. 88–111; Elizabeth Butler Cullingford, *Ireland's Others: Ethnicity and Gender in Irish Literature and Popular Culture* (Cork: Cork University Press, 2001); Colin Graham, *Deconstructing Ireland: Identity, Theory, Culture* (Edinburgh: Edinburgh University Press, 2001); Gerardine Meaney, *Gender, Ireland and Cultural Change: Race, Sex and Nation* (London: Routledge, 2010); Joseph Valente, *The Myth of Manliness in Irish National Culture, 1880–1922* (Champaign, IL: University of Illinois Press, 2011).

5 Wanda Balzano, Anne Mulhall and Moynagh Sullivan, 'Introduction', in Balzano et al. (eds), *Irish Postmodernisms and Popular Culture* (Basingstoke: Palgrave Macmillan, 2007), p. xviii.

CHAPTER ONE (Carville)

1 V.N. Vološinov, *Marxism and the Philosophy of Language*, trans. Ladislav Matejka and I.R. Titunik (Cambridge, MA: Harvard University Press, 1986), p. 9.

2 For a range of literature across the areas see the essays collected in: Adele M. Dalsimer (ed.), *Visualizing Ireland: National Identity and the Pictorial Tradition* (Boston and London: Faber & Faber 1993); Brian P. Kennedy and Raymond Gillespie (eds), *Ireland: Art into History* (Dublin: Town House, 1994); Lawrence W. McBride (ed.), *Images, Icons and the Irish Nationalist Imagination* (Dublin: Four Courts Press, 1990); *Third Text: Special Issue on Irish Culture*, vol. 19, no. 5, 2005; *Early Popular Visual Culture, Special Issue Popular Visual Culture in Ireland*, vol. 5, no. 3, 2007; *The Irish Review*, Contemporary Visual Arts, vol. 39, 2008; and Eóin Flannery and Michael Griffin (eds), *Ireland in Focus: Film, Photography, and Popular Culture* (Syracuse, NY: Syracuse University Press, 2009).

3 The anxiety thus lies in the uncertainty as to whether or not Irish visual culture is merely an emphasis within a broader field of theories of representation of Irish cultural life, that is to say a passing trend within arts and humanities scholarship, or if it is an emergent sub-discipline that requires a distinctive set of methods and models of theoretical analysis. If the latter is the case, the question that may be posed is what is Irish visual culture a sub-discipline of? Is it a sub-discipline of Irish studies, itself a sub-discipline of literary, media, cultural studies and historiography, or is it a re-branding of Irish art historical scholarship?

4 I am interpreting visual culture very broadly here, cognisant of the fact that disciplines such as art history and arts criticism have their own historical methods and forms of writing which are very different from the aspirations of visual culture or visual studies as an academic discipline. My point here is to draw attention to the difficulties associated with employing the term as a signifier of newness of both the subject of inquiry and methods used to discuss visual representations.

5 The most prominent example and contribution to the discussion of the complexities of the visual within Irish cultural life remains David Brett's *The Construction of Heritage* (Cork: Cork University Press, 1996), especially the chapter 'The Picturesque and the Sublime: Toward the Aestheticisation of History'.

6 For a brief overview of the incorporation of photography in physical anthropology see Frank Spencer, 'Some Notes on the Attempt to Apply Photography to Anthropometry during the Second Half of the Nineteenth Century', in Elizabeth Edwards (ed.), *Anthropology & Photography: 1860–1920* (New Haven, CT: Yale University Press, 1992), pp. 99–107.

7 Nicholas Mirzoeff, *An Introduction to Visual Culture*, 1st edn (London: Routledge, 1999), pp. 3–5.

8 Such observations are not new and have been identified by Arjun Appadurai as the 'two diacritics of migration and media'. See *Modernity at Large: Cultural Dimensions of Globalization* (Minneapolis, MN: University of Minnesota Press, 1997), pp. 2–3.

9 A sub-discipline of what is not very clear – although the lead appears to have been taken by literary and cultural Irish studies orientated towards colonial and postcolonial theory.

10 Adele M. Dalsimer and Vera Kreilkamp, 'Introduction', in *Visualizing Ireland*, pp. 3–8.

11 Máire de Paor, 'Irish Antiquarian Artists', in *Visualizing Ireland*, pp. 119–20.

12 Ibid., p. 120.

13 Walter Benjamin, *Illuminations: Essays and Reflections*, trans. Harry Zohn (London: Fontana, 1973), p. 96.

14 Luke Gibbons, 'Alien Eye', *Circa*, vol. 12, 1986, p. 10.

15 Mick Wilson, 'Terms of Art and Tricks of Trade: A Critical Look at the Irish Art Scene Now', *Third Text*, vol. 19, no. 5, 2005, pp. 535–43.

16 On a recent examination by Gibbons of absences in Irish visual culture in Ireland which pursue this theme, see the excellent essay 'Words Upon the Windowpane: Image, Text and Irish Culture', in James Elkins (ed.), *Visual Cultures* (Bristol: Intellect, 2010), pp. 43–56.

17 See de Paor, 'Irish Antiquarian Artists', p. 119.

18 Brett, *The Construction of Heritage*, p. 48. Barbara O'Connor, 'Myths and Mirrors: Tourist Images and National Identity', in Barbara O'Connor and Michael Cronin (eds), *Tourism in Ireland: A Critical Analysis* (Cork: Cork University Press, 1993), pp. 69–85.

19 Homi Bhabha, 'The Other Question ... Homi Bhabha Reconsiders the Stereotype and Colonial Discourse', *Screen*, vol. 24, no. 6, 1983, p. 25.

20 The standard biography of Haddon is A. Hingston Quiggin, *Haddon the Head-Hunter: A Short Sketch of the Life of A.C. Haddon* (Cambridge: Cambridge University Press, 1942).

21 On photography and the Bertillon method see Allan Sekula, 'The Body and the Archive', *October*, vol. 39, 1986, pp. 3–64.

22 Haddon wrote about these ruses in several texts on ethnology, including his entry on photography for *Notes and Queries in Anthropology*, 3rd edn (London: Royal Anthropological Institute, 1899), pp. 237–40.

23 W.J.T. Mitchell, 'There are no Visual Media', *Journal of Visual Culture*, vol. 4, no. 2, 2005, p. 257.

24 The indexical semiotic model I am following is Peirce's. See Charles S. Peirce, 'Logic as Semiotic: The Theory of Signs', in Robert E. Innis (ed.), *Semiotics: An Introductory Anthology* (Bloomington, IN: Indiana University Press, 1985), pp. 4–22.

25 Michel Foucault, *Discipline and Punish: The Birth of the Prison*, trans. Allan Sheridan (New York: Pantheon, 1977), pp. 170–1.

26 The dominant model of the Foucauldian social power model is John Tagg's *The Burden of Representation: Essays on Photographies and Histories* (London: Macmillan, 1988).

27 'Disciplinary power [. . .] is exercised through its invisibility; at the same time it imposes on those whom it subjects a principle of compulsory visibility.' Foucault, *Discipline and Punish*, p. 187.

28 Roland Barthes, *Camera Lucida: Reflections on Photography*, trans. Richard Howard (London: Flamingo, 1982), p. 76.

29 On the relationship between textuality and anthropology see James Clifford's essay 'On Ethnographic Authority', in *The Predicament of Culture: Twentieth-Century Ethnography, Literature and Art* (Cambridge, MA: Harvard University Press, 1988), pp. 21–54.

30 For an account of the emergence of the 'type' photograph in anthropology see Elizabeth Edwards, 'Photographic "Types": The Pursuit of Method', *Visual Anthropology*, vol. 3, 1990, pp. 235–56.

31 Martha Macintyre and Maureen Mackenzie, 'Focal Length as an Analogue of Cultural Distance', in Elizabeth Edwards (ed.), *Anthropology and Photography, 1860–1920* (New Haven, CT: Yale University Press, 1991), pp. 158, 160.

32 Roland Barthes, 'The Photographic Message', in *Image, Music, Text*, trans. Stephen Heath (London: Fontana, 1977).

33 Peter Galison and Lorraine Datson, *Objectivity* (Cambridge, MA: MIT Press, 2007), pp. 121, 139.

34 There is not the space here to do justice to a discussion of the disciplinary politics of the term 'culture'; however, it would appear that a particular model of 'culture' has been adopted in discussions of Irish visual representations which place an abstract aesthetic value on the visual. To quote Terry Eagleton, what 'at first denoted a thoroughly material process was then metaphorically transposed to affairs of the spirit', *The Idea of Culture* (Oxford: Blackwell, 2000), p. 1. The field of visual cultural studies has followed a similar model of culture in which even popular forms of culture have been 'elevated' to the aesthetic. During the last decade, alternative conceptions of visual 'culture', which have emerged from such diverse fields as the history of science, sociology and anthropology and which have questioned an evaluative model of culture, have influenced my discussion here. On the politics of 'culture' see also Chris Jenks, *Culture*, 2nd edn (London: Routledge, 2005); Raymond Williams, *Keywords* (London: Fontana, 1976).

35 Martin Jay, 'Scopic Regimes of Modernity', in Hal Foster (ed.), *Vision and Visuality* (Seattle: Bay Press, 1988), pp. 3–23.

36 Mitchell, 'There are no Visual Media', p. 257.

37 Gilles Deleuze and Félix Guattari, *A Thousand Plateaus: Capitalism and Schizophrenia*, trans. Brian Massumi (London: Continuum, 2001), p. 13.

38 My use of the term 'observer' here is deliberate so as to distinguish between the different agencies of looking between those represented within the photograph and the viewer of the photographic image. Jonathan Crary has identified the observer as meaning '"To conform one's action, to comply with", as in observing rules, codes, regulations and practices. Though obviously one who sees, an observer is more importantly one who sees within a prescribed set of possibilities, one who is embedded in a system of conventions and limitations', *Techniques of the Observer: On Vision and Modernity in the Nineteenth Century* (Cambridge, MA: MIT Press, 1993), p. 6.

39 Mikhail Bakhtin, *Art and Answerability: Early Philosophical Essays by M.M Bakhtin*, trans. Vadim Liapunov (Austin: University of Texas Press, 1990), p. 22.

40 Mikhail Bakhtin, *The Dialogic Imagination: Four Essays by M.M Bakhtin*, trans. Caryl Emerson and Michael Holquist (Austin: University of Texas Press, 1981), p. 324. Italics in original.

41 Bakhtin, *Art and Answerability*, p. 23.

42 For an account of the visual spectacles established to commemorate the Eucharistic Congress see Gary Boyd, 'Supernational Catholicity: Dublin and the 1932 Eucharistic Congress', *Early Popular Culture*, vol. 5, no. 3, 2007, pp. 317–33.

43 Eamonn Slater, 'Contested Terrain: Differing Interpretations of the Co. Wicklow Landscape', *Irish Journal of Anthropology*, vol. 3, 1993, p. 45.

44 I am borrowing Deleuze and Guattari's phrase 'deterritorializing lines of flight' here from *A Thousand Plateaus*, p. 224.

45 W.J.T. Mitchell, *Picture Theory* (Chicago: University of Chicago Press, 1994), p. 11.

46 Ibid., p. 13.

47 Vološinov, *Marxism and the Philosophy of Language*, p. 23.

CHAPTER TWO (Herr)

1 Kevin Rockett, Luke Gibbons and John Hill, *Cinema and Ireland* (Syracuse, NY: Syracuse University Press, 1988), p. 134.
2 Ibid., p. 245.
3 Ibid.
4 Martin McLoone, *Irish Film: The Emergence of a Contemporary Cinema* (London: British Film Institute, 2000), p. 185; Lance Pettitt, *December Bride* (Cork: Cork University Press, 2001), p. 31.
5 First published in the 1948 collection entitled *The Man Who Invented Sin* (New York: Devon-Adair, 1948).
6 Sean O'Faoláin, *The Collected Stories of Sean O'Faoláin* (Boston: Little Brown, 1983), p. 423.
7 Ibid., p. 423.
8 Ibid., p. 425.
9 Ibid., p. 426.
10 Ibid., p. 426.
11 Ibid., p. 428.
12 *The Field* (Cork: Cork University Press, 2002); 'Re-Imagining *Man of Aran*', *Canadian Journal of Irish Studies*, vol. 29, 2003, pp. 11–16; 'Thinking Inside the Box', in Brian McIlroy (ed.), *Genre and Cinema: Ireland and Transnationalism* (London: Routledge, 2007), pp. 111–22.
13 Pierre Bourdieu and Loïc J.D. Wacquant, *An Invitation to Reflexive Sociology* (Chicago: University of Chicago Press, 1992), p. 19.
14 Richard Jenkins, *Pierre Bourdieu* (London and New York: Routledge, 1992), pp. 89, 69, 71.
15 Pierre Bourdieu, *The Logic of Practice*, trans. Richard Nice (Palo Alto, CA: Stanford University Press, 1990), p. 14.
16 Jacques Lacan, 'Of Structure as the Inmixing of an Otherness Prerequisite to Any Subject Whatever', in Richard Macksey and Eugenio Donato (eds), *The Structuralist Controversy: The Languages of Criticism and the Sciences of Man* (Baltimore and London: Johns Hopkins University Press, 2007), pp. 186–95.

CHAPTER THREE (Monahan)

1 For example see Julia Kristeva, *Revolution in Poetic Language*, trans. Leon S. Roudiez (New York: Columbia University Press, 1984).
2 Constance Penley and Janet Bergstrom, 'The Avant-Garde: Histories and Theories', in Bill Nichols (ed.), *Movies and Methods, Volume 2* (Berkeley, CA: University of California Press, 1985), p. 292.
3 Daniel Herwitz, 'Screening Rothman's The "I" of the Camera', *Film and Philosophy*, vol. 2, 1996, p. 24.
4 Christian Metz, 'The Imaginary Signifier', *Screen*, vol. 16, no. 2, 1975, p. 55.
5 Vivian Sobchack, *The Address of the Eye: A Phenomenology of Film Experience* (Princeton, NJ: Princeton University Press, 1992), p. 168.
6 Daniel Frampton, *Filmosophy* (London and New York: Wallflower, 2006), p. 40.
7 Emile Benveniste, *Problèmes de Linguistique Générale* (Paris: Gallimard, 1974) p. 85.
8 Edward Branigan, *Narrative Comprehension and Film* (London and New York: Routledge, 1992), p. 94.
9 Ibid., p. 29.
10 Ibid., p. 101.

11 Timothy Mooney and Dermot Moran (eds), *The Phenomenology Reader* (London and New York: Routledge, 2002), p. 270.

12 Ibid.

13 Noël Carroll, *Interpreting the Moving Image* (Cambridge: Cambridge University Press, 1998), pp. 64–79.

14 Branigan, *Narrative Comprehension and Film*, p. 65.

15 Christian Metz, *Film Language: A Semiotics of the Cinema* (Oxford: Oxford University Press, 1974), pp. 21–2.

16 Quoted in Peter Brunette, *The Films of Michel Antonioni* (Cambridge: Cambridge University Press, 1998), pp. 120–1.

17 Stanley Cavell, *The World Viewed* (Cambridge, MA: Harvard University Press, 1979), p. 12.

18 Ibid., p. 25.

19 For a useful discussion on 'structuring absences' see Melvyn Stokes, 'Structuring Absences: Images of America Missing from the Hollywood Screen', *Revue Français D'Études Américaines*, vol. 89, 2001, pp. 43–53.

CHAPTER FOUR (Brown)

1 My title is indebted to David Lloyd, *Anomalous States: Irish Writing and the Post-Colonial Moment* (Durham, NC: Duke University Press, 1993), pp. 125–62.

2 For a more complete list see John Hill, *Cinema and Northern Ireland: Film, Culture, and Politics* (London: British Film Institute, 2006), pp. 190–243.

3 Marcia Landy, 'The International Cast of Irish Cinema', *boundary 2*, vol. 27, no. 2, 2000, pp. 22–3. See also John Hill, 'Images of Violence', in Kevin Rockett, Luke Gibbons and John Hill (eds), *Cinema and Ireland* (Syracuse, NY: Syracuse University Press, 1988), pp. 147–93.

4 Frederic Jameson, *Signatures of the Visible* (London: Routledge, 1992), pp. 2–3.

5 Laura Mulvey, *Death 24x a Second: Stillness and the Moving Image* (London: Reaktion Books, 2006), p. 7.

6 See Jane Giles, *The Crying Game* (London: British Film Institute, 1997), p. 47.

7 Slavoj Žižek, *Looking Awry: An Introduction to Jacques Lacan through Popular Culture* (Cambridge, MA: MIT Press, 1992), p. 112.

8 Steven Shaviro, *The Cinematic Body* (Minneapolis, MN: University of Minnesota Press, 1993), p. 257.

9 Ibid., p. 33.

10 Francis Bacon, *The Works of Francis Bacon, Lord Chancellor of England*, vol. 1, Basil Montagu (ed.) (Philadelphia: Hart, 1850), p. 206.

11 Sigmund Freud, *Group Psychology and the Analysis of the Ego*, trans. and ed. James Strachey (New York and London: Norton, 1959), p. 11.

12 Ibid., p. 57.

13 I take this sense of 'transitive fascination' from Steven Connor, 'Fascination, Skin and the Screen', *Critical Quarterly*, vol. 40, no. 1, 1998, pp. 9–24.

14 Freud, *Group Psychology*, p. 76.

15 Ackbar Abbas, 'On Fascination: Walter Benjamin's Images', *New German Critique*, vol. 48, 1989, p. 50; Theodor Adorno, *Minima Moralia: Reflections from Damaged Life*, trans. E.F.N. Jephcott (London: Verso, 1978), p. 238.

16 Ackbar, 'On Fascination', p. 51.

17 Walter Benjamin, 'Central Park', trans. Lloyd Spencer, Mark Harrington, *New German Critique*, vol. 34, 1985, p. 38.

18 Connor, 'Fascination, Skin and the Screen', p. 12, emphasis in original.

19 Maurice Blanchot, *The Space of Literature*, trans. Ann Smock (Lincoln, NE: University of Nebraska Press, 1982), p. 33.

20 Ibid., p. 32.

21 Laura Mulvey, 'Visual Pleasure and Narrative Cinema', in Leo Braudy and Marshall Cohen (eds), *Film Theory and Criticism* (Oxford: Oxford University Press, 2004), p. 847.

22 Blanchot, *Space of Literature*, p. 32.

23 Mulvey, *Death 24x a Second*, p. 187.

24 Ibid., p. 191.

25 ODC stands for Ordinary Decent Criminal, a colloquial term for non-political prisoners.

26 Hill, *Cinema and Ireland*, p. 184.

27 I refer to Derry/Londonderry not for political reasons but because this is the convention used in the film.

28 See Joseph Moser, 'Genre Politics: *Bloody Sunday* as Documentary and Discourse', in Brian McIlroy (ed.), *Genre and Cinema: Ireland and Transnationalism* (New York and London: Routledge, 2007), pp. 246–7.

29 Mulvey, *Death 24x a Second*, p. 192.

CHAPTER FIVE (Macdougall)

1 Teilifís na Gaeilge was originally abreviated as TnaG, but was rebranded as TG4 in 1999 to reflect its position on the dial. For the sake of convenience, I will use the abbreviation TG4 for all periods in the station's history.

2 'This is Ireland: Highlights from Census 2011, Part I', p. 40. Available online through the Central Statistics Office Ireland: http://www.cso.ie/en/census/census2011reports/ [accessed 1 August 2012].

3 Iarfhlaith Watson, *Broadcasting in Irish: Minority Language, Radio, Television and Identity* (Dublin: Four Courts Press, 2003), pp. 50–2.

4 See Article 8 of the Constitution of Ireland/Bunreacht na hÉireann (1937). A full version of the constitution may be downloaded from the website of the All-Party Oireachtas Committee on the Constitution: http://www.constitution.ie [accessed 10 January 2012].

5 Ruth Lysaght, 'Súil Eile, Dúil Nua (Another Perspective, a New Desire): Short Films in the Irish Language since the Advent of TG4', in Neal Alexander, Shane Murphy and Anne Oakman (eds), *To the Other Shore: Cross-Currents in Irish and Scottish Studies* (Béal Feirste: Cló Ollscoil na Banríona/Queen's University Press, 2004), p. 88.

6 Andrea Byrne, 'The Cupla Focal's Conquest', *Sunday Independent*, 13 May 2007, p. 16.

7 Interview between the author and Pádhraic Ó Ciardha, deputy CEO of TG4, 28 July 2009, Galway city, Ireland.

8 Richard Abel, Giorgio Bertellini and Rob King, *Early Cinema and the 'National'* (Bloomington, IN: Indiana University Press, 2008), p. 1.

9 Stephen Crofts, 'Concepts of National Cinema', in John Hill and Pamela Church Gibson (eds), *World Cinema: Critical Approaches* (Oxford: Oxford University Press, 2000), p. 1–3.

10 Andrew Higson, 'The Concept of National Cinema', *Screen*, vol. 30, no. 4, 1989, p. 39.

11 Ibid., p. 38.

12 Ibid., p. 38.

13 Benedict Anderson, *Imagined Communities: Reflections on the Origin and Spread of Nationalism*, 2nd edn (New York: Verso, 2006), p. 77.

14 Albert Moran, 'Terms for a Reader: Film, Hollywood, National Cinema, Cultural Identity and Film Policy', in Albert Moran (ed.), *Film Policy: International, National and Regional Perspectives* (New York: Routledge, 1996), p. 4.

15 Ibid., p. 4.

16 Martin McLoone, *Irish Film: The Emergence of a Contemporary Cinema* (London: British Film Institute, 2000), p. 116.

17 Ruth Barton, *Irish National Cinema* (London: Routledge, 2004), p. 105.

18 B. Mairéad Pratschke, 'A Look at Irish-Ireland: Gael-Linn's *Amharc Éireann* Films, 1956–64', *New Hibernia Review/Iris Éireannach Nua*, vol. 9, no. 3, 2005, p. 38.

19 Harvey O'Brien, 'Ghosts of Empire: *Mitchell and Kenyon in Ireland* and *Saoirse?* on DVD', *Estudios Irlandeses*, vol. 3, 2008, p. 254.

20 Michael Gray, '*Mise Éire*', Review, *Cineaste*, vol. 32, no. 2, 2007, p. 77.

21 Harvey O'Brien, *The Real Ireland: The Evolution of Ireland in Documentary Film* (Manchester: Manchester University Press, 2004), pp. 107–8.

22 Gerry McCarthy, 'George Morrison, Pioneer of Irish Film, Isn't Stuck in the Past', *Sunday Times*, 15 February 2009, p. 15 (Culture section).

23 Martin Doyle, 'Reel Hero of Irish History', *Irish Times*, 4 January 2008, p. 12.

24 Jerry White, 'Translating Ireland Back into Éire: Gael Linn and Film Making in Irish', *Éire-Ireland*, vol. 38, nos 1–2, 2003, p. 114.

25 O'Brien remarks that some of the scenes of Éamon de Valera evoke 'memories of similar footage of Lenin and Hitler in the propaganda films which had accompanied their respective rises to power'. 'Projecting the Past: Historical Documentary in Ireland', *Historical Journal of Film, Radio and Television*, vol. 20, no. 3, 2000, p. 342.

26 McLoone, *Irish Film*, p. 17.

27 Ibid., p. 133.

28 Quoted in Debbie Ging, 'Screening the Green Cinema under the Celtic Tiger', in Peadar Kirby, Luke Gibbons and Michael Cronin (eds), *Reinventing Ireland: Culture, Society, and the Global Economy* (Sterling, VA: Pluto Press, 2002), p. 179.

29 McLoone, *Irish Film*, p. 133.

30 Ross Whittaker, 'Short Film Fluency', *Film Ireland*, vol. 101, November/December 2004, p. 21.

31 Lysaght, 'Súil Eile, Dúil Nua', p. 89.

32 Niamh Creely, 'Schemers', *Film Ireland*, vol. 119, November/December 2007, p. 16. (This statement is somewhat misleading, as the other schemes were never limited to English-language submissions).

33 Cathal Goan, 'Teilifís Na Gaeilge: Ten Years A-Growing', *New Hibernia Review*, vol. 11, no. 2, 2007, p. 107.

34 Ruth Lysaght, 'Ar Oscailt – New Openings: Short Films in the Irish Language since the Advent of TG4', in R. González (ed.), *The Representation of Ireland/s: Images from Outside and from Within* (Barcelona: Promociones y Publicaciones Universitarias, 2003), p. 159.

35 Aodán Mac Póilin and Liam Andrews, *BBC agus an Ghaeilge/BBC and the Irish Language* (Belfast: Iontaobhas Ultach, 1993), p. 9.

36 Eithne O'Connell, 'Subtitles on Screen: Something for Everyone in the Audience?', *Teanga*, vol. 18, 1999, p. 87.

37 Ibid., p. 88.

38 Michael Cronin, *Translation goes to the Movies* (New York: Routledge, 2009), p. 106.

39 Toby Miller, 'Screening the Nation: Rethinking Options', *Cinema Journal*, vol. 38, no. 4, 1999, p. 97.

CHAPTER SIX (McFadden)

1 James Joyce, *A Portrait of the Artist as a Young Man* (Ware: Wordsworth Editions, 1992), p. 167. Translated by Jacqueline Belanger: 'I believe the life of the poor is simply atrocious, simply bloody atrocious, in Liverpool', p. 231.
2 Patrick O'Sullivan, 'General Introduction to the Series', in Patrick O'Sullivan (ed.), *The Irish World Wide: History, Heritage, Identity. Volume 1, Patterns of Migration* (Leicester: Leicester University Press, 1992), pp. xix.
3 Robert Stam, *Literature through Film: Realism, Magic, and the Art of Adaptation* (Oxford: Blackwell, 2005), p. 5.
4 Gérard Genette, *Palimpsests: Literature in the Second Degree*, trans. Channa Newman, Claude Doubinsky (Lincoln, NE: University of Nebraska Press, 1997), pp. 1–3.
5 Catherine Grant, 'Recognising Billy Budd in *Beau Travail*: Epistemology and Hermeneutics of an Auteurist "Free" Adaptation', *Screen*, vol. 43, no. 1, 2002, pp. 57–9.
6 John Ellis, 'The Literary Adaptation: An Introduction', *Screen*, vol. 23, no. 1, 1982, p. 3.
7 Suzanne Speidel quoted in Grant, 'Recognising Billy Budd', p. 57.
8 Stam extends Genette's concept of paratextuality to film adaptation by adding posters, trailers, reviews, interviews and so forth as the 'accessory messages' that constitute a film's paratexts: Robert Stam, 'Introduction: The Theory and Practice of Adaptation', in Robert Stam and Alessandra Raengo (eds), *Literature and Film: A Guide to the Theory and Practice of Film Adaptation* (Oxford: Blackwell, 2005), p. 28.
9 Neil Smith, 'Liam', *BBC Home*, 22 February 2001, http://www.bbc.co.uk/films/2001/02/14/liam_2001_review.shtml [accessed 10 January 2012].
10 Charles Taylor, 'Liam', *Salon: Arts and Entertainment*, 26 September 2001, http://www.salon.com/2001/09/26/liam [accessed 10 January 2012].
11 Peter Bradshaw, 'Liam', *The Guardian*, 23 February 2001, http://www.guardian.co.uk/film/2001/feb/23/1 [accessed 10 January 2012].
12 Steve Rhodes, 'Liam', http://www.allmovieportal.com/m/2001_Liam61.html [accessed 10 January 2012].
13 Roger Ebert, 'Liam', *Chicago Sun-Times*, 5 October 2001, http://rogerebert.sun-times.com/apps/pbcs.dll/article?AID=/20011005/REVIEWS/110050302/1023 [accessed 10 January 2012].
14 Charles Whitehouse, 'The London Film Festival: Capital Gains', *Sight and Sound*, vol. 10, no. 11, 2000, p. 18.
15 Joseph McKeown, *Back Crack Boy* (London: Corgi, 1986), p. 9.
16 Ibid., pp. 10–19.
17 Ibid., p. 23.
18 Ibid., p. 63.
19 Ibid., p. 139.
20 Ibid., p. 74.
21 Ibid., p. 22.
22 Ibid., p. 142.
23 Ibid., p. 143.
24 Ibid., p. 145.
25 Joyce, *Portrait*, p. 4.
26 Ibid., p. 10.

27 Ibid.

28 Ibid., p. 146.

29 Seamus Deane (ed.), 'Introduction', James Joyce, *A Portrait of the Artist as a Young Man* (Harmondsworth: New Penguin Books, 2003), p. xix.

30 Joyce, *Portrait*, p. 157.

31 Paul Gilroy, *Between Camps: Nations, Cultures and the Allure of Race*, 2nd edn (London: Routledge, 2004), p. 101.

32 O'Sullivan, 'Patterns of Migration', p. xix.

33 Declan Kiberd, *Inventing Ireland: The Literature of the Modern Nation* (London: Vintage 1996), p. 289.

34 Joyce, *Portrait*, p. 196.

35 Ibid., pp. 92–3.

36 Ibid., p. 95.

37 Ibid., p. 102.

38 Ibid., p. 101.

39 Ibid., p. 93.

40 Ibid., p. 92.

41 Ibid., p. 98.

42 T.S. Eliot, '*Ulysses*, Order and Myth', *The Dial*, vol. 75, no. 5, 1923, pp. 480–3.

43 Genette, *Palimpsests*, p. 400.

CHAPTER SEVEN (Radley)

1 Indeed, in a (highly critical) review of the film, Niall Kitson derisively refers to Wycherley only as 'the guy who does the MyHome ads on the radio', and not by name or reference to his other film and television work. 'Open Up and Say AAAAAAAAAGGGGGGGHHHHHHHHHH', *Film Ireland*, 2007, http://www.film ireland.net/exclusives/horrorthon2007.htm [accessed 19 March 2012].

2 Christine Gledhill, 'Genre and Nation', in Brian McIlroy (ed), *Genre and Cinema: Ireland and Transnationalism* (London: Routledge, 2007), p. 16.

3 Julia Kristeva, *Desire in Language*, trans. Thomas Gora, Alice Jardine and Leon S. Roudiez (New York: Columbia University Press, 1980), p. 130.

4 Barry Monahan, 'Playing Cops and Robbers: Recent Irish Cinema and Genre Performance', in McIlroy (ed), *Genre and Cinema*, p. 54.

5 This is a term used by Mikhail Bakhtin to describe writing or discourse that is dialogic, in other words, making deliberate reference to another's words. The uncanny referential relationship between the text and its 'origin' undermines the authority of epistemological certainty in communication and language. See Christine Gledhill, 'Genre and Nation', in McIlroy (ed.), *Genre and Cinema*, for a detailed analysis of Bakhtin's literary theory and Irish national cinema.

6 Julia Kristeva, *Revolution in Poetic Language*, trans. Margaret Waller (New York: Columbia University Press, 1984), p. 59.

7 See also Dervila Layden, 'Discovering and Uncovering Genre in Irish Cinema', in McIlroy (ed.), *Genre and Cinema*, pp. 27–44, for an 'excavation' of genre in Irish classic film.

8 This is not to suggest that only younger filmmakers deploy generic structures. The work of Neil Jordan, for example, has often been read with reference to his generic sensibility, although this is often (incongruously) seen as a reflection of 'genuine cinematic thinking' (Kevin Rockett and Emer Rockett, *Neil Jordan: Exploring Boundaries* (Dublin: Liffey Press, 2003), p. 8) rather than as a crisis in cinematic imagination.

9 For a comprehensive list of films produced that fall broadly under the category of horror, see Sean Crosson's review of Irish-language horror feature *Na Cloighne* in *Estudios Irlandeses*, vol. 6, 2011, pp. 202–4.

10 The horror genre, particularly, closely maps the traumas that shadow socio-cultural reality: the development of the 'slasher' genre in the 1970s and '80s has been read as a response to and a backlash against feminism, and more recently the increasingly graphic turn in horror (often called 'horror porn') has been linked to cultural trauma around the war on terror, border security, and torture. See Carol J. Clover, *Men, Women and Chainsaws* (Princeton, NJ: Princeton University Press, 1992); Gabrielle Murray, 'Hostel II: Representations of the Body in Pain and the Cinema Experience in Torture Porn', *Jump Cut*, vol. 59, 2008, http://www.ejump cut.org/archive/jc50.2008/TortureHostel2/text.html [accessed 16 January 2012].

11 Philip Brophy, 'Horrality: The Textuality of Contemporary Horror Films', in Ken Gelder (ed.), *The Horror Reader* (London: Routledge, 2000), p. 279.

12 Kristeva, *Desire in Language*, p. 36.

13 Roddy Flynn, 'Altered Images: *Shrooms* and Irish Cinema', *Estudios Irlandeses*, vol. 3, 2008, p. 229.

14 Tony Tracy, 'Introduction: Irish Film and Television, 2006', *Estudios Irlandeses*, vol. 2, 2007, p. 253.

15 Flynn, 'Altered Images', p. 229.

16 For a useful summary of the various approaches, see Michael Gillespie, *The Myth of an Irish Cinema: Approaching Irish-Themed Films* (Syracuse, NY: Syracuse University Press, 2008), pp. 29–53.

17 Andrew Higson, 'The Limiting Imagination of National Cinema', in Mette Hjort and Scott MacKenzie (eds), *Cinema and Nation* (London: Routledge, 2000), p. 67. at the beginning. See Gledhill, 'Genre and Nation' for more on national cinema and cultural differentiation.

18 Higson, ibid.

19 Des O'Rawe, 'Origins and Orientations: An Interview with Kevin Rockett, on Irish Film Studies', *The Canadian Journal of Irish Studies*, vol. 29, no. 2, 2003, p. 60.

20 Martin McLoone, *Irish Film: The Emergence of a Contemporary Cinema* (London: British Film Institute, 2000), p. 205; Ruth Barton, *Irish National Cinema* (London: Routledge, 2004), p. 184. While both critics perform useful and insightful readings of these films, their analyses remain predicated on an understanding of genre in and of itself as not 'properly' Irish.

21 Tracy, 'Introduction', p. 253.

22 Kristeva, *Revolution*, pp. 19–21.

23 Julia Kristeva, *Powers of Horror: An Essay in Abjection*, trans. Leon S. Roudiez (New York: Columbia University Press, 1982), p. 1. Horror, of course, is always already intimate with abjection and the 'dirty' spaces of signification – the permeable body, madness and carnality.

24 Kristeva, *Revolution*, p. 45.

25 Graham Allen, *Intertextuality* (London: Routledge, 2000), p. 36.

26 Kristeva quoted in Leon S. Roudiez, 'Introduction', *Revolution*, p. 3.

27 Kristeva, *Revolution*, p. 58.

28 Ibid., p. 59.

29 Allen, *Intertextuality*, p. 36.

30 Kristeva, *Desire in Language*, pp. 36–7.

31 Of course, the herding of frightened people into overcrowded trucks also recalls the visual iconography of the Holocaust.

32 See comments from Rockett, McLoone and Barton, cited above.

33 Flynn, 'Altered Images', p. 229.

34 As noted previously, horror is closely linked to periods of ideological anxiety. Other genres such as the Western and science-fiction have also historically been read as ideological investigations of American imperialism and national identity.

35 Allen, *Intertextuality*, p. 36.

36 For example, see films such as *Into the West* (Mike Newell, 1992), *The War of the Buttons* (John Roberts, 1994), and *The Butcher Boy* (Jordan, 1998).

37 Kristeva, *Desire in Language*, p. 125.

CHAPTER EIGHT (Mentxaka)

1 Kate O'Brien, *Mary Lavelle* (London: Virago, 2000). First published in 1936.

2 Virginia Woolf, 'The Cinema', in *The Crowded Dance of Modern Life. Selected Essays: Volume Two*, Rachel Bowlby (ed.) (Harmondsworth: Penguin, 1993), p. 56.

3 See Kamilla Elliott, *Rethinking the Novel/Film Debate* (Cambridge: Cambridge University Press, 2009), p. 124; Sergei Eisenstein, *Film Form: Essays in Film Theory*, trans. Jay Leyda (New York: Harcourt Brace,1977), p. 4; Nicci Gerrard, 'What! No Sound and Fury?' *The Observer*, 11 April 1999, http://www.guardian.co.uk/film/1999/apr/11/shakespeare [accessed 17 January 2012].

4 Bernard Smyth, *Modernism's History: A Study in Twentieth-Century Art and Ideas* (Sydney: University of New South Wales Press, 1998), pp. 5, 103.

5 See Lillian Faderman, *Surpassing the Love of Men: Romantic Friendship and Love between Women from the Renaissance to the Present* (London: The Women's Press, 1985), pp. 399–405.

6 See Vincent Gille, 'Love of Books, Love Books', in Jennifer Mundy (ed.), *Surrealism: Desire Unbound* (London: Tate Publications, 2001), pp. 130–1.

7 Smyth, *Modernism's History*, p. 17.

8 For example, see Irish art historian Brian Fallon's admiration for 'virility' in national movements freed from the 'Parisian' influence. Brian Fallon, *Irish Art 1830–1990* (Belfast: Appletree Press, 1994), pp. 16, 125.

9 They provided the context for the notorious 1914 attack on Diego Velazquez's painting *Rockeby Venus* (c. 1650), by a suffragette wielding a meat chopper.

10 Karl Radek, 'Contemporary World Literature and the Tasks of Proletarian Art', in Maxim Gorky et al., *Soviet Writers' Congress 1934: The Debate on Socialist Realism and Modernism in the Soviet Union* (London: Lawrence & Wishart, 1977), p. 153.

11 W.M. Letts, *Songs of Leinster* (London: Murray, 1913).

12 Blanaid Salkeld, *Hello, Eternity!* (London: E. Mathews Marrot, 1933).

13 Declan Kiberd, *Inventing Ireland: The Literature of the Modern Nation* (London: Vintage, 1996), p. 478; Patrick Kavanagh, *The Great Hunger* (Shannon: Irish University Press, 1971).

14 Elizabeth Bowen, *The Last September* (London: Vintage, 1988), p. 116.

15 See Jürgen Habermas, 'Modernity's Consciousness of Time and its Need for Self-reassurance', *The Philosophical Discourse of Modernity: Twelve Lectures*, trans. Frederick Lawrence (Cambridge, MA: MIT Press, 1981), p. 3. See also Cecil Salkeld and Francis Stuart, 'To All Artists and Writers', in David Pierce (ed.), *Irish Writing in the Twentieth Century: A Reader* (Cork: Cork University Press, 2000). In the late nineteenth century, the term 'modernist' was used to describe a person who believed that god was not the object of science, because god was beyond reason. This was referred to as 'the modernist view'.

16   Quoted by Bruce Arnold, *Mainie Jellett and the Modern Movement in Ireland* (New Haven, CT: Yale University Press, 1991), p. 181.

17   Kate O'Brien, *My Ireland* (London: Batsford, 1962), p. 25. On Clarke, see Kiberd, p. 464. Romanesque is said to adopt a different way of representation – a symbolic, subjective mode ('spiritual'), opposed to the pursuit of realism ('materialistic') in the visual art of the Italian Renaissance. See Jellet, quoted in Arnold, p. 101.

18   Mark Mulqueen, 'IFI – The Story So Far', *Irish Film Institute Programme: January– February 2005* (Dublin: Irish Film Institute, 2005), p. 23.

19   See David Monahan et al. (eds), *The Cinematic Jane Austen: Essays on the Filmic Sensibility of the Novels* (Jefferson, NC: McFarland, 2009).

20   There have been two film adaptations of Kate O'Brien novels to date: *For One Sweet Grape*, directed by Terence Young in 1955 and based on *That Lady* (New York: Penguin, 1985) and *Talk of Angels*, directed by Nick Hamm in 1998 and based on *Mary Lavelle*.

21   Kate O'Brien, *Presentation Parlour* (London: House of Stratus, 2001), p. 37.

22   Kate O'Brien, *Pray for the Wanderer* (London: Heinemann, 1938), p. 120.

23   Ibid., p. 184 [emphasis added].

24   For example, see *Distinguished Villa: A Play in Three Acts* (London: Ernest Benn, 1926).

25   Alison Butler, *Women's Cinema: The Contested Screen* (London and New York: Wallflower, 2005), p. 26.

26   Eugene Vale, *Tecnicas del Guion para Cine y Television* (Barcelona: Gedisa, 1989), p. 69.

27   Kate O'Brien, 'Why the Rage for French Films?', *The Star*, 1 February 1938, Kate O'Brien Papers, University of Limerick, doc. 134, p. 12.

28   Ibid.

29   Kate O'Brien, 'A Broken Song', Kate O'Brien Papers (n.d.), University of Limerick, doc. 185.

30   See Eibhear Walshe, *Kate O'Brien: A Writing Life* (Dublin: Irish Academic Press, 2006), p. 162.

31   Kate O'Brien, 'Mary Magdalen' (n.d.), National Library of Ireland, doc. 19, p. 703.

32   Jean-Paul Sartre, *Being and Nothingness: An Essay on Phenomenological Ontology*, trans. Hazel E. Barnes (London: Methuen, 1957).

33   Kate O'Brien, 'Gloria Gish' (n.d.), Kate O'Brien Papers, National Library of Ireland.

34   For example: Patricia Coughlan, 'Kate O'Brien: Feminine Beauty, Feminist Writing and Sexual Role', in Eibhear Walshe (ed.), *Ordinary People Dancing: Essays on Kate O'Brien* (Cork: Cork University Press, 1993), p. 60; Gerardine Meaney, 'Regendering Modernism: The Woman Artist in Irish Women's Fiction', *Women: A Cultural Review*, vol. 15, no. 1, 2004, p. 81; Sharon Tighe-Mooney, 'Sexuality and Religion in Kate O'Brien's Fiction', in Deirdre Quinn et al. (eds), *Essays in Irish Literary Criticism: Themes of Gender, Sexuality, and Corporeality* (Lewiston, NY: Edwin Mellen Press, 2008) p. 125.

35   Kate O'Brien, *Pray for the Wanderer*, p. 1. Joan Ryan describes this as 'photographic detail'. Joan Ryan, 'Class and Creed in Kate O'Brien', in Maurice Harmon (ed.), *The Irish Writer and the City* (Gerrards Cross: Colin Smythe, 1984), pp. 132, 127.

36   Richard Pine, 'Where is This Place? Kate O'Brien, Autism and Modern Literature', in John Logan (ed.), *With Warmest Love: Lectures for Kate O'Brien 1984–93*

(Limerick: Mellick Press, 1994), p. 95; Kate O'Brien, *The Land of Spices* (London: Virago, 2006).

37 Kate O'Brien, *As Music and Splendour* (Dublin: Penguin, 2005), p. 1.

38 Kate O'Brien, *Mary Lavelle*, p. 120.

39 Alexander Doty, 'Queer Theory', in John Hill et al. (eds), *The Oxford Guide to Film Studies* (Oxford: Oxford University Press, 1998), p. 150.

40 Alexander Doty, *Making Things Perfectly Queer: Interpreting Mass Culture* (Minneapolis, MN: University of Minessota Press, 1993), p. 3.

41 Quoted in ibid., p. xiii.

42 Noreen Giffney, 'Quare Theory', in Wanda Balzano et al. (eds), *Popular Culture and Postmodern Ireland* (London: Palgrave Macmillan, 2007), p. 202.

43 Judith Butler, *Gender Trouble* (New York and London: Routledge, 1990), p. 141. [emphasis in the original].

44 Elliott, p. 212.

45 Judith Butler, 'Imitation and Gender Insubordination', in Diana Fuss (ed.), *Inside/Out – Lesbian Theories, Gay Theories* (New York and London: Routledge, 1991), p. 22.

46 Ernest Hemingway, *Death in the Afternoon* (New York: Charles Scribner's Sons, 1960), p. 99; O'Brien, *Mary Lavelle*, p. 227.

47 Ibid., p. 309.

48 Ibid., p. 114.

49 Ibid., p. 309.

50 Ibid., p. 309.

51 Ibid., p. 153.

52 Ibid., p. 331.

53 Ibid., p. 307.

54 Hemingway, *Death in the Afternoon*, p. 145.

55 O'Brien, *Mary Lavelle*, p. 85.

56 Ibid., p. 200.

57 See Aintzane Legarreta Mentxaka, 'La Belle – Kate O'Brien and Female Beauty', in Sarah O'Connor et al. (eds), *Women, Social and Cultural Change in Twentieth-Century Ireland: Dissenting Voices?* (Newcastle: Cambridge Scholars' Press, 2008).

58 O'Brien, *Mary Lavelle*, p. 38.

59 Ibid., p. 143.

60 Ibid., p. 189.

61 Ibid., p. 185.

62 Kate O'Brien is modifying a famous coinage of 1914 by art critic Clive Bell, who claimed that modernism in the visual arts is a quest for 'significant form'. Clive Bell, *Art* (London: BiblioBazaar, 2007).

63 O'Brien, 'Why the Rage for French Films?'

64 Ibid. [emphasis in the original].

65 See Butler, 'Imitation and Gender Insubordination', p. 23.

66 Ibid., p. 24.

CHAPTER NINE (Mulhall)

1 Will Gesler, 'Lourdes: Healing in a Place of Pilgrimage', *Health & Place*, vol. 2, no. 2, 1996, p. 96.

2 Laurence Cox and Maria Griffin, 'Border Country Dharma: Buddhism, Ireland and Peripherality', *Journal of Global Buddhism*, vol. 10, 2009, p. 93.

3 Ibid., p. 114.

4 Edward Said, *Orientalism* (New York: Vintage, 1979).

5 Joseph Lennon, *Irish Orientalism: A Literary and Intellectual History* (Syracuse, NY: Syracuse University Press, 2004), p. 1.

6 Ibid., p. 374.

7 Ibid., p. 2.

8 Ibid., p. 311.

9 For an excellent account of 'the new age ethic' that includes a sociological account of some Irish variations, see Carmel Kuhling, *The New Age Ethic and the Spirit of Postmodernity* (Creskill, NJ: Hampton Press, 2004).

10 J.J. Clarke, *Oriental Enlightenment: The Encounter Between Asian and Western Thought* (London and New York: Routledge, 1997), p. 307.

11 Ibid., p. 302.

12 Jennifer Lea, 'Retreating to Nature: Rethinking Therapeutic Landscapes', *Area*, vol. 40, no. 1, 2008, p. 90.

13 Gesler, 'Lourdes', p. 96.

14 See Ronan Foley, *Healing Waters: Therapeutic Landscapes in Historic and Contemporary Ireland* (London: Ashgate, 2010); Gesler, 'Lourdes', p. 97.

15 Gesler, 'Lourdes', p. 99.

16 Peggy O'Brien, *Writing Lough Derg: From William Carleton to Seamus Heaney* (Syracuse, NY: Syracuse University Press, 2006), pp. 4–6.

17 In fact, the website as of 5 February 2012 has undergone further alterations. There is now no image of the monsignor on the homepage, and it is difficult to find any reference to him anywhere on the site. We are told that a new, redesigned website will be launched in 2012. See http://www.loughderg.org [accessed 5 February 2012].

18 The Ryan Report, which gives an account of the extensive abuse suffered by children in Catholic-run industrial schools, was published in May 2009. The Murphy Report details the way in which the Catholic Church dealt with complaints of abuse during the period 1975 to 2004, revealing secrecy and cover-ups as the mainstay of the church's administration. This report was released in November 2009.

19 See http://www.loughderg.org [accessed 5 February 2012].

20 Conor Feehan, 'Lough Derg Revival: Pilgrim's Progress', *Irish Independent*, 15 June 2004.

21 Ibid. Similar testimonials couched in New Age and mind, body and spirit vocabulary were quoted on the 2007 website, but interestingly none of these remained in the 2010 website, which had a corresponding section called 'Reflections' rather than 'Testimonials', which has now become 'Pilgrims' Reflections' on the version accessed on 5 February 2012.

22 David McKittrick, 'God and the Celtic Tiger: Pilgrims in Retreat from Progress', *The Independent*, 10 August 2006.

23 Joyce Davidson and Christine Milligan, 'Editorial: Embodying Emotion Sensing Space: Introducing Emotional Geographies', *Social & Cultural Geography*, vol. 5, no. 4, 2004, p. 523.

24 Moya Kneafsey, 'Tourism Images and the Construction of Celticity in Ireland and Britain', in David Harvey et al. (eds), *Celtic Geographies: Old Culture, New Times* (London: Routledge, 2001), p.123.

25 Ibid., p.127.

26 Kim Knott, *Hinduism: An Introduction* (Oxford: Oxford University Press, 1998), p. 94.

27 Anne-Cécile Hoyez, 'The "World of Yoga": The Production and Reproduction of Therapeutic Landscapes', *Social Science & Medicine*, vol. 65, 2007, p. 122.

28 Thanks to Aintzane Legarreta Mentxaka for bringing this leaflet to my attention.

29 The website for 'Krishna Island' can be found at http://www.krishnaisland.com and is the 'version' of Inis Rath linked to via the main ISKCON UK and Ireland website, http://iskconuk.com. 'Lake Isle Retreats' comes up in Google searches for ISKCON UK and Krishna Island, but appears, in terms of the absence of interconnecting weblinks, like an entirely different location, http://www.lakeisleretreats.com [accessed 5 February 2012].

30 http://www.lakeisleretreats.com [accessed 9 August 2010].

31 http://www.krishnaisland.com [accessed 9 August 2010].

32 Slavoj Žižek, *On Belief* (London and New York: Routledge, 2001), p.12.

CHAPTER TEN (Graham)

1 Joe Duggan, *Family Man*, Limerick City Art Gallery, 6 July–28 August 2007. This exhibition consisted of two related sets of work, 'Family Man' and 'Like Father, Like Son'.

2 Theodor Adorno, *Minima Moralia: Reflections on a Damaged Life*, trans. E.F.N. Jephcott (London: Verso, 2005), p. 112.

3 Ibid., p. 111.

4 Ibid., p. 111.

5 Ibid., p. 111. (The anecdote begins on p. 110.)

6 Ibid., p. 113.

7 Ibid., p. 113.

8 Ibid., p. 113.

9 The term famously associated with the photographic technique of Henri Cartier-Bresson. See Cartier-Bresson, *The Decisive Moment* (London: Simon & Schuster, 1952).

10 Adorno, *Minima Moralia*, p. 109.

11 Ibid., p. 109.

12 Ibid., p. 111.

13 Theodor Adorno, *The Culture Industry* (London: Routledge, 2001), p. 76.

14 Ibid., p. 59.

15 'Mass culture treats conflicts but in fact proceeds without conflict', *The Culture Industry*, p. 71.

16 The second paragraph of 'Second Harvest' is one sentence: 'Nowadays most people kick with the pricks', Adorno, *Minima Moralia*, p. 109.

17 See Nicolas Bourriaud, *The Radicant* (New York: Lukas & Sternberg, 2009) for a discussion of the role of identity politics in the formation of recent art practice and in particular a critique of the failure of 'radical' identity politics to maintain a distance from the identity politics utilised by late capitalist governance and the art market.

18 Hal Foster, *The Return of the Real* (Cambridge, MA: MIT Press, 1996), p. 82.

19 Ernest Bloch, *The Spirit of Utopia*, trans. Anthony A. Nassar (Palo Alto, CA: Stanford University Press, 2000), p. 33.

20 Ibid., p. 30.

21 Vilém Flusser, *Towards a Philosophy of Photography* (London: Reaktion, 2007), p. 36.

22 Jean Baudrillard, 'For Illusion is not the Opposite of Reality', in David Campany (ed.), *Art and Photography* (London: Phaidon, 2007), p. 236.

23 Adorno, *Minima Moralia*, p. 113.

24 Ibid., p. 113.
25 Ibid., p. 112.
26 Ibid., p. 113.
27 Vilém Flusser, *Writings* (Minneapolis, MN: University of Minnesota Press, 2002), p. 129.
28 Adorno, *Minima Moralia*, p. 113.

CHAPTER ELEVEN (Bracken)

 1 As an audience, we are encouraged to laugh at both Rats and Jeremy, though while Rats is constructed as a loveable fool, Jeremy is given a much more negative construction. His racism (he refuses to acknowledge the paralysis he has caused an immigrant man in a hit and run), misogyny and blatant class snobbery consistently presents him as a laughable character in all his repulsiveness.
 2 See actor Deirdre O'Kane's comments in Mick Heaney, 'Marriage of Convenience: Interview', *Sunday Times*, 9 June 2002.
 3 Liam Fay, 'Sex and the Single Microwave', *Sunday Times*, 16 December 2001.
 4 For an analysis of Deirdre O'Kane's stand-up comedy see Claire Bracken and Emma Radley, 'A Mirror up to Irishness: Hollywood Hardmen and Witty Women', in Wanda Balzano, Anne Mulhall and Moynagh Sullivan (eds), *Irish Postmodernisms and Popular Culture* (Basingstoke: Palgrave, 2007), pp. 157–68.
 5 Heaney, 'Marriage of Convenience', p. 2.
 6 Angela McRobbie, *The Aftermath of Feminism: Gender, Culture and Social Change* (London: Sage, 2009), pp. 54–72.
 7 For a perceptive analysis of contemporary Ireland and the positioning of women, see the opening sections of Patricia Coughlan's article 'Irish Literature and Feminism in Postmodernity', *Hungarian Journal of English and American Studies*, vol. 10, nos 1–2, 2004, pp. 175–81. Furthermore, Debbie Ging provides an excellent analysis of post-feminism and gender constructions in Ireland in 'All-Consuming Images: New Gender Formations in Post-Celtic-Tiger Ireland', in Debbie Ging, Michael Cronin and Peadar Kirby (eds), *Transforming Ireland: Challenges, Critiques and Resources* (Manchester: Manchester University Press, 2009), pp. 52–70.
 8 Luce Irigaray, *This Sex Which is Not One*, trans. Catherine Porter and Carolyn Burke (Ithaca, NY: Cornell University Press, 1985), p. 72.
 9 Ging, 'All-Consuming Images', p. 56.
10 Yvonne Tasker and Diane Negra, 'Introduction: Feminist Politics and Postfeminist Culture', in Yvonne Tasker and Diane Negra (eds), *Interrogating Postfeminism: Gender and the Politics of Popular Culture* (Durham, NC: Duke University Press, 2007), p. 2.
11 I am taking the term 'beauty myth' from American author Naomi Wolf's influential book *The Beauty Myth* (London: Vintage, 1991).
12 Wanda Balzano and Moynagh Sullivan, 'Editorial: The Contemporary Ballroom of Romance', special issue: Irish Feminisms, *Irish Review*, vol. 35, 2007, p. 1.
13 McRobbie, *The Aftermath of Feminism*, p. 57.
14 Ibid., p. 72.
15 In addition to Tasker and Negra's *Interrogating Postfeminism* and McRobbie's *The Aftermath of Feminism*, see Imelda Whelehan, *The Feminist Bestseller: From Sex and the Single Girl to Sex and the City* (Basingstoke: Palgrave Macmillan, 2005).
16 McRobbie, *The Aftermath of Feminism*, p. 58.
17 Luce Irigaray, *Speculum of the Other Woman*, trans. Gillian C. Gill (Ithaca, NY: Cornell University Press, 1985).

246 Notes to Pages 174–181

18 Irigaray, *Speculum*, p. 133.

19 Ibid., p. 144.

20 For an exploration of the process whereby the mother's birthing body is appropriated in Irish criticism and Irish culture see Moynagh Sullivan, 'Boyz to Menz(own): Irish Boy Bands and the Alternative Nation', *Irish Review*, vol. 34, 2006, pp. 58–78 and 'The Treachery of Wetness: Irish Studies, Seamus Heaney and the Politics of Parturition', *Irish Studies Review*, vol. 13, no. 4, 2005, pp. 451–68.

21 Luce Irigaray, 'Veiled Lips', trans. Sara Spiedal, *Mississippi Review*, vol. 11, no. 3, 1983, pp. 93–131.

22 Ibid., p. 99.

23 Ibid., p. 110.

24 In *The Aftermath of Feminism*, McRobbie uses the term 'masquerade' to refer to performances of femininity by young women in contemporary late capitalist culture.

25 Irigaray, 'Veiled Lips', p. 99.

26 For a similar point, see Tasker and Negra, 'Introduction', p. 8.

27 McRobbie, *The Aftermath*, p. 61.

28 Ibid.

29 Ibid.

30 One of the members of the documentary crew makes a point about the expense involved in beauty care. This is a particularly important comment given that the previous scene is an interview with the wife/partner of the man who Jeremy paralysed in the hit and run. The contrast between the two women's realities (she states how they have no money to pay the medical bills) points very clearly to the way post-feminism is marked by class and racial exclusions.

31 Irigaray, 'Veiled Lips', p. 111.

32 Ibid.

33 Laura Mulvey, 'Visual Pleasure and Narrative Cinema', in Amelia Jones (ed.), *The Feminism and Visual Culture Reader* (London: Routledge, 2008), p. 47.

34 The scene is very reflexive in this respect. The camera crew are in the room with Helen, framing her within the gaze of the spectator, thus the process which Mulvey talks about is actually revealed in the process of its operation.

35 The paternity question gestures towards questions of racial difference in Celtic Tiger Ireland. In a previous episode, in a swinging club scene, there is a (brief) shot of a black man, establishing the possibility that Penny's child could be mixed-race, thus destabilising a traditional construction of Irishness as defined by racial whiteness. However, this 'glance' is effectively left unexplored – a never-realised potential in the show's narrative.

36 During Penny's hen (bachelorette) party, Lorraine discovers the S&M room in her house; later, she is seen there in handcuffs, enjoying a 'whipping' from Fergus's sister Gráinne. In the final episode of *Paths to Freedom*, Helen removes her shirt and asks both the camera crew and Rats (who is visiting) to have sex with her, a request that is not fulfilled. What these two examples register is that the post-feminist woman has the potential to act for the self, and that is fundamentally threatening to a system which requires her to be object of support. However, rather than fully explore this, both series remove this suggestive threat by excising Lorraine and Helen at their conclusion.

37 Margaret Whitford, *Luce Irigaray: Philosophy in the Feminine* (London: Routledge, 1991), p. 114.

38 Fintan Walsh makes a similar point regarding neo-liberalism and queer culture in

the opening of his essay in this collection (p. 217) when he notes, 'the figure of the homosexual has stood in as a symbol of Irish cosmopolitanism.' For an important discussion of this in the intersecting contexts of sexuality and race see Anne Mulhall's essay 'Queer in Ireland: "Deviant" Filiation and the (Un)holy Family', in Lisa Downing and Robert Gillett (eds), *Queer in Europe* (Surrey: Ashgate, 2011), pp. 99–112.

39 Moynagh Sullivan, '"I Am Not Yet Delivered of the Past": The Poetry of Blanaid Salkeld', *Irish University Review*, vol. 33, no. 1, 2003, p. 190.

40 McRobbie, *The Aftermath of Feminism*, p. 4.

41 Patricia Coughlan, '"The Whole Strange Growth": Heaney, Orpheus and Women', *Irish Review*, vol. 35, 2007, p. 41.

42 'Renewing the Republic' is the title of a series of articles responding to the post-Tiger recession run in the national *Irish Times* newspaper in 2010. It is also the title of a book by Irish President Michael D. Higgins: *Renewing the Republic* (Dublin: Liberties Press, 2011).

CHAPTER TWELVE (Asava)

1 Pavel Barter, 'Irish Horror', *Sunday Times*, 21 October 2007, p. 4 (Culture section).

2 The female figure in horror film has been understood alternately as a victim (Laura Mulvey reads Hitchcock's heroines as the object of the male gaze), a symbol of abjection (Barbara Creed reads horror films like *Carrie* (Brian de Palma, 1976) and *Alien* (Ridley Scott, 1979) as rooted in fear of the 'monstrous feminine', i.e. the female body and its menstrual emissions as abject), and a 'final girl' (the last survivor of the slasher film who lives to tell the tale, as explored by Carol Clover). See Laura Mulvey, *Visual and Other Pleasures* (Bloomington, IN: Indiana University Press, 1989); Barbara Creed, *The Monstrous Feminine: Film, Feminism, Psychoanalysis* (London: Routledge, 1993); Carol Clover, *Men, Women and Chainsaws: Gender and the Modern Horror Film* (Princeton, NJ: Princeton University Press, 1992).

3 The 'tragic mulatta' is an exposition of the perceived divided nature of mixed-race people; it is a body at war with itself as its black and white elements conflict, thus it is tragic and doomed to failure. See Mary Beltràn and Camilla Fojas, *Mixed Race Hollywood* (New York: New York University Press, 2008); Suzanne Bost, *Mulattas and Mestizas: Representing Mixed Identities in the Americas, 1850–2000* (Athens, GA: University of Georgia Press, 2003). Although there are exceptions, mixed-race women have traditionally been overrepresented as 'tragic mulattas': see American films like *In Humanity's Cause* (James Hendrie, 1911), *The Birth of a Nation* (D.W. Griffith, 1915), *Showboat* (James Whale, 1936/George Sidney, 1951), *Imitation of Life* (John M. Stahl, 1934/Douglas Sirk, 1959) and *Carmen Jones* (Otto Preminger, 1954). The stereotype can still be read into modern American representations, e.g. Halle Berry in *Things We Lost in the Fire* (Susanne Bier, 2007) or *Monster's Ball* (Marc Forster, 2001).

4 The American hypodescent practice (whereby one is white if one has no black ancestry and black if one does) can be traced back to slavery: a mixed-race child was likely to have a mother who was a slave and a father who was a slave master. In order to protect property rights from slaves, the child would be classified as black (which equated to slave) and thus denied the rights of inheritance, ownership or citizenship. For more on this topic see Naomi Zack, *Race and Mixed Race* (Philadelphia: Temple University Press, 1993).

5 Known as 'The Celtic Tiger', this boom led to Ireland's first experience of

immigrants outnumbering emigrants, but many of the 'immigrants' until 2001 were actually Irish people who had been living abroad (see Steve Garner, *Whiteness: An Introduction* (London: Routledge, 2007)). The 2006 census of Ireland recorded that 10 per cent of the population was made up of non-nationals. Immigration led to an upsurge in racism: an Amnesty International 2001 study found that while blacks, Romas and Travellers were the groups most likely to suffer verbal/physical abuse, the black Irish expressed the highest rate of discrimination suffered – 88.6 per cent (Garner, 2007). Garner notes, 'By the beginning of the twenty-first century, racist abuse had become endemic in Ireland and its victims could be anyone who is not white, regardless of their nationality or immigration status' (p. 131).

6 Ronit Lentin, 'Black Bodies and Headless Hookers: Alternative Global Narratives for Twenty-First Century Ireland', *The Irish Review*, vol. 33, 2005, p. 7.

7 Gerardine Meaney, 'Race, Sex and Nation', *The Irish Review*, vol. 35, 2007, p. 50.

8 Negga's screen debut was as a Nigerian trafficked into Ireland and forced into prostitution in *Capital Letters* (Ciarán O'Connor, 2004), re-released in May 2010 under the title *Trafficked*. She plays an Irish single mother in *Isolation* and in *Breakfast on Pluto* (Neil Jordan, 2005).

9 In an interview with Irish TV show *Xposé* (TV3, 25 May 2010), Negga was asked the question, 'do you fly the flag for Ireland?' She responded by asserting her position as an Irish actress: 'that's how I identify myself.' When asked if American casting agents were surprised that she does not have 'red hair and freckles', Negga responded, 'they're always very surprised', and expressed dismay that such outdated stereotypes endure. Laughing, she continued, 'well I'm here and there's lots of us!'

10 For a detailed reading on the Othering of Travellers as part of the process of state nationalism, see Bryan Fanning, *Racism and Social Change in the Republic of Ireland* (Manchester: Manchester University Press, 2002).

11 In 2008 UK scientists created embryos using human and animal material, with eggs taken from a cow.

12 LeiLani Nishime, 'The Mulatto Cyborg: Imagining a Multiracial Future', *Cinema Journal*, vol. 44, no. 2, 2005, p. 35.

13 The criminalisation of interracial sex endured longest in America. It was illegal in various states between 1661 and 1967.

14 Donna Haraway, *Modest_Witness@Second_Millennium. Femaleman©_Meets_Oncomouse™* (London: Routledge, 1997), p. 258.

15 See Mary Foster, 'Interracial Couple Denied Marriage License in LA', *Associated Press*, 16 October 2009, http://www.thegrio.com/news/interracial-couple-denied-marriage-license-in-louisiana.php [accessed 15 January 2012].

16 The monster has been used as a tool to read non-normative and non-hegemonical identities through horror, e.g. the female as abject, see Barbara Creed, *The Monstrous Feminine*, 1993; the coloniser as vampire, see Luise White, *Speaking with Vampires: Rumor and History in Colonial Africa* (Berkeley, CA: University of California Press, 2000); the homosexual/lesbian as transgressive, see Harry M. Benshoff, *Monsters in the Closet: Homosexuality and the Horror Film* (Manchester: Manchester University Press, 1997).

17 This association is reinforced by a September 2009 radio ad funded by independent Irish stations and RTÉ, which encourages the use of radio for advertising by asserting the visual nature of the aural medium. A man describes

himself from head to toe, conjuring up a monstrous image of a sweating, 300-pound, 7-foot tall, naked, Samoan-Tongalese man raised in Ireland, with a ginger moustache and a rash on his upper thigh in the shape of a face. Disease, unattractive features, obesity, abnormality and bad smells are evoked in this narrative, all reinforced by his mixed-race identity.

18 Julia Kristeva, *Powers of Horror: An Essay on Abjection*, trans. Leon S. Roudiez (New York: Columbia University Press, 1982), p. 4.

19 See Bost, *Mulattas and Mestizas*, 2003.

20 Mary Beltràn, 'The New Hollywood Racelessness: Only the Fast, Furious (and Multiracial) Will Survive', *Cinema Journal*, vol. 44, no. 2, 2005, p. 50.

21 With the exception of their leads, both *Isolation* and *Boy Eats Girl* have all-white casts.

22 Ruth Barton, 'Boy Eats Girl', *Estudios Irlandeses*, vol. 1, 2006, p. 162.

23 Steve Garner, *Racism in the Irish Experience* (London: Pluto Press, 2003); Garner, *Whiteness*.

24 See Barton, 'Boy Eats Girl'.

25 Ibid.

26 Ibid.

27 See Emer Rockett and Kevin Rockett, *Neil Jordan: Exploring Boundaries* (Dublin: Liffey Press, 2003), p. 193.

28 Haraway, *Modest_Witness*, p. 258.

29 See Nira Yuval-Davis, *Gender and Nation* (London: Sage, 1997).

30 In his work *On the Phenomena of Hybridity in the Genus Homo* (London: Longman, Green, Longman & Roberts, 1864), French anthropologist Paul Broca endorsed procreation between black women and white men as he claimed their offspring would inherit more of the father's racial superiority, thus improving the status of humanity by elevating the perceived inferior races.

31 For more on the 'phallocular' gaze see Martin Jay, *Downcast Eyes: The Denigration of Vision in Twentieth-Century French Thought* (Berkeley, CA: University of California Press, 1993), pp. 493–542.

32 Anne McClintock, 'Family Feuds: Gender, Nationalism and the Family', *Feminist Review*, vol. 44, 1993, p. 61.

33 Shelly Feldman, 'Feminist Interruptions: The Silence of Easy Bengal in the Story of Partition', *Interventions: International Journal of Postcolonial Studies*, vol. 1, no. 2, 1999, p. 178.

34 Sigmund Freud, *The Uncanny*, trans. David McLintock (London: Penguin, 2003).

35 Beltràn, 'The New Hollywood Racelessness', pp. 50, 56.

36 Clover, *Men, Women and Chainsaws*.

37 Mia Mask, 'Monster's Ball', *Film Quarterly*, vol. 58, no. 1, 2004, p. 45.

38 Meaney, 'Race, Sex and Nation'.

39 Ibid., p. 61.

CHAPTER THIRTEEN (O'Connor)

1 See Emer Rockett and Kevin Rockett, *Neil Jordan: Exploring Boundaries* (Dublin: Liffey Press, 2003), and Martin McLoone, *Irish Film: The Emergence of a Contemporary Cinema* (London: British Film Institute, 2000).

2 Deleuze's understanding of physiological and cerebral connections to cinematic images is explored in his books on cinema: Gilles Deleuze, *Cinema 1: The Movement-Image*, trans. Hugh Tomlinson and Barbara Habberjam (London: Continuum, 2005) and *Cinema 2: The Time-Image*, trans. Hugh Tomlinson and

Robert Galeta (London: Continuum, 2005). It is also the subject of a collection of essays by Deleuzian scholars: Gregory Flaxman (ed.), *The Brain is the Screen: Deleuze and the Philosophy of Cinema* (Minneapolis, MN: University of Minnesota Press, 2000).

3 Claire Colebrook, *Gilles Deleuze* (Oxford and New York: Routledge, 2005), pp 1–8.

4 Ibid., p. 6 [emphasis in original].

5 The fact that 'becoming-woman' is the concept of two male philosophers is not lost on feminists. Claire Colebrook asserts that 'when Deleuze and Guattari address feminism, as the possibility for a new form of address or relation, they are at once drawn into the difficult relation between the becoming of feminism and the identity of the tradition'. Claire Colebrook, 'Introduction', in Ian Buchanan and Claire Colebrook (eds), *Deleuze and Feminist Theory* (Edinburgh: Edinburgh University Press, 2001), p. 4.

6 During Kitten's period as a peep-show performer, she explains to a punter why her 'bazoozoms' are not as voluptuous as those of her co-workers by describing herself as 'svelte' and 'gamine'.

7 Lir Mac Cárthaigh, 'Songs of Innocence', *Film Ireland*, vol. 108, January/February 2006, pp. 12–13. This performativity of femininity (and particularly the pursuit of glamour) recalls Judith Butler's work on gender construction in *Gender Trouble* (London: Routledge, 1990) and *Bodies That Matter* (London: Routledge, 1993). While Butler repudiates any rhizomatic links between her work and that of Deleuze, gender performativity enables the actor to play with the idea of gender as a process of construction.

8 Rosi Braidotti, *Metamorphoses: Towards a Materialist Theory of Becoming* (Cambridge: Polity Press, 2002), p. 69.

9 Deleuze and Guattari, *A Thousand Plateaus: Capitalism and Schizophrenia*, trans. Brian Massumi (London: Continuum, 2001), p. 267.

10 Slavoj Žižek, 'The Inaccessible Lady: From Courtly Love to *The Crying Game*', *New Left Review*, vol. 202, 1993, p. 105.

11 Ibid., p. 101.

12 Deleuze and Guattari, *A Thousand Plateaus*, p. 275.

13 Deleuze's phrase 'becoming-woman' uses the term 'woman' to express molecular becoming. There is no such thing as 'becoming-man' because man is molar and cannot truly become. Woman exists in the interstices, between molar entities, 'between orders, acts, ages, sexes' (*A Thousand Plateaus*, p. 305). Molar entities are those that reinforce the homosocial status quo; molecular entitities are in constant movement, changing and forming connections with other entities in a process that has no end (i.e. becoming).

14 Deleuze and Guatttari, *A Thousand Plateaus*, p. 305.

15 Ibid.

16 Braidotti, *Metamorphoses*, p. 97.

17 Deleuze and Guattari, *A Thousand Plateaus*, p. 35.

18 Ibid., p. 35.

19 Ibid., p. 305.

20 Luce Irigaray, *This Sex Which is Not One*, trans. Caroline Porter (Ithaca, NY: Cornell University Press, 1985), p. 77 [emphasis in original].

21 Žižek, 'The Inaccessible Lady', p. 96.

22 Žižek also discusses rape fantasies in 'How to Read Lacan. From *Che Vuoi?* to Fantasy: Lacan with *Eyes Wide Shut*', http://www.lacan.com/zizkubrick.htm

[accessed 16 January 2011]. He notes that 'There is a gap which forever separates the fantasmatic kernel of the subject's being from the more superficial
modes of his or her symbolic or imaginary identifications.' Kitten does not see
herself as the product of rape, nor does she truly accuse Fr Liam of committing
a heinous act. However, she retains the rape on the page of her copybook, as a
dramatic fiction, a spicy accoutrement to her otherwise banal existence. For
Kitten, 'fantasy is the screen which protects [her] from the encounter with the
Real'.
23 Žižek, 'The Inaccessible Lady', p. 95.
24 Gilles Deleuze and Felix Guattari, *Anti-Oedipus: Capitalism and Schizophrenia*, trans.
   Robert Hurley, Mark Seem and Helen R. Lane (London: Continuum, 2004),
   p. 326.
25 Braidotti, *Metamorphoses*, p. 82.
26 Ibid.
27 Ibid., pp. 105–6.
28 Ibid., p. 69.
29 Žižek, 'The Inaccessible Lady', p. 104.
30 Rockett and Rockett, *Neil Jordan*, p. 133.
31 Deleuze and Guattari, *A Thousand Plateaus*, p. 322.
32 Ibid., p. 304.
33 Ibid.

CHAPTER FOURTEEN (Walsh)

1 Leo Bersani and Ulysse Dutoit, *Forms of Being: Cinema, Aesthetics, Subjectivity*
  (London: British Film Institute, 2004), p. 9.
2 Mark O'Halloran, 'Editorial', special issue: 'Sex Please, We're Irish', *Film Ireland*,
  vol. 120, January/February, 2008, p. 5.
3 Ibid.
4 Ibid.
5 Fintan Walsh, 'Cock Tales: Homosexuality, Trauma, and the Cosmopolitan
  Queer', special issue: 'Sex Please, We're Irish', *Film Ireland*, vol. 120,
  January/February, 2008, pp. 16–18.
6 In addition to *Adam & Paul* and *Garage*, Abrahamson and O'Halloran respectively directed and wrote the television drama *Prosperity*, shown by RTÉ in 2007.
  The four one-hour long dramas were based around characters living in Ireland
  at the time, who were definitely not benefiting from the country's economic
  boom.
7 Implicit in this assertion is the belief that the development of a queer representational aesthetic in film and visual culture impacts upon the cultural imaginary
  on a broader plane, by creating space for the figuration and mediation of history
  and possibility.
8 Lance Pettitt, 'Pigs and Provos, Prostitutes and Prejudice: Gay Representation in
  Irish Film, 1984–1995', in Eibhear Walsh (ed.), *Sex, Nation and Dissent in Irish
  Writing* (Cork: Cork University Press, 1997), p. 253.
9 The traumatic figuration of sexuality, especially homosexuality, can be discerned
  in films as diverse as Liam McGrath's *Male Rape* (1996), Jimmy Smallhorne's
  2By4 (1998) and Neil Jordan's *The Crying Game* (1992) and *Breakfast on Pluto*
  (2005). Even in features that deal with institutional abuse, such as Peter Mullan's
  The Magdalene Sisters (2002) and Aisling Walsh's *Song for a Raggy Boy* (2003), paedophilia and an implied homosexuality are uncomfortably conflated.

10 Not only can the films be considered art house in terms of their subjects and aesthetic choices, but they primarily tour the European film circuit.

11 While Abrahamson's and O'Halloran's films are unusually accomplished in this respect, the short films of Ken Wardrop are similarly aesthetically interesting, in particular *Undressing My Mother* (2004).

12 Bersani and Dutoit reclaim the Lacanian concept of *joussiance* (variously understood as the subject's excess or death-drive) to designate the pleasure of resisting subjectivity or becoming a non-subject, however temporarily. In their discussion of *The Thin Red Line* the authors suggest that the film's trajectory not only mobilises the dispersal of subjectivity in the context of war, but makes visible the extensibility of a wide range of human and non-human networks.

13 Bersani and Dutoit, *Forms of Being*, pp. 8–9.

14 Leo Bersani, *The Culture of Redemption* (Cambridge, MA: Harvard University Press, 1990), p. 4.

15 Ibid.

16 Calvin Thomas, *Masculinity, Psychoanalysis, Straight Queer Theory: Essays on Abjection in Literature, Mass Culture and Film* (New York: Palgrave Macmillan, 2008), p. 85.

17 Examples include *Breakfast on Pluto* (Neil Jordan, 2005); *Kisses* (Lance Daly, 2008).

18 Bersani and Dutoit, *Forms of Being*, pp. 176–7.

19 On the film's Ulyssean inflection see Michael Patrick Gillespie, 'The Odyssey of Adam and Paul: A Twenty-First-Century Irish Film', *New Hibernia Review*, vol. 12, no. 1, 2008, pp. 41–53.

20 Bersani and Dutoit, *Forms of Being*, p. 169.

21 Luciana Parisi, *Abstract Sex: Philosophy, Bio-Technology and the Mutations of Desire* (New York: Continuum, 2004), pp. 171–93.

22 Ibid., p. 189.

23 See Jane Bennett, *Vibrant Matter: A Political Ecology of Things* (Durham, NC: Duke University Press, 2010).

24 Patricia MacCormack, *Cinesexuality* (Aldershot: Ashgate, 2008), p. 149.

25 Ibid., p. 2.

26 Ibid., p. 3.

27 Ibid.

28 See Jacques Rancière, *The Politics of Aesthetics: The Distribution of the Sensible*, trans. Gabriel Rockhill (London and New York: Continuum, 2004).

29 Michael O'Rourke, 'For the Love of Cinema', Series Editors' Preface, in Patricia MacCormack, *Cinesexuality*, pp. ix–xi, x–xi.

BIBLIOGRAPHY

Abbas, Ackbar, 'On Fascination: Walter Benjamin's Images', *New German Critique*, vol. 48, 1989, pp. 43–62

Abel, Richard, Giorgio Bertellini and Rob King (eds), *Early Cinema and the 'National'* (Bloomington, IN: Indiana University Press, 2008)

Adorno, Theodor, *Minima Moralia: Reflections from Damaged Life*, trans. E.F.N. Jephcott (London: Verso, 1978, 2005)

Adorno, Theodor, *The Culture Industry* (London: Routledge, 2001)

Allen, Graham, *Intertextuality* (London: Routledge, 2000)

Anderson, Benedict, *Imagined Communities: Reflections on the Origin and Spread of Nationalism*, 2nd edn (New York: Verso, 2006)

Appadurai, Arjun, *Modernity at Large: Cultural Dimensions of Globalization* (Minneapolis, MN: University of Minnesota Press, 1997)

Arnold, Bruce, *Mainie Jellett and the Modern Movement in Ireland* (New Haven, CT: Yale University Press, 1991)

Bakhtin, Mikhail, *Art and Answerability: Early Philosophical Essays by M.M Bakhtin*, trans. Vadim Liapunov (Austin, TX: University of Texas Press, 1990)

Bakhtin, Mikhail, *The Dialogic Imagination: Four Essays by M.M Bakhtin*, trans. Caryl Emerson and Michael Holquist (Austin, TX: University of Texas Press, 1981)

Wanda Balzano, Anne Mulhall, and Moynagh Sullivan, 'Introduction', in Balzano et al (eds.), *Irish Postmodernisms and Popular Culture* (Basingstoke, Hampshire: Palgrave Macmillan, 2007), pp. xii–xix

Balzano, Wanda and Moynagh Sullivan, 'Editorial: The Contemporary Ballroom of Romance', special issue: Irish Feminisms, *Irish Review*, vol. 35, 2007, pp. 1–6

Barter, Pavel, 'Irish Horror', *Sunday Times*, 21 October 2007, p. 4 (Culture section)

Barthes, Roland, *Camera Lucida: Reflections on Photography*, trans. Richard Howard (London: Flamingo, 1982)

Barthes, Roland, *Image, Music, Text*, trans. Stephen Heath (London: Fontana, 1977)

Barton, Ruth, *Irish National Cinema* (London: Routledge, 2004)

Barton, Ruth, 'Boy Eats Girl', *Estudios Irlandeses*, vol. 1, 2006, pp. 162–3

Baudrillard, Jean, 'For Illusion is Not the Opposite of Reality', in David Campany (ed.), *Art and Photography* (London: Phaidon, 2007), pp. 234–8

Bell, Clive, *Art* (London: BiblioBazaar, 2007)

Beltràn Mary, 'The New Hollywood Racelessness: Only the Fast, Furious (and Multiracial) Will Survive', *Cinema Journal*, vol. 44, no. 2, 2005, pp. 50–67

Beltràn Mary and Camilla Fojas, *Mixed Race Hollywood* (New York: New York University Press, 2008)

Benjamin, Walter, 'Central Park', trans. Lloyd Spencer, Mark Harrington, *New German Critique*, vol. 34, 1985, pp. 32–58

Benjamin, Walter, *Illuminations: Essays and Reflections*, trans. Harry Zohn (London: Fontana, 1973)

Bennett, Jane, *Vibrant Matter: A Political Ecology of Things* (Durham, NC: Duke University Press, 2010)

Benshoff, Harry M., *Monsters in the Closet: Homosexuality and the Horror Film* (Manchester: Manchester University Press, 1997)

Benveniste, Emile, *Problèmes de Linguistique Générale* (Paris: Gallimard, 1974)

Bersani, Leo, *The Culture of Redemption* (Cambridge, MA: Harvard University Press, 1990)

Bersani, Leo and Ulysse Dutoit, *Forms of Being: Cinema, Aesthetics, Subjectivity* (London: British Film Institute, 2004)

Bhabha, Homi, 'The Other Question ... Homi Bhabha Reconsiders the Stereotype and Colonial Discourse', *Screen*, vol. 24, no. 6, 1983, pp. 13–36

Blanchot, Maurice, *The Space of Literature*, trans. Ann Smock (Lincoln, NE: University of Nebraska Press, 1982)

Bloch, Ernest, *The Spirit of Utopia*, trans. Anthony A. Nassar (Palo Alto, CA: Stanford University Press, 2000)

Bost, Suzanne, *Mulattas and Mestizas: Representing Mixed Identities in the Americas, 1850–2000* (Athens, GA: University of Georgia Press, 2003)

Bourdieu, Pierre, *The Logic of Practice*, trans. Richard Nice (Palo Alto, CA: Stanford University Press, 1990)

Bourdieu, Pierre and Loïc, J.D. Wacquant, *An Invitation to Reflexive Sociology* (Chicago: University of Chicago Press, 1992)

Bourriaud, Nicolas, *The Radicant* (New York: Lukas & Sternberg, 2009)

Bowen, Elizabeth, *The Last September* (London: Vintage, 1988)

Boyd, Gary, 'Supernational Catholicity: Dublin and the 1932 Eucharistic Congress', *Early Popular Culture*, vol. 5, no. 3, 2007, pp. 317–33

Bracken, Claire and Emma Radley, 'A Mirror up to Irishness: Hollywood Hardmen and Witty Women', in Wanda Balzano, Anne Mulhall and Moynagh Sullivan (eds), *Irish Postmodernisms and Popular Culture* (Basingstoke: Palgrave, 2007), pp. 157–68

Bradshaw, Peter, 'Liam', *The Guardian*, 23 February 2001, http://www.guardian. co.uk/film/2001/feb/23/1

Braidotti, Rosi, *Metamorphoses: Towards a Materialist Theory of Becoming* (Cambridge: Polity Press, 2002)

Branigan, Edward, *Narrative Comprehension and Film* (London and New York: Routledge, 1992)

Brett, David, *The Construction of Heritage* (Cork: Cork University Press, 1996)

Brophy, Philip, 'Horrality: The Textuality of Contemporary Horror Films', in Ken Gelder (ed.) *The Horror Reader* (London: Routledge, 2000), pp. 276–84

Brunette, Peter, *The Films of Michel Antonioni* (Cambridge: Cambridge University Press, 1998)

Buchanan, Ian and Claire Colebrook (eds), *Deleuze and Feminist Theory* (Edinburgh: Edinburgh University Press, 2001)

Butler, Alison, *Women's Cinema: The Contested Screen* (London and New York: Wallflower, 2005)

Butler, Judith, *Bodies That Matter* (London: Routledge, 1993)

Butler, Judith, *Gender Trouble* (London: Routledge, 1990)

Butler, Judith, 'Imitation and Gender Insubordination', in Diana Fuss (ed.), *Inside/Out – Lesbian Theories, Gay Theories* (New York and London: Routledge, 1991), pp. 13–31

Byrne, Andrea, 'The Cupla Focal's Conquest', *Sunday Independent*, 13 May 2007, p. 16

Carroll, Noël, *Interpreting the Moving Image* (Cambridge: Cambridge University Press, 1998)

Cartier-Bresson, Henri, *The Decisive Moment* (London: Simon & Schuster, 1952)

Cavell, Stanley, *The World Viewed* (Cambridge, MA: Harvard University Press, 1979)

Clarke, J.J., *Oriental Enlightenment: The Encounter Between Asian and Western Thought* (London and New York: Routledge, 1997)

Clifford, James, *The Predicament of Culture: Twentieth-Century Ethnography, Literature and Art* (Cambridge, MA: Harvard University Press, 1988), pp. 21–54

Clover, Carol, *Men, Women and Chainsaws: Gender and the Modern Horror Film* (Princeton, NJ: Princeton University Press, 1992)

Colebrook, Claire, *Gilles Deleuze* (Oxford and New York: Routledge, 2005)

Connor, Steven, 'Fascination, Skin and the Screen', *Critical Quarterly*, vol. 40, no. 1, 1998, pp. 9–24

Constitution of Ireland/Bunreacht na hÉireann, http://www.constitution.ie

Coughlan, Patricia, '"Bog Queens": The Representation of Women in the Poetry of John Montague and Seamus Heaney,' in Toni O'Brien Johnson and David Cairns (eds.), *Gender and Irish Writing* (Milton Keynes: Open University Press, 1991), pp. 88–111

Coughlan, Patricia, 'Irish Literature and Feminism in Postmodernity', *Hungarian Journal of English and American Studies*, vol. 10, nos. 1–2, 2004, pp. 176–202

Coughlan, Patricia, 'Kate O'Brien: Feminine Beauty, Feminist Writing and Sexual Role', in Eibhear Walshe (ed.), *Ordinary People Dancing: Essays on Kate O'Brien* (Cork: Cork University Press, 1993), pp. 59–85

Coughlan, Patricia, '"The Whole Strange Growth": Heaney, Orpheus and Women', *Irish Review*, vol. 35, 2007, pp. 25–45

Cox, Laurence and Maria Griffin, 'Border Country Dharma: Buddhism, Ireland and Peripherality', *Journal of Global Buddhism*, vol. 10, 2009, pp. 93–126

Crary, Jonathan, *Techniques of the Observer: On Vision and Modernity in the Nineteenth Century* (Cambridge, MA: MIT Press, 1993)

Creed, Barbara, *The Monstrous Feminine: Film, Feminism, Psychoanalysis* (London: Routledge, 1993)

Creely, Niamh, 'Schemers', *Film Ireland*, vol. 119, November/December 2007, pp. 16–17

Crofts, Stephen, 'Concepts of National Cinema', in John Hill et al. (eds), *World Cinema: Critical Approaches* (Oxford: Oxford University Press, 2000), pp. 1–10

Cronin, Michael, *Translation Goes to the Movies* (New York: Routledge, 2009)

Crosson, Sean, '*Na Cloighne*', *Estudios Irlandeses*, vol. 6, 2011, pp. 202–4

Cullen, Fintan. *Visual Politics: Representation of Ireland 1750-1950* (Cork: Cork University Press, 1995)

Cullen, Fintan and John Morrison (eds.), *A Shared Legacy: Essays on Irish and Scottish Art and Visual Culture* (Aldershot, UK: Ashgate, 2005)

Cullingford, Elizabeth Butler, *Ireland's Others: Ethnicity and Gender in Irish Literature and Popular Culture* (Cork University Press, 2001)

Dalsimer, Adele M. (ed.), *Visualizing Ireland: National Identity and the Pictorial Tradition* (Boston and London: Faber & Faber 1993)

Dalsimer, Adele M. and Vera Kreilkamp, 'Introduction', in Adele M. Dalsimer (ed.) *Visualizing Ireland* (Boston and London: Faber & Faber 1993), pp. 3–8

Davidson, Joyce and Christine Milligan, 'Editorial: Embodying Emotion, Sensing Space: Introducing Emotional Geographies', *Social & Cultural Geography*, vol. 5, no. 4, 2004, pp. 523–32 de Paor, Máire, 'Irish Antiquarian Artists', in Adele M. Dalsimer (ed.), *Visualizing Ireland* (Boston and London: Faber & Faber 1993), pp. 119–32

Deane, Seamus, 'Introduction', in Seamus Deane (ed.), James Joyce, *A Portrait of the Artist as a Young Man* (Harmondsworth: New Penguin Books, 2003), pp. vii–xxix

Deleuze, Gilles, *Cinema 1: The Movement-Image*, trans. Hugh Tomlinson and Barbara Habberjam (London: Continuum, 2005)

Deleuze, Gilles, *Cinema 2: The Time-Image*, trans. Hugh Tomlinson and Robert Galeta (London: Continuum, 2005)

Deleuze, Gilles and Félix Guattari, *Anti-Oedipus: Capitalism and Schizophrenia*, trans. Robert Hurley, Mark Seem and Helen R. Lane (London: Continuum, 2004)

Deleuze, Gilles, *A Thousand Plateaus: Capitalism and Schizophrenia*, trans. Brian Massumi (London: Continuum, 2001)

Doty, Alexander, *Making Things Perfectly Queer: Interpreting Mass Culture* (Minneapolis, MN: University of Minnesota Press, 1993)

Doty, Alexander, 'Queer Theory', in John Hill et al. (eds), *The Oxford Guide to Film Studies* (Oxford University Press, 1998), pp. 148–52

Doyle, Martin, 'Reel Hero of Irish History', *Irish Times*, 4 January 2008

Eagleton, Terry, *The Idea of Culture* (Oxford: Blackwell, 2000)

Ebert, Roger, 'Liam', *Chicago Sun-Times,* 5 October 2001, http://rogerebert.suntimes.com/apps/pbcs.dll/article?AID=/20011005/REVIEWS/11005 0302/1023

Edwards, Elizabeth, 'Photographic "Types": The Pursuit of Method', *Visual Anthropology*, vol. 3, 1990, pp. 235–56

Eisenstein, Sergei, *Film Form: Essays in Film Theory*, trans. Jay Leyda (New York: Harcourt Brace, 1977)

Elliott, Kamilla, *Rethinking the Novel/Film Debate* (Cambridge: Cambridge University Press, 2009)

Eliot, T.S., '*Ulysses*, Order and Myth', *The Dial*, vol. 75, no. 5, 1923, pp. 480–3

Ellis, John, 'The Literary Adaptation: An Introduction', *Screen*, vol. 23, no. 1, 1982, pp. 3–5

Faderman, Lillian, *Surpassing the Love of Men: Romantic Friendship and Love between Women from the Renaissance to the Present* (London: The Women's Press, 1985)

Fallon, Brian, *Irish Art 1830–1990* (Belfast: Appletree Press, 1994)

Fanning, Bryan, *Racism and Social Change in the Republic of Ireland* (Manchester: Manchester University Press, 2002)

Fay, Liam, 'Sex and the Single Microwave', *Sunday Times*, 16 December 2001

Feehan, Conor, 'Lough Derg Revival: Pilgrim's Progress', *Irish Independent*, 15 June 2004

Feldman, Shelly, 'Feminist Interruptions: The Silence of Easy Bengal in the Story of Partition', *Interventions: International Journal of Postcolonial Studies*, vol. 1, no. 2, 1999, pp. 167–82

Flannery, Eóin and Michael Griffin (eds), *Ireland in Focus: Film, Photography, and Popular Culture* (Syracuse, NY: Syracuse University Press, 2009)

Flaxman, Gregory (ed.), *The Brain is the Screen: Deleuze and the Philosophy of Cinema* (Minneapolis, MN: University of Minnesota Press, 2000)

Flusser, Vilém, *Towards a Philosophy of Photography* (London: Reaktion, 2007)

Flusser, Vilém, *Writings* (Minneapolis, MN: University of Minnesota Press, 2002)

Flynn, Roddy, 'Altered Images: *Shrooms* and Irish Cinema', *Estudios Irlandeses*, vol. 3, 2008, pp. 229–32

Foley, Ronan, *Healing Waters: Therapeutic Landscapes in Historic and Contemporary Ireland* (London: Ashgate, 2010)

Foster, Hal, *The Return of the Real* (Cambridge, MA: MIT Press, 1996)

Foster, Mary, 'Interracial Couple Denied Marriage License in LA', *Associated Press*, 16 October 2009, http://www.thegrio.com/news/interracial-couple-denied-marriage-license-in-louisiana.php

Foucault, Michel, *Discipline and Punish: The Birth of the Prison*, trans. Allan Sheridan (New York: Pantheon, 1977)

Frampton, Daniel, *Filmosophy* (London and New York: Wallflower, 2006)

Freud, Sigmund, *Group Psychology and the Analysis of the Ego*, trans. and ed. James Strachey (New York and London: Norton, 1959)

Freud, Sigmund, *The Uncanny*, trans. David McLintock (London: Penguin, 2003)

Galison, Peter and Peter Datson, *Objectivity* (Cambridge, MA: MIT Press, 2007)

Garner, Steve, *Racism in the Irish Experience* (London: Pluto Press, 2003)

Garner, Steve, *Whiteness: An Introduction* (London: Routledge, 2007)

Genette, Gérard, *Palimpsests: Literature in the Second Degree*, trans. Channa Newman and Claude Doubinsky (Lincoln, NE: University of Nebraska Press, 1997)

Genz, Stéphanie and Benjamin A. Brabon, *Postfeminism: Cultural Texts and Theories* (Edinburgh: Edinburgh University Press, 2009)

Gerrard, Nicci, 'What! No Sound and Fury?' *The Observer*, 11 April 1999, http://www.guardian.co.uk/film/1999/apr/11/shakespeare

Gesler, Will, 'Lourdes: Healing in a Place of Pilgrimage', *Health & Place*, vol. 2, no. 2, 1996, pp. 95–105

Gibbons, Luke, 'Alien Eye', *Circa*, vol. 12, 1986, p. 10

Gibbons, Luke, 'Words Upon the Windowpane: Image, Text and Irish

Culture', in James Elkins (ed.), *Visual Cultures* (Bristol: Intellect, 2010), pp. 43–56

Giffney, Noreen, 'Quare Theory', in Wanda Balzano, Anne Mulhall, and Moynagh Sullivan (eds), *Popular Culture and Postmodern Ireland* (London: Palgrave Macmillan, 2007), pp. 197–209

Giles, Jane, *The Crying Game* (London: British Film Institute, 1997)

Gille, Vincent 'Love of Books, Love Books', in Jennifer Mundy (ed.), *Surrealism: Desire Unbound* (London: Tate Publications, 2001), pp. 125–35

Gillespie, Michael Patrick, 'The Odyssey of Adam and Paul: A Twenty-First-Century Irish Film', *New Hibernia Review*, vol. 12, no. 1, 2008, pp. 41–53

Gilroy, Paul, *Between Camps: Nations, Cultures and the Allure of Race*, 2nd edn (London: Routledge, 2004)

Ging, Debbie, 'All-Consuming Images: New Gender Formations in Post-Celtic-Tiger Ireland', in Debbie Ging, Michael Cronin and Peadar Kirby (eds), *Transforming Ireland: Challenges, Critiques and Resources* (Manchester: Manchester University Press, 2009), pp. 52–70

Ging, Debbie, 'Screening the Green Cinema under the Celtic Tiger', in Peadar Kirby, Luke Gibbons and Michael Cronin (eds), *Reinventing Ireland: Culture, Society, and the Global Economy* (Sterling, VA: Pluto Press, 2002), pp. 177–95

Gledhill, Christine, 'Genre and Nation', in Brian McIlroy (ed), *Genre and Cinema: Ireland and Transnationalism* (London: Routledge, 2007), pp. 11–26

Goan, Cathal, 'Teilifís na Gaeilge: Ten Years A-Growing', *New Hibernia Review*, vol. 11, no. 2, 2007, pp. 101–15

Graham, Colin, *Deconstructing Ireland: Identity, Theory, Culture* (Edinburgh University Press, 2001)

Grant, Catherine, 'Recognising Billy Budd in *Beau Travil*: Epistemology and Hermeneutics of Auteurist "Free" Adaptation', *Screen*, vol. 43, no. 1, 2002, pp. 57–73

Habermas, Jürgen, *The Philosophical Discourse of Modernity: Twelve Lectures*, trans. Frederick Lawrence (Cambridge, MA: MIT Press, 1981)

Haddon, A.C., *Notes and Queries in Anthropology*, 3rd edn (London: The Anthropological Institute, 1899)

Haraway, Donna, *Modest_Witness@Second_Millennium. Femaleman©_Meets_Oncomouse™* (London: Routledge, 1997)

Heaney, Mick, 'Marriage of Convenience: Interview', *Sunday Times*, 9 June 2002

Hemingway, Ernest, *Death in the Afternoon* (New York: Charles Scribner's Sons, 1960)

Herr, Cheryl, *The Field* (Cork: Cork University Press, 2002)

Herr, Cheryl, 'Re-Imagining *Man of Aran*', *Canadian Journal of Irish Studies*, vol. 29, no. 2, 2003, pp. 11–16

Herr, Cheryl, 'Thinking Inside the Box', in Brian McIlroy (ed.) *Genre and Cinema: Ireland and Transnationalism* (London: Routledge, 2007), pp. 111–22

Herwitz, Daniel, 'Screening Rothman's The "I" of the Camera', *Film and Philosophy*, vol. 2, 1996

Higgins, Michael D. *Renewing the Republic* (Dublin: Liberties Press, 2011)

Higson, Andrew, 'The Concept of National Cinema', *Screen*, vol. 30, no. 4, 1989, pp. 36–47

Hill, John, *Cinema and Northern Ireland: Film, Culture, and Politics* (London: British Film Institute, 2006)

Hill, John, 'Images of Violence', in Kevin Rockett, Luke Gibbons and John Hill (eds), *Cinema and Ireland* (Syracuse, NY: Syracuse University Press, 1988), pp. 147–93

Hoyez, Anne-Cécile, 'The "World of Yoga": The Production and Reproduction of Therapeutic Landscapes', *Social Science & Medicine*, vol. 65, 2007, pp. 112–24

Irigaray, Luce, 'Veiled Lips', trans. Sara Spiedal, *Mississippi Review*, vol. 11, no. 3, 1983, pp. 93–131

Irigaray, Luce, *Speculum of the Other Woman*, trans. Gillian C. Gill (Ithaca, NY: Cornell University Press, 1985)

Irigaray, Luce, *This Sex Which is Not One*, trans. Caroline Porter (Ithaca, NY: Cornell University Press, 1985)

Jameson, Frederic, *Signatures of the Visible* (London: Routledge, 1992)

Jay, Martin, *Downcast Eyes: The Denigration of Vision in Twentieth-Century French Thought* (Berkeley, CA: University of California Press, 1993)

Jay, Martin, 'Scopic Regimes of Modernity', in Hal Foster (ed.), *Vision and Visuality* (Seattle: Bay Press, 1988), pp. 3–23

Jenkins, Richard, *Pierre Bourdieu* (London and New York: Routledge, 1992)

Jenks, Chris, *Culture*, 2nd edn (London: Routledge, 2005)

Joyce, James, *A Portrait of the Artist as a Young Man* (Ware: Wordsworth Editions, 1992)

Kavanagh, Patrick, *The Great Hunger* (Shannon: Irish University Press, 1971)

Kennedy, Brian P. and Raymond Gillespie (eds), *Ireland: Art into History* (Dublin: Town House, 1994)

Kiberd, Declan, *Inventing Ireland: The Literature of the Modern Nation* (London: Vintage 1996)

King, Linda and Elaine Sisson (eds.), *Ireland, Design and Visual Culture: Negotiating Modernity, 1922-1992* (Cork University Press, 2011)

Kirby, Peadar, Luke Gibbons and Michael Cronin (eds), *Reinventing Ireland: Culture, Society, and the Global Economy* (Sterling, VA: Pluto Press, 2002)

Kitson, Niall, 'Open Up and Say AAAAAAAAAGGGGGGGHHHHHH-HHHH', *Film Ireland*, 2007, http://www.filmireland.net/exclusives/horrorthon 2007.htm

Kneafsey, Moya, 'Tourism Images and the Constructions of Celticity in Ireland and Britain', in David Harvey, Rhys Jones, Neil McInroy and Christine Milligan (eds), *Celtic Geographies: Old Culture, New Times* (London: Routledge, 2001), pp. 123–38

Knott, Kim, *Hinduism: An Introduction* (Oxford: Oxford University Press, 1998)

Kristeva, Julia, *Desire in Language*, trans. Tomas Gora, Alice Jardine (New York: Columbia University Press, 1980)

Kristeva, Julia, *Powers of Horror: An Essay on Abjection*, trans. Leon S. Roudiez (New York: Columbia University Press, 1982)

Kristeva, Julia, *Revolution in Poetic Language*, trans. Margaret Waller (New York: Columbia University Press, 1984)

Kuhling, Carmen, *The New Age Ethic and the Spirit of Postmodernity* (New Jersey: Hampton Press, 2004)

Lacan, Jacques, 'Of Structure as the Inmixing of an Otherness Prerequisite to Any Subject Whatever', in Richard Macksey and Eugenio Donato (eds), *The Structuralist Controversy: The Languages of Criticism and the Sciences of Man* (Baltimore and London: Johns Hopkins University Press, 2007), pp. 186–95

Landy, Marcia, 'The International Cast of Irish Cinema', *boundary 2*, vol. 27, 2000, pp. 22–3

Layden, Dervila, 'Discovering and Uncovering Genre in Irish Cinema', in Brian McIlroy (ed), *Genre and Cinema: Ireland and Transnationalism* (London: Routledge, 2007), pp. 27–44

Lea, Jennifer, 'Retreating to Nature: Rethinking "Therapeutic Landscapes"', *Area*, vol. 40, no. 1, (2008), pp. 90–8

Lennon, Joseph, *Irish Orientalism: A Literary and Intellectual History* (Syracuse, NY: Syracuse University Press, 2004)

Lentin, Ronit, 'Black Bodies and Headless Hookers: Alternative Global Narratives for Twenty-First-Century Ireland', *The Irish Review*, vol. 33, 2005, pp. 1–12

Letts, W.M., *Songs of Leinster* (London: Murray, 1913)

Lloyd, David, *Anomalous States: Irish Writing and the Post-Colonial Moment* (Durham, NC: Duke University Press, 1993)

Lysaght, Ruth, 'Súil Eile, Dúil Nua (Another Perspective, a New Desire): Short Films in the Irish Language since the Advent of TG4', in Neal Alexander, Shane Murphy, and Anne Oakman (eds), *To the Other Shore: Cross-Currents in Irish and Scottish Studies* (Béal Feirste: Cló Ollscoil na Banríona/Queen's University Press, 2004)

Lysaght, Ruth, 'Ar Oscailt – New Openings: Short Films in the Irish Language since the Advent of TG4', in Rosa González (ed.), *The Representation of Ireland/s: Images from Outside and from Within* (Barcelona: Promociones y Publicaciones Universitarias, 2003)

Mac Cárthaigh, Lir, 'Songs of Innocence', *Film Ireland*, vol. 108, January/February 2006, pp. 12–15

MacCormack, Patricia, *Cinesexuality* (Aldershot: Ashgate, 2008)

Macintyre, Martha and Maureen Mackenzie, 'Focal Length as an Analogue of Cultural Distance', in Elizabeth Edwards (ed.), *Anthropology and Photography, 1860–1920* (New Haven, CT: Yale University Press, 1991), pp. 158–64

Mac Póilin, Aodán and Liam Andrews, *BBC agus an Ghaeilge/BBC and the Irish Language* (Béal Feirste: Iontaobhas Ultach, 1993)

McBride, Lawrence W. (ed.), *Images, Icons and the Irish Nationalist Imagination* (Dublin: Four Courts Press, 1990)

McCarthy, Gerry, 'George Morrison, Pioneer of Irish Film, Isn't Stuck in the Past', *Sunday Times*, 15 February 2009, p. 15 (Culture section)

McClintock, Anne, 'Family Feuds: Gender, Nationalism and the Family', *Feminist Review*, vol. 44, 1993, pp. 61–80

McKeown, Joseph, *Back Crack Boy* (London: Corgi, 1986)

McKittrick, David, 'God and the Celtic Tiger: Pilgrims in Retreat from Progress', *The Independent*, 10 August 2006

McLoone, Martin, *Irish Film: The Emergence of a Contemporary Cinema* (London: British Film Institute, 2000)

McRobbie, Angela, *The Aftermath of Feminism: Gender, Culture and Social Change* (London: Sage, 2009)

Mask, Mia, 'Monster's Ball', *Film Quarterly*, vol. 58, no. 1, 2004, pp. 44–55

Meaney, Gerardine, *Gender, Ireland and Cultural Change: Race, Sex and Nation* (London: Routledge, 2010)

Meaney, Gerardine, 'Race, Sex and Nation', *The Irish Review*, vol. 35, 2007, pp. 46–63

Meaney, Gerardine, 'Regendering Modernism: The Woman Artist in Irish Women's Fiction', *Women: A Cultural Review*, vol. 15, no. 1, 2004, pp. 67–82

Mentxaka, Aintzane Legarreta, 'La Belle – Kate O'Brien and Female Beauty', in Sarah O'Connor et al. (eds), *Women, Social and Cultural Change in Twentieth-Century Ireland: Dissenting Voices?* (Newcastle: Cambridge Scholars' Press, 2008), pp. 183–98

Metz, Christian, *Film Language: A Semiotics of the Cinema* (Oxford: Oxford University Press, 1974)

Metz, Christian, 'The Imaginary Signifier', *Screen*, vol. 16, no. 2, 1975, pp. 14–76

Miller, Toby, 'Screening the Nation: Rethinking Options', *Cinema Journal*, vol. 38, no. 4, 1999, pp. 93–7

Mirzoeff, Nicholas, *An Introduction to Visual Culture*, 1st edn (London: Routledge, 1999)

Mitchell, W.J.T., *Picture Theory: Essays on Verbal and Visual Representation* (Chicago: University of Chicago Press, 1994)

Mitchell, W.J.T., 'There are no Visual Media', *Journal of Visual Culture*, vol. 4, no. 2, 2005, pp. 257–66

Monahan, Barry, 'Playing Cops and Robbers: Recent Irish Cinema and Genre Performance', in Brian McIlroy (ed), *Genre and Cinema: Ireland and Transnationalism* (London: Routledge, 2007), pp. 45–58

Monahan, David et al. (eds), *The Cinematic Jane Austen: Essays on the Filmic Sensibility of the Novels* (Jefferson, NC: McFarland, 2009)

Mooney, Timothy and Dermot Moran (eds), *The Phenomenology Reader* (London and New York: Routledge, 2002)

Moran, Albert, *Film Policy: International, National and Regional Perspectives* (New York: Routledge, 1996)

Moser, Joseph, 'Genre Politics: *Bloody Sunday* as Documentary and Discourse', in Brian McIlroy (ed.), *Genre and Cinema: Ireland and Transnationalism* (New York and London: Routledge, 2007), pp. 245–59

Mulhall, Anne, 'Queer in Ireland: "Deviant" Filiation and the (Un)holy Family', in Lisa Downing and Robert Gillett (eds), *Queer in Europe* (Surrey: Ashgate, 2011), pp. 99–112

Mulqueen, Mark, 'IFI – The Story So Far', *Irish Film Institute Programme: January–February 2005* (Dublin: Irish Film Institute, 2005), p. 23

Mulvey, Laura, *Death 24x a Second: Stillness and the Moving Image* (London: Reaktion Books, 2006)

Mulvey, Laura, *Visual and Other Pleasures* (Bloomington, IN: Indiana University Press, 1989)

Mulvey, Laura, 'Visual Pleasure and Narrative Cinema', in Leo Braudy and Marshall Cohen (eds), *Film Theory and Criticism* (Oxford: Oxford University Press, 2004), pp. 837–48

Mulvey, Laura, 'Visual Pleasure and Narrative Cinema', in Amelia Jones (ed.), *The Feminism and Visual Culture Reader* (London: Routledge, 2008), pp. 44–53

Murray, Gabrielle, '*Hostel II*: Representations of the Body in Pain and the Cinema Experience in Torture Porn', *Jump Cut*, vol. 59, 2008, http://www.ejumpcut.org/archive/jc50.2008/TortureHostel2/text.html

Negra, Diane, *What a Girl Wants? Fantasizing the Reclamation of the Self in Postfeminism* (London: Routledge, 2009)

Nishime, LeiLani, 'The Mulatto Cyborg: Imagining a Multiracial Future', *Cinema Journal*, vol. 44, no. 2, 2005, pp. 34–49

O'Brien, Harvey, 'Ghosts of Empire: *Mitchell and Kenyon in Ireland* and *Saoirse?* on DVD', *Estudios Irlandeses*, vol. 3, 2008, pp. 252–4

O'Brien, Harvey, *The Real Ireland: The Evolution of Ireland in Documentary Film* (Manchester: Manchester University Press, 2004)

O'Brien, Harvey, 'Projecting the Past: Historical Documentary in Ireland', *Historical Journal of Film, Radio and Television* vol. 20, no. 3, 2000, pp. 335–50

O'Brien, Peggy, *Writing Lough Derg: From William Carleton to Seamus Heaney* (Syracuse, NY: Syracuse University Press, 2006)

O'Brien, Kate, *As Music and Splendour* (Dublin: Penguin, 2005)

O'Brien, Kate, *Distinguished Villa: A Play in Three Acts* (London: Ernest Benn, 1926)

O'Brien, Kate, 'Gloria Gish' (n.d.), Kate O'Brien Papers, National Library of Ireland

O'Brien, Kate, *The Land of Spices* (London: Virago, 2006)

O'Brien, Kate, *Mary Lavelle* (London: Virago, 2000)

O'Brien, Kate, 'Mary Magdalen' (n.d.), National Library of Ireland, doc. 19

O'Brien, Kate, *My Ireland* (London: Batsford, 1962)

O'Brien, Kate, *Pray for the Wanderer* (London: Heinemann, 1938)

O'Brien, Kate, *Presentation Parlour* (London: House of Stratus, 2001)

O'Brien, Kate, 'Why the Rage for French Films?', *The Star*, 1 February 1938 [no p.], Kate O'Brien Papers, University of Limerick, doc. 134

O'Connell, Eithne, 'Subtitles on Screen: Something for Everyone in the Audience?', *Teanga*, vol. 18, 1999, pp. 85–91

O'Connor, Barbara, 'Myths and Mirrors: Tourist Images and National Identity', in Barbara O'Connor and Michael Cronin (eds), *Tourism in Ireland: A Critical Analysis* (Cork: Cork University Press, 1993), pp. 69–85

O'Faoláin, Sean, *The Collected Stories of Sean O'Faoláin* (Boston: Little Brown, 1983)

O'Halloran, Mark, 'Editorial', special issue: Sex Please, We're Irish, *Film Ireland*, vol. 120, January/February 2008, p. 5

O'Rourke, Michael, 'For the Love of Cinema', Series Editors' Preface, in Patricia MacCormack, *Cinesexuality* (Aldershot: Ashgate, 2008), pp. ix–xi

O'Sullivan, Patrick, 'General Introduction to the Series', in Patrick O'Sullivan (ed.), *The Irish World Wide: History, Heritage, Identity. Volume 1, Patterns of Migration* (Leicester: Leicester University Press, 1992), pp. xiii–xxiv

Parisi, Luciana, *Abstract Sex: Philosophy, Bio-Technology and the Mutations of Desire* (New York: Continuum, 2004), pp. 171–93

Penley, Constance and Janet Bergstrom, 'The Avant-Garde: Histories and Theories', in Bill Nichols (ed.), *Movies and Methods, Volume 2* (Berkeley, CA: University of California Press, 1985), pp. 287–99

Peirce, Charles S., 'Logic as Semiotic: The Theory of Signs', in Robert E. Innis (ed.), *Semiotics: An Introductory Anthology* (Bloomington, IN: Indiana University Press, 1985), pp. 4–22

Pettitt, Lance, *December Bride* (Cork: Cork University Press, 2001)

Pettitt, Lance, 'Pigs and Provos, Prostitutes and Prejudice: Gay Representation in Irish Film, 1984–1995', in Eibhear Walsh (ed.), *Sex, Nation and Dissent in Irish Writing* (Cork: Cork University Press, 1997), pp. 252–85

Pine, Richard, 'Where is This Place? Kate O'Brien, Autism and Modern Literature', in John Logan (ed.), *With Warmest Love: Lectures for Kate O'Brien, 1984–93* (Limerick: Mellick Press, 1994), pp. 77–98

Pratschke, B. Mairéad, 'A Look at Irish-Ireland: Gael-Linn's *Amharc Éireann* Films, 1956–64', *New Hibernia Review/Iris Éireannach Nua*, vol. 9, no. 3, 2005, pp. 17–38

Quiggin, A. Hingston, *Haddon the Head-Hunter: A Short Sketch of the Life of A.C. Haddon* (Cambridge: Cambridge University Press, 1942)

Radek, Karl, 'Contemporary World Literature and the Tasks of Proletarian Art', in Maxim Gorky et al., *Soviet Writers' Congress 1934: The Debate on Socialist Realism and Modernism in the Soviet Union* (London: Lawrence & Wishart, 1977), pp. 73–162

Rancière, Jacques, *The Politics of Aesthetics: The Distribution of the Sensible*, trans. Gabriel Rockhill (London and New York: Continuum, 2004)

Rhodes, Steve, 'Liam', http://www.allmovieportal.com/m/2001_Liam61.html

Rockett, Emer and Kevin Rockett, *Neil Jordan: Exploring Boundaries* (Dublin: Liffey Press, 2003)

Rockett, Kevin, Luke Gibbons and John Hill, *Cinema and Ireland* (Syracuse, NY: Syracuse University Press, 1988)

Roudiez, Leon S. 'Introduction', Julia Kristeva, *Revolution in Poetic Language*, trans. Margaret Waller (New York: Columbia University Press, 1984), pp. 1–12

Ryan, Joan, 'Class and Creed in Kate O'Brien', in Maurice Harmon (ed.), *The Irish Writer and the City* (Gerrards Cross: Colin Smythe, 1984), pp. 125–35

Said, Edward, *Orientalism* (London: Vintage, 1979)

Salkeld, Blanaid, *Hello, Eternity!* (London: E. Mathews Marrot, 1933)

Salkeld, Cecil and Francis Stuart, 'To All Artists and Writers', in David Pierce (ed.), *Irish Writing in the Twentieth Century: A Reader* (Cork: Cork University Press, 2000), pp. 290–1

Sartre, Jean-Paul, *Being and Nothingness: An Essay on Phenomenological Ontology*, trans. Hazel E. Barnes (London: Methuen, 1957)

Schatzki, Theodore R., Karin Knorr Cetina and Eike Von Savigny (eds), *The Practice Turn in Contemporary Theory* (London and New York: Routledge, 2001)

Sekula, Allan, 'The Body and the Archive', *October*, vol. 39, 1986, pp. 3–64

Shaviro, Steven, *The Cinematic Body* (Minneapolis, MN: University of Minnesota Press, 1993)

Slater, Eamonn, 'Contested Terrain: Differing Interpretations of the Co. Wicklow Landscape', *Irish Journal of Anthropology*, vol. 3, 1993, pp. 23–55

Sobchack, Vivian, *The Address of the Eye: A Phenomenology of Film Experience* (Princeton, NJ: Princeton University Press, 1992)

Smith, Neil, 'Liam', *BBC Home*, 22 February 2001, http://www.bbc.co.uk/films/2001/02/14/liam_2001_review.shtml

Smyth, Bernard, *Modernism's History: A Study in Twentieth-Century Art and Ideas* (Sydney: University of New South Wales Press, 1998)

Spencer, Frank, 'Some Notes on the Attempt to Apply Photography to Anthropometry during the Second Half of the Nineteenth Century', in Elizabeth Edwards (ed.), *Anthropology & Photography: 1860–1920* (New Haven, CT: Yale University Press, 1992), pp. 99–107.

Stam, Robert, 'Introduction: The Theory and Practice of Adaptation', in Robert Stam and Alessandra Raengo (eds), *Literature and Film: A Guide to the Theory and Practice of Film Adaptation* (Oxford: Blackwell, 2005), pp. 1–52

Stam, Robert, *Literature through Film: Realism, Magic, and the Art of Adaptation* (Oxford: Blackwell, 2005)

Stokes, Melvyn, 'Structuring Absences: Images of America Missing from the Hollywood Screen', *Revue Français D'Études Américaines*, vol. 89, 2001, pp. 43–53

Sullivan, Moynagh, 'Boyz to Menz(own): Irish Boy Bands and the Alternative Nation', *Irish Review*, vol. 34, 2006, pp. 58–78

Sullivan, Moynagh, '"I Am Not Yet Delivered of the Past": The Poetry of Blanaid Salkeld', *Irish University Review*, vol. 33, no. 1, 2003, pp. 182–200

Sullivan, Moynagh, 'The Treachery of Wetness: Irish Studies, Seamus Heaney and the Politics of Parturition', *Irish Studies Review*, vol. 13, no. 4, 2005, pp. 451–68

Tagg, John, *The Burden of Representation: Essays on Photographies and Histories* (London: Macmillan, 1988)

Tasker, Yvonne and Diane Negra, 'Introduction: Feminist Politics and Postfeminist Culture', in Yvonne Tasker and Diane Negra (eds), *Interrogating Postfeminism: Gender and the Politics of Popular Culture* (Durham, NC: Duke University Press, 2007), pp. 1–25

Taylor, Charles, 'Liam', *Salon: Arts and Entertainment*, 26 September 2001, http://www.salon.com/2001/09/26/liam

This is Ireland: Highlights from Census 2011, http://www.cso.ie/en/census/census2011reports/

Thomas, Calvin, *Masculinity, Psychoanalysis, Straight Queer Theory: Essays on Abjection in Literature, Mass Culture and Film* (New York: Palgrave Macmillan, 2008)

Tighe-Mooney, Sharon, 'Sexuality and Religion in Kate O'Brien's Fiction', in Deirdre Quinn et al. (eds), *Essays in Irish Literary Criticism: Themes of Gender, Sexuality, and Corporeality* (Lewiston, NY: Edwin Mellen Press, 2008), pp. 125–40

Tracy, Tony, 'Introduction: Irish Film and Television, 2006', *Estudios Irlandeses*, vol. 2, 2007, pp. 251–4

Vale, Eugene, *Tecnicas del Guion para Cine y Television* (Barcelona: Gedisa, 1989)

Valente, Joseph, The Myth of Manliness in Irish National Culture, 1880-1922 (University of Illinois Press, 2011).

Vološinov, V.N., *Marxism and the Philosophy of Language*, trans. Ladislav Matejka and I.R. Titunik (Cambridge, MA: Harvard University Press, 1986)

Walsh, Fintan, 'Cock Tales: Homosexuality, Trauma, and the Cosmopolitan Queer', special issue: Sex Please, We're Irish, *Film Ireland*, vol. 120, January/February, 2008, pp. 16–18

Walshe, Eibhear, *Kate O'Brien: A Writing Life* (Dublin: Irish Academic Press, 2006)

Watson, Iarfhlaith, *Broadcasting in Irish: Minority Language, Radio, Television and Identity* (Dublin: Four Courts Press, 2003)

Whelehan, Imelda, *The Feminist Bestseller: From Sex and the Single Girl to Sex and the City* (Basingstoke: Palgrave Macmillan, 2005)

White, Jerry, 'Translating Ireland Back into Éire: Gael Linn and Film Making in Irish', *Éire-Ireland*, vol. 38, nos. 1–2, 2003, pp. 106–22

White, Luise, *Speaking with Vampires: Rumor and History in Colonial Africa* (Berkeley, CA: University of California Press, 2000)

Whitehouse, Charles, 'The London Film Festival: Capital Gains', *Sight and Sound*, vol. 10, no. 11, 2000, pp. 18–19

Whitford, Margaret, *Luce Irigaray: Philosophy in the Feminine* (London: Routledge, 1991)

Whittaker, Ross, 'Short Film Fluency', *Film Ireland*, vol. 101, November/December 2004, pp. 20–2

Williams, Raymond, *Keywords* (London: Fontana, 1976)

Wilson, Mick, 'Terms of Art and Tricks of Trade: A Critical Look at the Irish Art Scene Now', *Third Text*, vol. 19, no. 5, 2005, pp. 535–43

Wolf, Naomi, *The Beauty Myth* (London: Vintage, 1991)

Woolf, Virginia, *The Crowded Dance of Modern Life. Selected Essays: Volume Two*, Rachel Bowlby (ed.) (Harmondsworth: Penguin, 1993)

Yuval-Davis, Nira, *Gender and Nation* (London: Sage, 1997)

Zack, Naomi, *Race and Mixed Race* (Philadelphia: Temple University Press, 1993)

Žižek, Slavoj, 'How to Read Lacan: From *Che Vuoi?* to Fantasy: Lacan with *Eyes Wide Shut*', www.lacan.com/zizkubrick.htm

Žižek, Slavoj, 'The Inaccessible Lady: From Courtly Love to The Crying Game', *New Left Review*, vol. 202, 1993, pp. 95–108

Žižek, Slavoj, *Looking Awry: An Introduction to Jacques Lacan through Popular Culture* (Cambridge, MA: MIT Press, 1992)

Žižek, Slavoj, *On Belief* (London and New York: Routledge, 2001)

Select Visual Texts

Adam & Paul, directed by Lenny Abrahamson, Element Pictures, 2004

Bloody Sunday, directed by Paul Greengrass, Bórd Scannán na hÉireann, 2002

Boy Eats Girl, directed by Stephen Bradley, Element Pictures, 2005

Breakfast on Pluto, directed by Neil Jordan, Pathé Pictures International, 2005

Browne, Charles R., from 'Ethnography of the Mullet' c. 1895, Proceedings of the Royal Irish Academy, ser. 3, vol. III, pp. 587–649 (Appendix) 1, pp. 173–5, 1,893–6

The Crying Game, directed by Neil Jordan, Palace Pictures, 1992

Dead Meat, directed by Conor McMahon, Three Way Productions, 2004

Duggan, Joe, *Family Man*, solo exhibition, Limerick City Art Gallery, 6 July–28 August 2007

Duggan, Joe, 'Family Man, No. 1', *Family Man*, solo exhibition, Limerick City Art Gallery, 6 July–28 August 2007

Duggan, Joe, 'Family Man, No. 5', *Family Man*, solo exhibition, Limerick City Art Gallery, 6 July–28 August 2007

Duggan, Joe, 'Like Father, Like Son (Ball)', *Family Man*, solo exhibition, Limerick City Art Gallery, 6 July–28 August 2007

Duggan, Joe, 'Like Father, Like Son (Kite)', *Family Man*, solo exhibition, Limerick City Art Gallery, 6 July–28 August 2007

Duggan, Joe, 'Like Father, Like Son (Kitchen)', *Family Man*, Limerick City Art Gallery, 6 July–28 August 2007

Fergus's Wedding, Grand Pictures, 2002

Fluent Dysphasia, directed by Daniel O'Hara, 2004

'The Fun Starts Here' (Red Rage Films, 2010), Fáilte Ireland advertisement, 2010

Garage, directed by Lenny Abrahamson, Element Pictures, 2007

Gerrard, John, 'Animated Scene (Oil Field)', Galerie Ernst Hilger, 2007

Gerrard, John, 'Dark Portraits', *Dark Portraits*, solo exhibition, RHA

Gallagher Gallery, Dublin, 17 November 2006–7 January 2007

Gerrard, John, 'Dust Storm', Galerie Ernst Hilger, 2007

Gerrard, John, One Thousand Year Dawn (Marcel), *Dark Portraits*, solo exhibition, RHA Gallagher Gallery, Dublin, 17 November 2006–7 January 2007

Gerrard, John, 'Portrait to Smile Once a Year (Mary)', Galerie Ernst Hilger, 2006

Gerrard, John, 'Saddening Portrait', *New Work in New Media*, solo exhibition, Gallery of Photography, Dublin, 23 October–30 November 2003

Haddon, Alfred Cort, 'Bertillonage Method, Ireland', c. 1890, Alfred Cort Haddon Collection, Museum of Archaeology and Anthropology, University of Cambridge

Hunger, directed by Steve McQueen, Film Four, 2008

International Society for Krishna Consciousness UK and Ireland, http://www.iskconuk.com

Isolation, directed by Billy O'Brien, Film Four, 2005

Krishna Island, ISKCON, http://www.krishnaisland.com

'Lake Isle Retreats', ISKCON Centre advertising flier, 2005

Lake Isle Retreats, ISKCON, http://www.lakeisleretreats.com

Liam, directed by Stephen Frears, BBC, 2001

Lough Derg, http://www.loughderg.org

Paths to Freedom, Grand Pictures, 2000

A Portrait of the Artist as a Young Man, directed by Joseph Strick, Ulysses Film Company, 1977

'Re-Kindle Your Spirit', Lough Derg marketing poster, 2004

Shrooms, directed by Paddy Breathnach, Capitol Films, 2007

'Soul Survival', Lough Derg marketing poster, 2004

Starkey, Hannah, 'Untitled – May 1997', c-type print, 122 x 152cm, 1997

Starkey, Hannah, 'Untitled – March 2002', c-type print, 122 x 183cm, 2002

Starkey, Hannah, 'Untitled – June 2007', c-type print, 122 x 183cm, 2007

The Woman Who Married Clark Gable, directed by Thaddeus O'Sullivan, Samson Films, b/w, 28m, 1985

Yu Ming is Ainm Dom, directed by Daniel O'Hara, Dough Productions, 2003

INDEX

*(An italic numeral denotes an
illustration on the page)*

271